L.I.F.E. MINISTRIES

"I HAVE COME TO GIVE LIFE AND TO GIVE IT MORE ABUNDANTLY"
JOHN 10:10

A Biblical Approach to Overcoming Addictions

A Forty Lesson Biblical Journey in Recovery

MICHAEL R. DIXON

ISBN: 978-1-09834-422-1

L.I.F.E. MINISTRIES

"I HAVE COME TO GIVE LIFE AND TO GIVE IT MORE ABUNDANTLY"
JOHN 10:10

This addiction recovery workbook is the result of over 30 years of study, a lifetime of experience, and the dedication and service of many individuals.

I dedicate this book for God's glory and I give special thanks to the original L.I.F.E. leadership team:

Pastor Glenn Howell and wife Renee, leaders in LIFE since the beginning, faithful servants
Justin Hipsky, onboard and active since the conception of L.I.F.E.
Scott & Michelle House, living examples of God's power
Maranda Horst, a dear friend, faithful servant and sweet sister
JoLynn Melton, who knows the impact addiction has on a home

To my wife, soul mate, best friend, proof-reader and editor,
Melissa Dixon

In memory of a dear brother in Christ, whose struggle is now over,
Jimmy Perry

Until we meet again my brother, guitars in hand, free from sin, in the Master's Land

Table of Contents

Welcome to the L.I.F.E. curriculum,

We know that you are probably dealing with a lot of issues and emotions right now. Whether you are going to be working through these lessons on your own, or as a member in a group, you have made a good and very wise choice in seeking help for your struggles. So, try to relax and remind yourself that your new life awaits, straight ahead! L.I.F.E. is an acrostic for "Living In Freedom Everyday." The name for the ministry derives from the words of Jesus recorded in John 10:10:

> **"The thief comes only to steal and kill and destroy. I came that they may have life and have it abundantly." (John 10:10 ESV)**

The LIFE program began in March of 2017 as a Christ-centered addiction recovery ministry, open to men and women seeking freedom from addiction. L.I.F.E. has since become a 501(c3) nonprofit ministry offering hope, encouragement, and direction to others.

From a LIFE member:

"LIFE Ministries means so much to me. I was a lost crackhead with no need to keep living. I started attending the LIFE meetings with my wife and I am now off crack for good. Thanks to the meetings and the people of LIFE, as well as to Pastor Mike and his desire to help others, these days are so much better then when I was chasing the demon of crack."

Patrick Holland, Member of LIFE Ministries for over 2 years

Our main goal is to help you understand what God says about your struggles. Only God offers the answers you seek for your deliverance. I believe and know, from my own personal struggles with addiction that God is able to set you free. He really does offer to you a new life, abundant life, overflowing with strength and the power that you seek right now. God has done this for me and He is more than willing and able to accomplish this deliverance in your life as well.

As you journey through this workbook you will notice that it contains forty biblical lessons. Why forty? The number forty appears in the Bible well over one hundred times. Numbers in scripture have significance. For example, the number one represents union and oneness. Galatians 3:20 tells us that "God is one." The number two speaks of companionship, as in marriage. Three speaks of divine design, as is seen in the Trinity, God in three persons yet one God. The number six is the number for man, created on the 6th day of creation and also is short on perfection and completion which the number seven represents. The number forty in the Bible often signifies very important time periods which are often difficult, or periods of testing. For example, Jesus fasted for forty days in the wilderness as he was tempted by Satan (Matthew 4:2, Mark 1:13, Luke 4:2). During the worldwide flood in Noah's day, it rained for forty days and forty nights (Genesis 7:4). God caused the Israelites to wander in the wilderness for forty years because of their disobedience (Numbers 32:13). The giant Goliath challenged the Israelites for forty days before David defeated him (1 Samuel 17:16).

As you discipline yourself to work through these forty lessons, whether you do this in forty days or over forty weeks, this is a very significant and important period of time for you. This could be the MOST important period of time in your life if you are willing to really listen to God and follow His will for your life. No doubt this will also be a time filled with many temptations to turn back. The battle is real but the victory is available for you through faith in Christ and obedience to God's Word. Jesus fasted for forty days and was tempted by Satan, yet He victoriously prevailed through total reliance and obedience to God's Word. We will follow Christ's example as we move through this important period of time ahead, immersing ourselves in what God says about our struggles, and fighting each temptation to turn back with the Word of God which is the sword of the Spirit (Ephesians 6:17).

There are two very important statements I want you to hear right from the beginning:

#1. You are eternally loved and cherished. God created you, loves you, and He has directed your path to this program. Know this before you begin allowing those old messages to creep back into your thinking; No one, whether it is your counselor, mentor, sponsor, or fellow group member is any better than anyone else. We all fall short of who we should be, yet God, our Father, continues to love us.

#2. It is vital that you make the decision right now to commit to this program and to take responsibility for your own personal growth and deliverance. This means actively attending all meetings and being prepared by having your assignments completed. God is offering you all you need for transformation. God offers you salvation, deliverance, freedom, and abundant life, but it is your responsibility to receive these gifts from Him. Sometimes this may come easy but often there will be intense struggles, even times of temporary defeat for some. I encourage you, urge you, plead with you, that you take this journey seriously. Be ready to fight, ready to resist, ready to change, and prepare for the victory which awaits. You can be delivered and changed forever. You do not have to remain who you have been nor who you are right now. Let's get serious because the issues we will be dealing with are not only about life and death but eternity is also at stake.

Living In Freedom Everyday,
Pastor Michael R Dixon
MDIV/CO, LCAS-A
Author, Founder and Executive Director of L.I.F.E. Ministries

"I was introduced to the LIFE program through my pastor at our church. Once I had my one on one with Pastor Mike I felt right at home. It was nice being around a Christian based program where I wasn't judged because of my struggles. I met some really nice people who instantly made me feel welcomed. The great thing is that it's not just a weekly meeting, it's an opportunity to enjoy a good meal while I fellowship with other people who share a similar story as mine. The LIFE group has become a tight family for me. I know that any of them are just a phone call away if I need them." Anthony Mills, Rocky Mount, N.C.

6 Basic Truths Necessary for LIFE

In the course of these 40 lessons we will discuss and seek to apply these 6 basic truths to our lives:

#1. Your Salvation – What is my spiritual condition? (My situation)

#2. Your Confession – Who am I? (My identity)

#3. Your Motivation –Why do I do what I do? (My goals)

#4. Your Repentance –Which direction should I be going? (My redirection)

#5. Your Transformation –What does change look like? (My personal results)

#6. Your Duplication-How can I help others? (My service)

Tips for you as you begin this forty-week journey:

#1. Get a Bible or download a Bible app. The scripture quoted in these lessons are drawn from two major translations: The New King James Version (NKJV) and the English Standard Version (ESV).

#2. Have a designated notebook where you can record your thoughts, prayers, and notes as God speaks to you through His Word.

#3. Seek out a prayer partner. Share with someone close to you that you are working through this material. Ask them to pray for you as you journey through each lesson.

CORE FOUNDATIONAL BELIEFS

The following core beliefs are interwoven within these lessons:

#1. We believe in the biblical teaching of the Trinity; God the Father, God the Son, and God the Holy Spirit, yet there is only one God in three persons.

We believe that God is the Supreme Ruler and Creator of all the universe and all that exists.

Jesus Christ (God in human flesh, presented as God's only Son in the Bible), was born into this world through the virgin Mary. Jesus lived a life free of sin, and gave His life freely for us that our sins could be forgiven. Jesus died, was buried, and arose on the third day. It is through faith in accepting Jesus as our substitute that we can receive and live in the abundant life that He offers.

We believe that as Jesus ascended back to the Father in Heaven that He sent His Spirit, the Holy Spirit, into the world to convict people of their sin, to draw people to Jesus for salvation, and to empower believers to live transformed lives.

#2. We believe that the Bible is our foundation for truth, authored by God Himself as He used human writers to record His words. We believe that God's Word offers us direction for life, solutions to our struggles, and most importantly it reveals to us how we can be made right with God, our Creator.

#3. We believe that drug and alcohol abuse, as well as all addictions, are not diseases in themselves. However, we do acknowledge that habitual use and continual active involvement in such lifestyles can and does lead to sickness and even disease, mental illness as well as shortened life spans and premature death. We believe that all addiction is the result of our sinful nature. Without a right relationship with God, who created us, we are left to our own schemes, plans, and devices.

#4. We believe that it is only through a personal relationship with Jesus Christ that we can receive the power we need to change. It is only with God's power that we are able to live a life free from addiction and free from the bondage of sin. Through God's power, which is available to you, we are able to live a full, abundant, free, purposeful and joy-filled life.

#5. We believe that there is hope for change in anyone's life! No one has fallen so low that they cannot be changed, restored, and transformed by God if they will come to Him in humility, calling upon Jesus for salvation. We believe that God is willing and ready to forgive, save, and deliver anyone. We believe recovery is possible and available for all. You do not have to stay the person you are right now!

#6. We believe in the local church. It is vital in our recovery and personal growth that we surround ourselves with other believers who are also desiring to live in the freedom and life that Christ offers. God has given the church the ministry of reconciliation (2 Corinthians 5:16) which means showing others how they can be in a right relationship with God. The local church is our best support group.

As you read and work through the following assignments you will notice these core beliefs in each lesson. Our foundation of truth is God's Word, the Holy Bible. Our transforming power for change is realized through the presence and power of the Holy Spirit. The only way to be reconciled with God, filled with the Holy Spirit, and empowered to live this abundant life is to come in faith to Jesus Christ in repentance and surrender.

OKAY. Now, I want you to pause just a moment. Take a deep breath, stop trying to figure it all out and commit today that you will remain active in this program. Listen for God's voice through each truth that is taught. Regardless of what you may be feeling right now, God has a tremendous plan for your deliverance and for your future. Let's begin the journey now!

"I have always said that the LIFE program and curriculum have been wonderful for just that; Life. Addiction is something that I have not personally battled, but it has ransacked my family for many years. So often we focus primarily upon the addiction itself and not upon the truth. The truth is the LIFE curriculum helps you stay focused and grounded by pointing you to the truth of Christ. This program helps you learn how to use the tools needed, grounded in scripture, to break free from the bondage of addiction. If you are like me and have had the horrible effects of addiction try to settle into your family's life, I encourage you to take the time and work through this curriculum. We often make excuses for the addiction and try to save our loved ones from the horrible pain of their own choices. There is only one who can save them and He is fully capable of doing just that; trust in Jesus Christ. These lessons will help you stand firm and teach you how to better serve your loved one by living in freedom every day in your own personal life."
Maranda Horst, Nashville, N.C.

Living Abundantly
Week #1

Would you prefer many blessings in your life or only a few? How about money? Recently the lottery system in North Carolina has been overwhelmed with huge jackpots, sometimes over 1 billion dollars, and long lines of people in stores trying to purchase tickets. So, based on that response I think it's safe to say that most people would like to have an abundance of money. This L.I.F.E. curriculum is about abundance. Our focus is to help people experience the good life, the full life, the abundant life that only Christ can bring. Reason with me just a moment, since God created us shouldn't He be the first one that we turn to for direction on how we should live? I mean, God had a purpose and plan in mind when He created us. Interesting enough, this abundant life has nothing to do with how much money you have or how many toys you own. Several years ago, I had the opportunity to meet Rick Stanley, the younger step-brother of Elvis Pressley. I remember Rick sharing with us his experiences growing up as the younger brother to Elvis. At Christmas, Elvis would bring home motorbikes, toys, and all kinds of expensive gifts for everyone. Elvis seemed to have it all. He was rich in wealth and recognized around the world. Yet, Rick said that he would often hear his brother say, "I'm lonely. I'm not happy. I'm struggling." You see contrary to what so many believe, it's not wealth or even being an iconic figure like Elvis that brings a full life. Let's begin our discussion today as we think about where this abundance can be found. We will continue to look at this subject during the next two weeks.

Listen to the words of Jesus:

John 10:10 (ESV)
"The thief comes only to steal and kill and destroy. I came that they may have life and have it abundantly."

Based upon that verse the thief comes to do what three things?

1. _____

2. _____

3. _____

Has the enemy been successful in your past in fulfilling one or more of his intentions? How? Please explain:

There is clearly good and evil present in this world. The battle between the two is evident and clear. The enemy desires to destroy and Jesus comes to bring us life and that we might "have it more abundantly." Abundant life offered by Jesus! I searched for that "life" for many years before coming to Christ for what only He could provide. You probably have as well. I tried so many things to try and fulfill a hunger I seemed to have deep within and nothing seemed to satisfy me for very long. The drugs and alcohol, the immoral lifestyle, the partying and life of crime, only brought me pain and trouble. I am excited to share with you in this lesson my experience that has ended my search and brought to me real life in Christ.

1 Thessalonians 3:7-12 (ESV)
"for this reason, brothers, in all our distress and affliction we have been comforted about you through your faith. ⁸ For now we live, if you are standing fast in the Lord. ⁹ For what thanksgiving can we return to God for you, for all the joy that we feel for your sake before our God, ¹⁰ as we pray most earnestly night and day that we may see you face to face and supply what is lacking in your faith? ¹¹ Now may our God and Father himself, and our Lord Jesus, direct our way to you, ¹² and may the Lord make you increase and abound in love for one another and for all, as we do for you,"

There are two words in verse 12 above that speak of abundance. What are these two words?

1. _____

2. _____

God doesn't want us to simply survive but He desires that we actually thrive! You were actually created to thrive. Isn't that good news? Often when I ask people, "How are you doing?" I hear the response, "Well, I'm making it." "I'm getting by." "I'm surviving." Wait! That doesn't sound like abundance of life to me! Today we will discuss the first thing that's needed for you to experience the abundant life of Christ:

#1. FAITH

Paul writes in **1 Thessalonians 3:7, "we have been comforted about you through your faith."**

What do you think faith means?

The word faith is translated from a Greek word which means, "trust," or "firm persuasion." Where do you ultimately place your trust? What is it that you are convinced is completely trustworthy? Paul found comfort in knowing that the people to whom he was writing had placed their faith in the right place. He identifies the object of their faith in **1 Thessalonians 3:8, "you are standing fast in the Lord."** This means that they were trusting God's Word to be completely reliable and trustworthy.

Psalm 119:105 (ESV)
"Your word *is* a lamp to my feet And a light to my path."

According to Psalm 119:105 God's Word is referred to as:

#1. _____

#2. _____

Matthew 4:4 (ESV)
"But He answered and said, "It is written, *'Man shall not live by bread alone, but by every word that proceeds from the mouth of God.'*""

According to Matthew 4:4, we need more than physical food. What else do we need?

Hebrews 11:6 (ESV)
"But without faith *it is* impossible to please *Him,* for he who comes to God must believe that He is, and *that* He is a rewarder of those who diligently seek Him."

As we place our faith in God, and live our lives trusting Him, God is pleased and we are blessed. Faith pleases God but faith also places us in the proper position in life to experience God's abundance. You must have faith in what God says in order to live victoriously in this abundant life. Grab these promises from God with your faith:

Romans 8:37 (ESV)

"Yet in all these things we are more than conquerors through Him who loved us."

How can trusting the above verse aid you in recovery?

1 Corinthians 10:13 (ESV)

"No temptation has overtaken you except such as is common to man; but God is faithful, who will not allow you to be tempted beyond what you are able, but with the temptation will also make the way of escape, that you may be able to bear it."

That is a promise from God! You can trust God and every promise He has ever made. How does 1 Cor. 10:13 give you strength to stay clean and sober?

Romans 8:16-17 (ESV)

"The Spirit Himself bears witness with our spirit that we are children of God, ^{17} and if children, then heirs--heirs of God and joint heirs with Christ, if indeed we suffer with *Him,* that we may also be glorified together."

We are called what? _____

Decide right now what will be the object of your faith. Are you going to continue to trust in yourself, your own ability, your own will-power, and self-determination to change? How has that worked for you in the past? Have you experienced long-term sobriety? Will you trust in man-made theories and philosophies to walk in victory? Listen to how God describes programs and methods that are void of His truth:

Romans 1:22 (ESV)

"Claiming to be wise, they became fools…"

God offers you all you need to be forever changed! He does not tell us that change will be easy but He does promise to give us all we need for change to be realized.

2 Peter 1:3 (NKJV)
"as His divine power has given to us all things that *pertain* to life and godliness,
through the knowledge of Him who called us by glory and virtue,"

Fill in the blank: "His divine power has given to us _____ that pertain to life and godliness…."

Take advantage of all the resources God has placed around you to aid you in recovery. Become active in a Bible believing church. Plug into the available support groups. Mediate on the prayers and steps that are taught. Do your homework. See your therapist or counselor. Do everything you can to stay clean but don't leave God out! Make sure that your number one priority is to have faith in what He says above all else. His Word is the foundational truth that we will look to together through this program.

A word of testimony:

"I started experimenting with drugs throughout high school. I ended up getting pregnant. I got really sick and was prescribed pain pills as well as other medications. I stayed on the pain pills for two years. I became addicted and my addiction led to heroin. I ended up losing full custody of my son. After I lost my son, I wanted my life back. I went to outpatient treatment and they prescribed me more medications. Honestly, the medications I was prescribed were worse on me than the drugs I had become addicted to. I began to self-medicate again because nothing else was working. All these secular programs, there is no real compassion and support there. During my first visit to the LIFE program everyone was welcoming. I could be myself. I could be real and honest about my struggles. Coming to LIFE has helped me." Ashley Pendergrass, Nash County, N.C.

Jesus offers you abundant life!

PRAYER: "Dear Heavenly Father, I long for the abundant life that only You can offer. Please help me to walk in your truth, applying Your resources to my daily life, that I will realize and experience real life. Thank-you for already providing all that I need to be changed forever. As I begin these lessons, please speak to me. Help me to hear your voice and give me faith to believe. In Christ's name I pray, Amen."

Living Abundantly Part 2
Week #2

We are studying how we can experience a life that is full, satisfying, and fulfilling. The L.I.F.E. ministry is founded upon Jesus' statement as recorded in John 10:10 that He had come to give abundant life. This full and rich life is available to you! Last week we focused on the vital aspect of faith. This is where real life begins, through placing our faith or trust in Jesus as our personal Lord and Savior. God created us for the purpose of bringing Him honor and glory. Sin has made this impossible for you and I to accomplish on our own. We simply do not have the strength within ourselves to live a life that honors God and in turn blesses us. This is how the Apostle Paul described his own inadequacies:

Romans 7:15-20 (ESV)

"For I do not understand my own actions. For I do not do what I want, but I do the very thing I hate. [16] Now if I do what I do not want, I agree with the law, that it is good. [17] So now it is no longer I who do it, but sin that dwells within me. [18] For I know that nothing good dwells in me, that is, in my flesh. For I have the desire to do what is right, but not the ability to carry it out. [19] For I do not do the good I want, but the evil I do not want is what I keep on doing. [20] Now if I do what I do not want, it is no longer I who do it, but sin that dwells within me."

Do you ever feel the way that Paul felt? He said that sometimes he couldn't figure out why he did the things that he did. Looking back over my life of substance abuse I can so identify with his statement! Why in the world would a person desire to keep going back into a lifestyle that has done nothing but brought pain and trouble? The pull of addiction is real just as this spiritual battle is real. If we attempt to live our lives without faith in God we are going to find nothing but repetitive failures, relapses, and a continual state of, "I just don't seem to have what it takes."

Describe a time in your life when you realized that you did not have the power you needed to accomplish change in your life:

There is a story of a little ten-year boy who was told by his father, "I want you to go outside and unload those boards off the back of my truck. Use every resource at your disposal." The boy went out to his father's truck and saw these ten feet long, heavy boards laying in the back of his father's truck. The boy, desiring to please his father attempted to pick up one of the boards but he could hardly budge it. After trying and trying, almost exhausting himself, he returned to his father, "I'm sorry dad but I can't, the boards are too heavy." The father asked his son, "Did you use every resource at your disposal?" The boy replied, "I guess I did." The father responded, "No son, you didn't. I am here and willing to help. You didn't come to me."

How do you think that story applies to your life?

What are the heavy boards in your life right now that you need help dealing with?

To whom should you turn to for help?

#1. Faith is vital if you will live out the abundant life that Christ is offering you. However, there is something else you need in your life. You need **#2. Prayer.** Prayer is simply talking to God. As you pray don't worry about the mechanics of prayer, the words you use, the length of your prayer, or what time of day or night it is. Just open your heart up to God. Be honest with your struggles. Be real with God. He already knows what you are dealing with anyway. He knows you better than you know yourself. Let's return to 1 Thessalonians 3:

1 Thessalonians 3:9-10 (ESV)
"For what thanksgiving can we return to God for you, for all the joy that we
feel for your sake before our God, as we pray most earnestly night and day that
we may see you face to face and supply what is lacking in your faith?"

Paul is writing to the church at Thessalonica as he inquires concerning any prayer needs that they may have. Look at verse 9. What two things should be a part of our prayers?

#1. _____

#2. _____

Let me tell you what will help you mentally, emotionally and spiritually to overcome your struggles: **Being thankful and being joyful!** Get your mind in line with what God says. Expect to be victorious and to conquer temptation! If you expect failure you will more than likely experience that in your life!

Make a list of things below that you can give thanks for right now in prayer:

Now take a few minutes and thank God in prayer for those things.

There needs to be thanksgiving in your prayers. There needs to be joy in your prayers. How can you have joy when things are not going your way? You *choose* to be joyful anyway! Begin by telling yourself, "Although I may have troubles to deal with right now I'm still going to be joyful because I know God is going to see me through. I'm going to rejoice because problems come but problems go. I choose joy."

Include thanksgiving and joy in your prayer life but also make sure you have a PURPOSE! Paul wrote in verse 9 that he longed to be with them and to see them face to face. Whatever your need is-take it to God in prayer! Be specific! Have a purpose as you speak with God. Sometimes my purpose is simply to praise my Lord and to give Him thanks. Paul also said that he prayed day and night. That means continually.

Use the space below to write a prayer from your heart to God. Include thanksgiving and joy in your prayer. Have a purpose as you write your prayer:

PRAYER: *"Dear God, it is in faith, believing, that I come to you today. I trust you and all that you are and in all that you do. I believe that you have already made a way for me through my struggles. I know that I will be victorious as I continue to trust you. My heart is filled with joy as I think of your great love, mercy and grace extended towards me. Thank-you for loving me."*

Living Abundantly Part 3
Week #3

As we continue studying this biblical teaching of abundant life we must realize that faith is needed, communication with God is needed, but we must also listen to God as He speaks. Listen and receive every word that God says and know that it is truth! This will be the focus of this week's lesson.

So often we can be guilty of hearing but not really listening. Can I get an amen? If you have been a parent you can no doubt remember occasions when you told your son or daughter to do something, only to discover later that the task was left undone. "Why didn't you take care of this?" you asked your child. "I didn't know I was suppose to," may have been the reply. Oh, yes, I remember those times. Yet how often God must feel the same frustrations when we act in the same manner towards His commands for us. My friend, ignorance is no excuse. We have the Word of God. So, I encourage you to not simply hear God's instructions to you but I want you to really listen to what God says. If you really listen, then God's Word will be seen through your life in the manner in which you live.

Listening to and heeding His voice is necessary for you to live in His abundance. I want you to receive **five clear statements from God**. Really listen. Receive these statements as truth from God because they are. Addictions break a person down in many ways. The struggle brings shame, guilt, feelings of low self-value and worthlessness. It is vital that you address the spiritual issues at the root of addiction. You need to know what God says about you. These truths can aid you in your recovery, give you peace and encouragement, and transform your state of mind. Listen as God speaks these truths to you:

Truth #1. "Don't question my love for you. I love you so much that I died for you. Just look at the cross. I did that for you, in your place, so you could be set free from every bondage."

Most people are familiar with **John 3:16, "For God so loved the world that he gave his one and only Son, that whoever believes in him shall not perish but have eternal life."** Here's the foundation for the Christian life! Since God loved you enough to die on the cross, please understand that He loves you in your struggles now.

Romans 8:38-39 (ESV)
"For I am sure that neither death nor life, nor angels nor rulers, nor things present

nor things to come, nor powers, nor height nor depth, nor anything else in all creation, will be able to separate us from the love of God in Christ Jesus our Lord."

What does that verse say to you about how much God loves you right now?

The love of God will never fail you! Isn't that wonderful news? You may feel like everyone else has failed you, and maybe you have even failed yourself, but God doesn't fail in anything, including His love for you. Often people who need help in recovery are ashamed to ask because they feel so undeserving of another chance. Many people spend years trying to make up for some failure in their past. But Jesus reminds us that even the addiction, the lies, and all the past wrongs can't keep Him from loving us. He reminds us in **Jeremiah 31:34** that **"I will forgive their wickedness and will remember their sins no more."**

God says this to you right now!

Truth #2. "Why don't you allow Me to carry your burden? I am here to help you."

We know that recovery is often a difficult journey, and many people grow tired of the fight. There are triggers and temptations that can pull us back into using again. We must always be on guard.

Matthew 11:28

"Come to me, all you who are weary and burdened, and I will give you rest."

Jesus spoke the words recorded above in Matthew 11:28. What does Jesus say He will do for you?

What is our responsibility according to Jesus' words?

Truth #3. "I came to heal the broken-hearted and to set the captives free (Isaiah 61:1, Luke 4:17-21). I want to set YOU free."

Sometimes the thought of maintaining a substance-free life is daunting, just as trying to live life free from lying, cheating, or stealing. Temptation can seem overwhelming. We all have sins that try to weigh us down, and it is a daily struggle to follow God's commands. But life is a lot harder when you don't listen and follow His commands. You know this is true! Through the Holy Spirit, we gain power and strength, and when we fall short, we can remember that God still forgives. Sometimes we may feel like God is far, far away but God's Word teaches us:

Psalm 34:18 (ESV)
"The LORD is near to the brokenhearted and saves the crushed in spirit."

According to the above verse, where is God in your pain?

As Christians we have the Holy Spirit who will empower and guide us, but we have to listen to his urging and humbly follow.

Truth #4. "The thief, Satan, came to steal, kill and destroy, but I came that you would have life abundantly." (John 10:10)

Finally, Jesus tells us that we can have new life through Him. Jesus desires that you experience a life of psychological and spiritual abundance and fulfillment. If you follow His teachings, they will set you free to live the abundant life He wants you to enjoy. He died to offer you access to this abundant life that God has designed you to live. These words are empowering to the addict in recovery, as he faces the daily struggles of life and learns to trust God's will for his life.

The final statement from God that I want you to listen to and receive is:

Truth #5. "I know you are overwhelmed and afraid, but I will bring you peace and stability."

Life can sometimes feel like we are constantly trying to dig our way out of trouble pits we have fallen into. These pits are sometimes created by our own decisions and sometimes not so. In an addiction, stopping the downward spiral is difficult. Each and every day we must be determined to make the right choices that lead to staying sober and moving forward. Caution: Making those decisions when stressed, hopeless, emotional, and mentally foggy usually lead to wrong choices. Peace to think clearly and not make knee-jerk or impulsive decisions is essential to start making one good decision after another.

Has there ever been times in your life that you made a hasty decision that you later regretted?

Reflecting back on those hasty decisions which led to regret, how would you choose differently now?

Isaiah 26:3 (ESV)
"You (God) keep him (addict) in perfect peace whose mind is
stayed (focused) on you (God), because he trusts in you."

Put your trust in God! Stop relying on yourself and stop totally relying on others. Take responsibility for your life. When troubles come, and difficulties arise, turn to our Rock, Jesus the Christ. Lean on Him. Trust Him. Draw closer to Him. Jesus is the rock on which you can build your peace upon. Keep your eyes and mind fixed upon Him and you will have the peace you need to begin a positive climb out of the hole of addiction and into the light of Jesus' love, grace, and freedom!

PRAYER: *"Dear God, my Savior and Lord, I confess that every word from you is true and trustworthy. I accept your truth into my life today. Help me Oh God, to rely on you for all I need to live in freedom from my struggles. I turn to you in my time of need and in my time of great blessing. You and you alone are all I need to experience freedom, peace, purpose and joy in my life. I trust you. In Jesus' name, Amen."*

Building Our Relationship with God
Week #4

"LIFE Ministries has helped me to establish a long term positive relationship with not only God but also with people who have always been there for me when I have struggled. LIFE has also helped my husband and I to remain grounded in Christ. We are more determined now, that we will not remain the same, but we will grow in our faith. Stick with Jesus! He will never ever let you go! Christ is the only way to beat addiction. My family is living proof."

Angela Yvette Holland, Tarboro, N.C.

Recently we have studied how to walk in the abundant life that Jesus has promised to give us. There must be faith, prayer, listening and obeying what God says, and we must have godly goals. Let's build upon this by considering how we can strengthen our relationship with God. None of us have perfectly arrived at the place we need to be. I can look back over my life, considering where I am now, and I can honestly say "I am not always where I need to be spiritually but I am so much more today than I have ever been before." It is my prayer that you can also say that. Is change in your life becoming a reality? If not, this process can begin right now.

A few weeks ago, we discussed the importance of faith in God. This is where our spiritual healing begins as we enter recovery. This however is only the beginning of a life-long change process that the Bible calls "sanctification." This word simply means that we are in the process of change, becoming more like Jesus. I want you to stop and think about your life and ask yourself, "How have I changed because of my faith and God's presence in my life?"

Can you describe some of those changes below? These may be recent changes or changes that you identify over a long-term period. What changes has God brought into your life?

The stronger our relationship with God, or the more intimate that relationship becomes, the more change I will realize in my life. We also know that in order to get to know someone better you must spend time with that person.

Describe below your regular time with God:

As I study the scriptures it seems to me that the strongest people of faith in the Gospels should have been the twelve apostles. These are the guys who spent the most time with Jesus during His short ministry on earth prior to the cross. Yet, we consistently see from the biblical accounts that these men were not always where they should have been spiritually. They struggled with doubts, temptations, and even addictions from time to time. One of those men was named Simon Peter. This man is a great encouragement to me because I can relate to Peter's actions many times. He often acted before carefully thinking through what he was doing. One of the greatest evidences that the Bible is God's Word is that we not only read of the great victories in the lives of the great biblical characters, but we are also given record of their terrible failures. We can learn from those as well. In the final chapters of Matthew's gospel we read of how Jesus was arrested, He faced a mock trial, and He was condemned to die. When Jesus was arrested all His followers fled, including His twelve Apostles! Notice in the verses below what Peter does:

Matthew 26:57-58 (ESV)
"Then those who had seized Jesus led him to Caiaphas the high priest, where the scribes and the elders had gathered. ⁵⁸ And Peter was following him at a distance, as far as the courtyard of the high priest, and going inside he sat with the guards to see the end."

Verse 58 above tells us that Peter followed at a _____.

I sometimes have flashbacks of old songs or old television shows when I study scripture. (I have no clue why). Do you remember the show "Lost in Space?" There was a robot on that show and a boy named Will Robinson. Whenever Will found himself in a dangerous situation the robot would warn, "Danger-Danger-Danger Will Robinson." I hear that message when I read verse 58. Whenever we are distant from God we are placing ourselves in a dangerous place.

Do you know what Peter did next?

Matthew 26:69-74 (ESV)
"Now Peter was sitting outside in the courtyard. And a servant girl came up to him and said, 'You also were with Jesus the Galilean.' ⁷⁰ But he denied it before them all, saying, 'I do not know what you mean.' ⁷¹ And when he went out to the entrance, another servant girl saw him, and she said to the bystanders, 'This man was with Jesus

of Nazareth.' [72] **And again he denied it with an oath: 'I do not know the man.' [73] After a little while the bystanders came up and said to Peter, 'Certainly you too are one of them, for your accent betrays you.' [74] Then he began to invoke a curse on himself and to swear, 'I do not know the man.' And immediately the rooster crowed."**

We could say that Peter experienced a relapse. The term relapse is defined as a turning back to what you have left behind. Peter slipped back and lied, even cursing, that he did not know Jesus.

What do you think was Peter's motivation for relapsing? In other words, why did he act this way?

When we become controlled by fear, worry, or any other emotional response we can easily fall into a state of relapse as well. Let's consider what God says to us about being victorious through these emotional events in life.

James 4:7-10 (ESV)
"Submit yourselves therefore to God. Resist the devil, and he will flee from you. [8] Draw near to God, and he will draw near to you. Cleanse your hands, you sinners, and purify your hearts, you double-minded. [9] Be wretched and mourn and weep. Let your laughter be turned to mourning and your joy to gloom. [10] Humble yourselves before the Lord, and he will exalt you."

#1. DRAW CLOSE TO GOD! Verse 7, 8

Often I hear people quote only part of verse 7 as they will say, "Resist the devil and he will flee from you." However, there is no way you will achieve this unless first of all you apply the first part of that verse. "Submit to God!" This word "submit" is a military term which means "to lineup under the command of your leader." Obey what God is telling you to do! Decide right now that you will draw close to Him. He promises in verse 8 that when we draw close to Him, He will draw near to _____.

How can you draw closer to God?

#2. RESIST THE DEVIL! Verse 7

Do not allow anything to remain in your life that will ultimately pull you away from God. Don't allow the enemy to even get his foot in the door. (For example, keeping a stash thinking, "I won't touch it.") Make a plan right now that will strengthen you to walk in victory!

#3. CLEANSE AND PURIFY YOURSELF! Verse 8

In verse 8 we find mentioned our hands, our hearts, and our minds. Our hands represent our actions. Our hearts represent what we believe. Our minds speak of how we think. Make sure you are believing right, which will lead to thinking right, which results in living right. This requires action and effort from us. Your recovery will require work on your part! Don't think for a minute that you are going to be clean yet it will not require any effort on your part. Don't be double-minded. Have a one-track mind, keeping your mind focused on God and His power at work in your life. This means I do not need to be involved in drinking alcohol, taking drugs, or engaging in past self-destructive practices. Each time I do so the bondage just gets stronger and I am opening myself up for failure.

#4. GET SERIOUS NOW! Verse 9-10

Verse 9 is reminding us that this is serious stuff. Don't play around with sin. There can be no room for lukewarmness in this endeavor to change. Do not make light of your sins of the past by thinking, "Well, it wasn't that bad. It didn't really hurt anyone. It all turned out alright in the end." See through the lies! That addiction that almost destroyed you, hate it, be broken about it now. Acknowledge as you draw close to God that you need Him. Humble yourself.

Matthew 6:33 (ESV)
"But seek first the kingdom of God and his righteousness,
and all these things will be added to you."

Write the above verse, Matthew 6:33, in your own words:

Summarize this lesson below. What did you learn today?

GOOD NEWS: Peter repented of his sin of denying Jesus and Jesus restored him. God also used the failures in Peter's life to make him stronger. We will discuss this more later. Think about how God has used your own failures to make you the person you are today.

PRAYER: "Dear Lord, I have messed up so many times in my life. I am just like Simon Peter in my failures. Help me I pray to draw close to you. I resist the enemy in the name of Jesus. I am now serious about living life in holiness and righteousness. I don't desire to simply be sober but I desire to be all that you desire for me to be. In Jesus' name, Amen."

The Problem With Idols
Week #5

Philippians 4:13 (ESV)
"I can do all things through Him *(Christ)* **who strengthens me."**

We live in an increasing liberal society with decaying morals and blatant rebellion. What was called "wrong" a few years ago is now deemed "acceptable." Many people now want to believe that truth is relative. Some even profess that there are no absolutes. People smugly state, "What is wrong for you may not be wrong for me." This is a clear indication of a civilization of people who are attempting to candy coat their sin and excuse their wrongs. The result is a people barreling off course and now heading at lightning speed away from God and head on into destruction. The Psalmist, referring to those who worship idols, wrote in **Psalm 16:4 (ESV) "The sorrows of those who run after another god shall multiply…"**

Yet idolatry is not only acceptable but it is also encouraged in today's world. It is interesting that one of the most viewed reality television shows in recent years in the United States has been "American Idol." We have become a nation that no longer recognizes there is a Creator and He deserves and commands our worship. Instead of worshipping God as God we have constructed our own false gods who offer us a bogus sense of security and well-being. These idols are not restricted to the United States of America. Idols are everywhere. They are also nothing new. There have been idols as long as there has been sin in the world. Idols have always been a spiritual problem between man and His Creator. We were created to worship God. The Bible declares this to be true.

1 Peter 2:9 (ESV)
"But you are a chosen race, a royal priesthood, a holy nation, a people
for his own possession, that you may proclaim the excellencies of him
who called you out of darkness into his marvelous light."

God declares as recorded in **Isaiah 43:7 (ESV) "everyone who is called by my name, whom I created for my glory, whom I formed and made."** There is an undeniable internal urge within mankind to worship. People attempt to satisfy that urge with activities, things, or people other than the God who created us. When this happens, idols are constructed and erected within the heart. Those idols begin to control and steer that person's life who now becomes an idolater and ultimately even a slave to their own false god.

There are many things that can become idols. In ancient days the Hebrews, who were under Aaron's leadership, melted down their precious metals and formed a golden calf that they began to worship. Once Moses came down off the mountain, with the Ten Commandments in hand, he was outraged that God's people would be guilty of such flagrant idolatry. Moses in his burning anger threw down the two stone tablets breaking them into pieces at the foot of the mountain. He then commanded that the golden calf be burned and crushed into power. In an attempt to teach the people a lesson Moses had the powder deposited into their drinking water (Exodus 32). It is astounding that even under the great leadership of Moses and Aaron, God's people were still pulled toward idolatry. We will indeed worship someone or something as god.

Again, as recorded in 2 Kings 18:4, God's people desired to worship the bronze serpent that Moses had erected for their deliverance from a plague of snakes (Numbers 21). Time and time again we find recorded on the pages of the Holy Bible the problem with idols even among God's people. Idols have always been a problem. They were not simply a problem a thousand years ago but they remain a real and serious problem today. We are created to worship. We need to understand that God is serious concerning His people worshipping only Him. When the Israelites were about to enter into the Land of Canaan God commanded them concerning the pagan and idolatrous people they would encounter.

Exodus 34:13-14 (ESV)
"You shall tear down their altars and break their pillars and cut down their Asherim (for you shall worship no other god, for the LORD, whose name is Jealous, is a jealous God),"

Deuteronomy 4:24 (ESV)
"For the LORD your God is a consuming fire, a jealous God."

The first of the Ten Commandments declares:

Exodus 20:3 (ESV)
"You shall have no other gods before Me." (Exodus 20:3). God is a jealous God.

When we begin to worship someone or something other than God we are giving our allegiance to a false god. False gods cannot bring protection, blessing, or any good thing because they are not gods at all. However, our enemy is a cunning expert at convincing us otherwise.

Every addiction, or spiritual idol, in the heart begins with deceptive messages. The Bible clearly identifies our enemy as a liar and the father of all liars (John 8:44). As the temptation is realized a person begins to believe that a substance, a drug, or even an activity can bring them happiness. This is the enemy's deceptive plan which leads a person into the bondage of drug addiction, alcoholism, and even into pornography and gambling addictions. We begin to tell ourselves, "This will make me feel better." "It isn't hurting anyone." "This will help me forget about my problems." In the end it is realized none of those promises are fulfilled. Instead of happiness there is only sadness. Instead of riches there is abject poverty. Instead of promised peace there is now only guilt and shame. The painful aftermath of addictive behavior has not only now consumed the addict but has also spilled over into the lives of everyone nearby. Tragically, it is usually those that we love the most, those closest to us, who bear the blunt of pain as result of these struggles.

It is not only drug addiction that we are talking about here. Pornography addiction usually begins with the idea that we can control others through images and use them to fulfill our own selfish desires. Too many have discovered that this activity begins to control them instead of them controlling it. This becomes an idol in the person's life. It is an idol that demands more and is never fully satisfied. The addiction draws the addict further down into the pit of despair and self-destruction.

An idol controls a person's thoughts, time, and resources. Isn't this also true of addictions? The addict begins to discover that an increasing amount of time, money, and resources is being directed toward the worship of their false god. The bondage of addiction seeks to consume all that a person is and ever hopes to become. The end result is a trail of broken lives, destroyed reputations, serious health problems, and even death. Addiction is a serious worship disorder.

What should we do with idols according to God?

Joshua 7:13 (ESV)
"Get up! Consecrate the people and say, 'Consecrate yourselves for tomorrow; for thus says the LORD, God of Israel, "There are devoted things in your midst, O Israel. You cannot stand before your enemies until you take away the devoted things from among you.'"

God is commanding us to get rid of the idols! Paul writes under the inspiration of the Holy Spirit and commands us to run from idols. Paul writes in **1 Corinthians 10:14 (ESV), "Therefore, my beloved, flee from idolatry."** Instead of running toward these idols we should run away from them! Our hearts are naturally turned away from our God. We so easily find ourselves moving in the wrong direction. Rebellion comes to the surface through our idolatrous affections. God is however very serious concerning this issue. What's the consequence if we don't flee these idols? What will happen if we continue on our rebellious path away from the worship of the one true God?

1 Corinthians 6:9-10 (ESV)

"Or do you not know that the unrighteous will not inherit the kingdom of God? Do not be deceived: neither the sexually immoral, nor idolaters, nor adulterers, nor men who practice homosexuality, nor thieves, nor the greedy, nor drunkards, nor revilers, nor swindlers will inherit the kingdom of God."

Idolatry is evidence of a heart that has not fully surrendered to the Lordship of Jesus Christ. It could also be evidence of an unregenerate heart. This issue must be dealt with if you desire to live the life that God desires for you. You must cast down those idols. This can only be accomplished through the power of the Gospel. It is not enough to simply stop ungodly behavior but we must replace it with godliness. We must stop bowing down and worshipping the false gods, whatever form they may take, and begin worshipping only God. This is the purpose for which you were created. It's only in fulfilling your intended purpose that you will find real life. Are you ready to begin?

"The Problem With Idols"
Week #5 assignment "Identifying Our Idols"

As recorded in John 4 Jesus was traveling through the region of Samaria when He came upon a well where He stopped to get a drink of water. It was here that Jesus, a Jew, met a Samaritan woman and He engaged her in a true recovery conversation.

John 4:7-30 (ESV)

Jesus said to her, "Give me a drink." [8] (For his disciples had gone away into the city to buy food.) [9] The Samaritan woman said to him, "How is it that you, a Jew, ask for a drink from me, a woman of Samaria?" (For Jews have no dealings with Samaritans.) [10] Jesus answered her, "If you knew the gift of God, and who it is that is saying to you, 'Give me a drink,' you would have asked him, and he would have given you living water." [11] The woman said to him, "Sir, you have nothing to draw water with, and the well is deep. Where do you get that living water? [12] Are you greater than our father Jacob? He gave us the well and drank from it himself, as did his sons and his livestock." [13] Jesus said to her, "Everyone who drinks of this water will be thirsty again, [14] but whoever drinks of the water that I will give him will never be thirsty again. The water that I will give him will become in him a spring of water welling up to eternal life." [15] The woman said to him, "Sir, give me this water, so that I will not be thirsty or have to come here to draw water." [16] Jesus said to her, "Go, call your husband, and come here." [17] The woman answered him, "I have no husband." Jesus said to her, "You are right in saying, 'I have no husband'; [18] for you have had five husbands, and the one you now have is not your husband. What you have said is true." [19] The woman said to him, "Sir, I perceive that you are a prophet. [20] Our fathers worshiped on this mountain, but you say that in Jerusalem is the place where people ought to worship." [21] Jesus said to her, "Woman, believe me, the hour is coming when neither on this mountain nor in Jerusalem will you worship the Father. [22] You worship what you do not know; we worship what we know, for salvation is from the Jews. [23] But the hour is coming, and is now here, when the true worshipers will worship the Father in spirit and truth, for the Father is seeking such people to worship him. [24] God is spirit, and those who worship him must worship in spirit and truth." [25] The woman said to him, "I know that Messiah is coming (he who is called Christ). When he comes, he will tell us all things." [26] Jesus said to her, "I who speak to you am he." [27] Just then his disciples came back. They marveled that he was talking with a woman, but no one said, "What do you seek?" or, "Why are you talking with her?" [28] So the woman left her water jar and went

away into town and said to the people, ²⁹ "Come, see a man who told me all that I ever did. Can this be the Christ?" ³⁰ They went out of the town and were coming to him.

From the biblical account above (John 4:1-30) what would you identify as the woman's idol?

Jesus offered this woman a gift. It wasn't going to cost her anything. This gift is free. What was it that Jesus offered her?

This same free gift is available to you but you must know what the gift is. How would you describe this gift offered to you today?

This woman at the well identified Jesus as a "Jew" in verse 9 and then as a "prophet" in verse 19. As the story progresses she finally comes to understand He is more than a Jewish prophet. According to verse 29 who does she begin to see Jesus as?

Mark 10:17-27 (ESV)

And as he was setting out on his journey, a man ran up and knelt before him and asked him, "Good Teacher, what must I do to inherit eternal life?" ¹⁸ And Jesus said to him, "Why do you call me good? No one is good except God alone. ¹⁹ You know the commandments: 'Do not murder, Do not commit adultery, Do not steal, Do not bear false witness, Do not defraud, Honor your father and mother.'" ²⁰ And he said to him, "Teacher, all these I have kept from my youth." ²¹ And Jesus, looking at him, loved him, and said to him, "You lack one thing: go, sell all that you have and give to the poor, and you will have treasure in heaven; and come, follow me." ²² Disheartened by the saying, he went away sorrowful, for he had great possessions. ²³ And Jesus looked around and said to his disciples, "How difficult it will be for those who have wealth to enter the kingdom of God!" ²⁴ And the disciples were amazed at his words. But Jesus said to them again, "Children, how difficult

it is to enter the kingdom of God! ²⁵ It is easier for a camel to go through the eye of a needle than for a rich person to enter the kingdom of God." ²⁶ And they were exceedingly astonished, and said to him, "Then who can be saved?" ²⁷ Jesus looked at them and said, "With man it is impossible, but not with God. For all things are possible with God.

From the biblical account above (Mark 10:17-27) what would you identify as the young man's idol?

What was this man's response when Jesus required him to turn from his idol?

How did this young man identify Jesus?

Who do you say that Jesus is?

Whatever is most important to you becomes your god. For many people they value their children more than anything, or their profession, or their hobby, or their spouse, but many worship self. God has created us to worship Him. If we worship anything or anyone other than Him, we are involved in idolatry. Idols must be cast down and turned away from. God promised His people that they would live in the land of Canaan, the Promised Land. In order to do so there were many enemies that would first need to be conquered. Those enemies worshipped idols, graven images. God warned them:

Deuteronomy 7:25-26 (ESV)
"The carved images of their gods you shall burn with fire. You shall not covet the silver or the gold that is on them or take it for yourselves, lest you be ensnared by it, for it is an abomination to the LORD your God. ²⁶ And you shall not bring an abominable thing into your house and become devoted to destruction like it. You shall utterly detest and abhor it, for it is devoted to destruction."

Identify some of the idols in your past. What are some of those things that you have allowed to control your life?

Make the decision right now to turn from those idols and turn your heart toward God. Write your prayer below that expresses your desire to worship only God. Ask God to forgive you and to help you leave those idols in the past as you begin to worship only Him:

PRAYER: *"My Lord God, right now I denounce any idols in my life. I am ready to cast those idols down right now. My desire is to worship only you. You are the only one true God. I have been created to worship you with my life. This is my heart's desire. I live to worship only you. In Jesus' name, Amen."*

We All Have a Story to Tell
Week #6

Ephesians 2:8-9 (NKJV)
"For by grace you have been saved through faith, and that not of yourselves;
it is the gift of God, not of works, lest anyone should boast."

If you are reading this, chances are you or someone you know, is struggling in the bondage of addiction. There is hope. The hope for freedom is offered through the power of God in the Person of Jesus. As the children of Israel were taken into bondage through slavery in Babylon, God spoke these words through the prophet Jeremiah: **"For I know the thoughts that I think toward you, says the LORD, thoughts of peace and not of evil, to give you a future and a hope." (Jeremiah 29:11 NKJV).** Those are God's words to you today. God desires to give you forgiveness and a new start. That new beginning can begin right now. It will not be easy BUT you can be set free and become a new person.

I know God can give you all that you need to be delivered. First of all, I know this is true because God promises to give us freedom and deliverance. God cannot lie (Numbers 23:19 NKJV). The Psalmist declared **"He is my loving God and my fortress, my stronghold and my deliverer, my shield, in whom I take refuge, who subdues peoples under me." (Psalm 144:2 NKJV).** There are many other promises recorded in the Holy Bible which we will study together in the coming chapters. These promises are from *God*! God's Word is always true and faithful.

Secondly, I also know from personal experience that God can deliver you. It was on a cold winter night in 1988 that God reached down and pulled my soul out from the pit of alcohol and drug addiction. Since that time, I have chosen to walk in deliverance and freedom in the power of the Holy Spirit who lives within me. There has been temptation, but I have chosen to be victorious over these. Do not tell yourself that you can't be set free. Listen my friend, God has not changed! **Hebrews 13:8** declares **"Jesus Christ is the same yesterday, today, and forevermore."** He is the same God with the same power for you as He is for me. Just as He has delivered me, He can deliver you. God shows no favoritism. It is God's desire that you walk in freedom and that you begin right now.

I know we all have a story to tell. Each one who has been touched by the invisible hand of almighty God knows the undeniable power that God offers for the believing sinner. It is my prayer that God can use a small part of my story, along with His infallible truths of Scripture, to speak to your heart. I pray that you will allow Him to transform you as we listen to His voice through this lesson. I give God all the glory, praise, and credit for what has taken place within me. This wonderful new life that I have received through Christ is what I desire for you as well. It is not only *available* for you, but God desires for you to *make it yours.*

My life has not always been a joyful experience. I have made many mistakes and chosen foolishness over godly wisdom many times over the years. There is so much in my past that I wish I could simply erase from my memory forever. Maybe you feel that way as well. Are there hidden skeletons in your closet—things which have happened in your life that you would never desire others to know? Some of these events in my past I had kept secret for many years. Some of these are shameful and to be honest I had never planned on ever telling this story. That is until the Holy Spirit taught me a very valuable lesson: God is so mighty and awesome that He can use even my failures and all of my past mistakes for His glory. What a mighty God we serve! He can use not only the good things in our lives but also those things that were meant to harm and even destroy us. Trust God with your story!

I also know that as I share what God has done, my heart is healed a bit more. We all need healing. We all yearn for freedom from our past mistakes and deliverance from the wickedness the enemy has thrown at us. Jesus promised that the Truth would bring us freedom (John 8:32). Truth is found in God. God is Truth. He is the giver of life and everything "good and perfect." **James 1:17 (NKJV)** reminds me that **"every good gift and every perfect gift is from above, and comes down from the Father of lights, with Whom there is no variation or shadow of turning."** I have found in God, through the Gospel of Christ, a good and blessed life. What a good God we serve! Many times in our church fellowship we will shout in unison, "God is good all the time! All the time God is good!"

As I look back over my life, I realize how God in His goodness has used every event in my past to draw me unto Himself. I must confess, I am not always all that I should be, even now, but I am so much more than I have ever been before. God has brought into my heart healing from the past, strength for the present, and a blessed hope for the future. It is my prayer that you too, experience this transformation.

We all have the same problem. It is not that some have a sickness which causes them to become addicts. Our problem is *sin* sickness. We are all sinners (Romans 3:23). Notice that my use of the word *sin* is in the singular and not the plural. Our greatest dilemma is not brought upon us because of the *sins* we commit, but rather from the inherently sinful nature that we all possess. The simple yet horrifying reality is that we are all born into a sin-cursed world with sinful hearts within. My heart was naturally turned away from God and against the life that only He offers. As a result, there was much loneliness, despair and pain within me, even as a child growing up in rural North Carolina.

My father was self-employed in his own heating and air conditioning business, located right beside our home. My dad was a hard worker and usually very busy maintaining his business. If he was at home he was usually resting, reading the newspaper, or watching the news. Often my dad received phone calls after hours which took him away on service calls to repair someone's heating or air conditioning unit. He was a good man who provided well for our family.

My father passed away on July 14, 1985 from a series of major heart attacks when I was twenty-four years old. There have been countless times that I have wished I could have rolled back time and enjoyed a closer relationship with my dad. There seemed to have been a great distance between us for most of my older childhood. I know that much of this distance was created as a result of my own rebellious attitude and foolish decisions. Indeed, my sinful heart had a way of drawing out my dad's faults which were usually expressed toward me in anger and frustration.

I am not a victim, nor do I blame anyone for the choices I have made personally. I was an adolescent boy in pain, empty inside and struggling to find my place in this world. My heart was screaming out for someone to just love me and affirm value and worth in me.

The enemy sent people into my life, into my pain, who influenced me into seeking comfort and relief through drugs and alcohol. There was much pain deep within me which I did not understand how to cope with. By the age of sixteen, I was huffing industrial chemicals, stealing and abusing valium, smoking, and even growing and selling marijuana. I thought I hated anyone in authority over me. As a seventeen-year-old, I had already been arrested, taken to jail for driving under the influence, had totaled my brother's car, lost my driving privileges because of fifteen traffic violations, was involved in all sorts of crimes-*and I really didn't care.* There was such an overwhelming darkness in my life, birthed deep within my heart and it was threatening to consume my very existence.

One evening, while at a friend's home, I stole half a bottle of his mother's valium. That night I ingested fifteen 10-mg valium pills, not really caring if I ever woke up again. In my perception of things, life seemed empty, useless, and too painful to offer any lasting hope of actually being something good. I do not remember anything else about that night of partying. The next thing I knew it was twenty hours later and I was facing my devastated mother and my enraged father who were now threatening to send me away to a reform school. I could not remember how I even made it home or what I had done the previous day or night. I later learned that my *friends* had loaded me into the trunk of a car and then dumped me in my front yard the night before. I could have died that night and my friends seemed to be oblivious to the dangers we were continually exposing ourselves to. My life was spiraling out of control.

I wish I could tell you that this event in my life convinced me that I needed help. It *did* unsettle me, however change would not be realized in my life until several years later. There were many times over those years of drugs and alcohol abuse that I promised myself I was going to change, turn over a new leaf, and become a better person. I remember many mornings waking up in a hangover, filled with regrets and shame, longing for my life to be different. I would try to be a better person but the results were always the same agonizing disappointment as I would very quickly slip right back into my old habits time after time. *Maybe this is where you are in your struggles? Have you failed in your past attempts to experience lasting change? Please continue reading because there is power available that can bring you to deliverance and healing.*

I wanted everyone to just leave me alone. I wished my parents would get off my back. I wanted the police to just give me a break. I did not want anyone telling me what to do or what I shouldn't be doing.

At the age of nineteen I saw a way out from under my dad's authority, marriage. I thought this would fulfill me and give me what I needed to have joy, peace and purpose. I married a childhood sweetheart who was only fifteen years old. Her father had to sign for her to get married because she was under the legal age in the state of North Carolina. I immediately moved out of my parent's home and into the home of my bride's father. My life continued as usual with one hang over after another. Following the birth of our child, our 3 year marriage ended in divorce.

At the age of twenty-two my life hit rock bottom. My wife had left me, our marriage was over, and my life was in shambles. The hopelessness in my heart plunged me into a dark emotional place where I began using drugs in a manner I had promised myself I never would. I began using a needle to shoot up cocaine intravenously. I thank God that He gave me enough sense that I realized I was headed for certain ruin and a premature death. Some of my drug buddies had already died. Some from overdoses and some were dying from the HIV/AIDS virus because of contaminated needles. I was still hurting, confused and even more lonely than ever before.

Into my painful existence God sent a special woman, Melissa, and in 1985 we were married. My substance abuse continued, however, and just two years into our marriage we were struggling to keep it all together. My mother has always been God's instrument in my life to point me back towards God and God has used her in a tremendous way to bring me to where I am today. Even after all the pain I had caused my mother through my teenage years and into young adulthood she was still there reminding me that God was waiting for my total surrender. My wife, Melissa, and I knew we needed a power beyond ourselves to heal our hearts and to save our marriage. Upon my mother's urging we visited her church for a midweek prayer meeting. It was in that service that the Holy Spirit broke through the hardness of our hearts. I remember an overwhelming sense of love and mercy just flooding over me that night. It was strangely comforting but also very violent within me. Walls of bitterness and pain were being demolished in the power of the Holy

Spirit. Melissa and I, kneeling together at the altar in brokenness, weeping and desperately attempting to speak words through the tears that were soaking the carpet beneath us, surrendered to Christ and received a forgiveness that we had never thought possible. Yes, there was a battle for our hearts that evening in that service, a battle that was victoriously won by God as He drew us to Himself.

I will never forget the flood of emotions that I experienced as that altar time ended. I don't know if we were kneeling for just a few minutes or several, but I did know we had been changed and our lives were now different somehow. For the first time in my life there was an overwhelming presence of love and hope within my soul. A great burden was lifted and an indescribable peace was realized at last. I knew when I rose to my feet that this twenty-seven-year-old man had received new power. I had been given power to change, power to love, power to forgive, the power of God to do what I had failed so many times to accomplish. Since that night in 1988 I have never turned back. I have been drug-free since that wonderful night when God touched me and filled me with His Spirit.

What made the difference between that night and all the other times in my life that I had attempted change? This time I was no longer looking to myself for the strength I needed. My past had taught me that *my* strength was not enough. Now I was totally relying upon God and I had finally opened my heart to the eternal impact of the Gospel of Christ. I understood in my inner man that Christ had not only died *for* me but *as* me. He was buried in a tomb in my place. Then on the third day, Jesus arose from the dead victorious over death, hell, and the grave. He did all this in my place, as my substitute! This was not only accomplished for me but as me. All I needed to do was place my faith in Christ, who is the Gospel, and my life would never be the same.

The Power of the Gospel is a soul-saving, life-changing, eternally-transforming power and that power is available to you right now. God's gift can bring you peace and healing. There is victorious power available for you through Christ's death, burial, and resurrection. Jesus did not die just so your sins could be forgiven. The Gospel of our Lord is also about living in the present. It is my sincere prayer that as you proceed through the following studies, you will have a responsive heart toward God as He does His work in your life. In your flesh you will only fail. In our resurrected Christ victory can be yours.

PRAYER: "Dear God in Heaven, thank-you for already writing my story of deliverance and recovery. I acknowledge that you are a good and gracious God who has a marvelous plan for my life. I know that in my own strength I will fail. I need you and your power to change. Please fill me with your presence. Help me to renew my mind with your truth. I desire and long for your story to come to pass in my life. In Jesus' name, Amen."

"We All Have a Story To Tell"
Week #6 assignment

Everyone has a story to tell. We have all had pain in our lives that we have had to face and overcome. I want you to write out your story below. Include those events in your life that have shaped you into the person you are today:

Be blessed by reading the testimony of a long-term LIFE member who is now living in victory, healed and delivered from his addictions:

The Testimony of Toney Maryland
Edgecombe County LIFE Chapter member

My name is Toney Maryland. My life before I surrendered was miserable and unstable. I felt like it was me against the world. I started drinking and smoking weed when I was around sixteen years old. At around nineteen this slowly progressed to smoking crack. I thought I was blending in with the crowd, that I was around, trying not to be different. I use to love to drink and get high. As the years passed by I got worse, so did my nerves. I worked during the day and chased drugs and girls into the wee hours of the morning. I lied on a daily basis, cheated when I could, and stole when the time was right. I told myself that I didn't need any help and that I could handle this. I told myself that I could slow down when I wanted to and stop when I got ready. I was bold and hard-headed. I only prayed when things got bad. I was stubborn, miserable, and regretful because I knew I was throwing my life away but I didn't care. I just wanted to smoke crack…A night stalker, I was.

I came to the point of surrender when I got tired of the cycle that I was in. I felt like I was a hamster in a cage on one of those spinning wheels. I got to the point that I had to admit that I had a problem. Plus, my marriage was going downhill. My wife was going to leave me if I didn't get help. I was tired and miserable and desperately needing a change. It was at that point that I surrendered my life to God. I was clean for two weeks when my wife, Kim, found L.I.F.E. Ministries. I have been attending ever since my first Tuesday night visit.

My life since trusting God can be described as free, humble, and thankful. My eyes are open to the world that I use to live in. My thought patterns have changed. I am filled with His Holy Spirit! God has renewed my strength. The LORD has brought me from darkness into light. My wife and I are finally together as one. I thank God for His grace and His mercy. In the mighty name of Jesus, He has delivered me!

AMEN! Toney Maryland, Rocky Mount, N.C.

Rahab's Rehab
Week #7

Here I am a Pastor of over 29 years and I am still amazed at what God has chosen to do in my life. It doesn't even seem like that was me years ago living under the chains of addiction. God has brought me from darkness into His glorious kingdom of light. Thinking back to my teenage years, I am certain that no one within my graduating class of 1979 would have ever imagined that I would one day be a minister of the Gospel. It is amazing to see whom God chooses for service in His kingdom. People tend to select those individuals whose appearance—looks, height, build—meets their standards. Ability and intelligence also play a part in the selection process. The best and the brightest are assumed to be the right individuals for the important tasks. In some cases, one's family name may be the factor in whether or not an individual receives a particular opportunity. Listen to what God tells you:

Isaiah 55:8-9 (NKJV)
⁸ "For My thoughts *are* not your thoughts,
Nor *are* your ways My ways," says the LORD.
⁹ For *as* the heavens are higher than the earth,
So are My ways higher than your ways,
And My thoughts than your thoughts."

Our God is so amazing! He doesn't use the same standards that the world does in choosing the people that He will work through. Such is the example of a woman named Rahab whose story we find recorded in the Book of Joshua. The title of this study is "Rahab's Rehab." Rahab was a harlot, a prostitute, living in Jericho, on the eastern edge of Canaan near the Jordan River. The amazing thing about Rahab is that she is in the lineage, the family line, of Jesus! God chose a prostitute to be in the same family heritage as the Messiah! Wow!

Now the word "rehab" is a word that refers to the process of helping someone become healthy. Let's see how God moved in the life of Rahab to bring her to health and well-being spiritually. How could God rehabilitate someone like Rahab?

Now, to set the text in context, Jericho was a major city in Canaan. It was a double-walled city with a population of about 3000 people. Jericho was a mighty fortress. Yet, this was the first city that the Israelites would conquer, under the leadership of Joshua, in taking possession of the Promised Land. First, Israel's great military leader Joshua, sent spies into Jericho:

Joshua 2:1-7 (ESV)

And Joshua the son of Nun sent two men secretly from Shittim as spies, saying, "Go, view the land, especially Jericho." And they went and came into the house of a prostitute whose name was Rahab and lodged there. ² And it was told to the king of Jericho, "Behold, men of Israel have come here tonight to search out the land." ³ Then the king of Jericho sent to Rahab, saying, "Bring out the men who have come to you, who entered your house, for they have come to search out all the land." ⁴ But the woman had taken the two men and hidden them. And she said, "True, the men came to me, but I did not know where they were from. ⁵ And when the gate was about to be closed at dark, the men went out. I do not know where the men went. Pursue them quickly, for you will overtake them." ⁶ But she had brought them up to the roof and hid them with the stalks of flax that she had laid in order on the roof. ⁷ So the men pursued after them on the way to the Jordan as far as the fords. And the gate was shut as soon as the pursuers had gone out.

God had promised this land to Israel. Now everything was ready for Israel to conquer and take possession of the Promised Land. At this point it appears God hadn't given Joshua any specific directions or battle plan. Being a military man, Joshua understood the need for inside information prior to attacking. So, Joshua sent two men to secretly gather information about the land and the city of Jericho. Upon arriving in Jericho, they stayed at the home of Rahab.

Here's a good question; "Why would these men go to the house of a prostitute?" At first this seems questionable to say the least. Allow me to set your mind at ease. Many women in this profession would have rooms for rent. Her services would be offered to those who stayed in her lodging if they so desired. Also, what could have been a better disguise than for two men to stay in the home of a prostitute? It seems to have been a good cover. However, it was not good enough because word of the spies' arrival came to the King and the King sent messengers to Rahab to question her. Would she obey the king of her city or take the risk of hiding the men who represented Israel? She decided to protect the Israelites, but what would she say in response to the king's men? Well, there is no way around it, she lied. So, this woman is guilty of sin in more than one way. She was a prostitute and a liar. However, God brings to Rahab rehab.

Rahab hides the spies on the roof among the bundles of flax that were there drying in the sun. She then sends the King's messengers on a wild goose chase through her lying. Nowhere does God condone lying. Although the result was the safety of the spies, God could have protected them with Rahab telling the truth instead. However, before we pass judgement upon Rahab we should be honest, there are many imperfections that God is still getting out of each one of us as Christians too.

Notice what happens next:

Joshua 2:8-11 (ESV)
"Before the men lay down, she came up to them on the roof
⁹ and said to the men, 'I know that the LORD has given you the land, and that the fear of
you has fallen upon us, and that all the inhabitants of the land melt away before you.
¹⁰ For we have heard how the LORD dried up the water of the Red Sea before you when
you came out of Egypt, and what you did to the two kings of the Amorites who were
beyond the Jordan, to Sihon and Og, whom you devoted to destruction. ¹¹ And as soon
as we heard it, our hearts melted, and there was no spirit left in any man because of you,
for the LORD your God, he is God in the heavens above and on the earth beneath.'"

In her process of rehab, what was it that concerned Rahab, regarding God? (verse 9)

What concerns you as you think of God?

What great event in the past concerning God's intervention for His people did Rahab reflect upon? (verse 10):

What was Rahab's response to God's greatness? (verse 11):

Rahab makes a great confession of whom she knows God to be in verse 11. She refers to God as the God in the _____ above and on the _____ beneath.

Think about God's intervention in your life. List ways that you see God's hand actively involved in your past:

As you remember God's great involvement in your life in the past, how does that help you see your future?

Rahab continued her conversation with the spies:

Joshua 2:12-13 (ESV)

**"Now then, please swear to me by the LORD that, as I have dealt kindly
with you, you also will deal kindly with my father's house, and give me a
sure sign ¹³ that you will save alive my father and mother, my brothers and
sisters, and all who belong to them, and deliver our lives from death."**

Another step in her rehab is that Rahab asked for mercy for her and her family. Mercy is not getting what we deserve. She also asked to be delivered from death. Jesus offers both of these blessings! Mercy and deliverance. Those bring us to good health spiritually.

Joshua 2:14-21 (ESV)

**"And the men said to her, 'Our life for yours even to death! If you do not tell this business
of ours, then when the LORD gives us the land we will deal kindly and faithfully with
you.' ¹⁵ Then she let them down by a rope through the window, for her house was built
into the city wall, so that she lived in the wall. ¹⁶ And she said to them, 'Go into the
hills, or the pursuers will encounter you, and hide there three days until the pursuers
have returned. Then afterward you may go your way.' ¹⁷ The men said to her, 'We will be
guiltless with respect to this oath of yours that you have made us swear. ¹⁸ Behold, when
we come into the land, you shall tie this scarlet cord in the window through which you
let us down, and you shall gather into your house your father and mother, your brothers,
and all your father's household. ¹⁹ Then if anyone goes out of the doors of your house
into the street, his blood shall be on his own head, and we shall be guiltless. But if a
hand is laid on anyone who is with you in the house, his blood shall be on our head. ²⁰
But if you tell this business of ours, then we shall be guiltless with respect to your oath**

that you have made us swear.' ²¹ And she said, 'According to your words, so be it.' Then she sent them away, and they departed. And she tied the scarlet cord in the window."

Rahab helped the spies escape by way of a rope out of her window because her dwelling was up high on the inside of the city wall. The spies made a promise that they would order the invading Israelites not to harm her or her family as long as they stayed inside their dwelling. The way the Israelites would be able to identify her house would be the scarlet cord she was to hang outside her window.

Did she believe the promise given to her by the spies? _____

How do you know?

What has God promised you?

What should be your response?

Rahab's rehab included growing in her understanding of who God was, what God had done, and the faithfulness of His Word. The rest of the story finds the Israelites taking Jericho captive and sparing Rahab and her family. However, that was not the only blessing that Rahab received. She was allowed to continue to live in the land and was incorporated into God's people. This is not the picture of an outcast being tolerated. No, Rahab was a woman who, by faith and action, bravely made a commitment to God and His people. She had heard of Israel's God and His mighty works, and when the opportunity arose, she began her walk of faith by the risky business of hiding the spies and aiding in their escape.

This is what happens within us when we accept Christ! As we understand who God is, what He has done, and His faithfulness to His Word we begin our rehab as well. Who is God? He is our Creator, our Savior, our Sustainer. He has all we need. When we cry out for mercy from Him we receive that mercy freely. What has God done? He has sent His only begotten Son to die in our place and rise again from the dead so that we can be forgiven. (John 3:16). What does the faithfulness of His Word do for your rehab? Understand that everything God has promised He is more than able to fulfill.

Rahab was a Canaanite, a prostitute, a liar, and so underserving of anything good from God. Yet the one thing that brought about her transformation was she had faith in a God who loved her. Oh yes, that scarlet cord hanging outside her window represented Jesus. He is our salvation. The cross is our scarlet cord. We discover the same blessings that Rahab experienced as we come by faith to the cross. We experience:

C ontinual love

R edeeming blood

O vercoming power

S ustaining strength

S upernatural compassion

> **Hebrews 11:31 (ESV)**
> **"By faith Rahab the prostitute did not perish with those who were disobedient, because she had given a friendly welcome to the spies."**

God's rehab offers us:

A place among God's people

Deliverance from judgement

A life secure and fulfilling

PRAYER: "God, please help me to learn the lessons from you that will enable me to live my life for you. I realize that I am in the process of change. I yield to you and your divine work. I desire the blessings that flow from a life transformed by you. Have your way, I pray. In Jesus' name, Amen."

First Things First
Week #8

Romans 1:16 (ESV)
"For I am not ashamed of the gospel, for it is the power of God for salvation
to everyone who believes, to the Jew first and also to the Greek."

Maybe you have already unsuccessfully attempted to change many times. You may be wondering, just as I was, where you should even begin this time. There must be a greater plan, a stronger power, than what you have attempted in the past. Sincerity has not been enough. Trying harder has brought only one failed attempt after another. Maybe you have even utilized rehab programs and detox facilities, only to find yourself falling right back into those relentless habits.

Proverbs 14:12 (NKJV) reminds us,
"There is a way that seems right to a man, but its end is the way of death."

If all of man's ways and plans have failed you in your attempts to break free from addiction, take heart my friend, for there is a greater power available.

God has given to us a Book which teaches us how to overcome sin in our lives and how to walk victoriously in this world. I know your heart longs for that victory. Our journey begins with this question; **"Where do you stand in relationship with God?"** This is where we must begin. If you are sincere about desiring lasting change in your life, there is a wonderful hope for you. This hope will not be found in your intelligence or strength, nor is it offered by the worldly experts among us. We must take first things first.

If you desire God's power to change you must first receive that power into your life. What does God say needs to happen in order for us to be right with Him? The Book of Romans is a great place to begin answering this very important question. God spoke through the Apostle Paul to write the Book of Romans. In fact, of the twenty-seven books which are found in the New Testament, God chose Paul to write at least thirteen of those books. What an honor that God chose Paul to write at least half of the New Testament! Paul was a person just like you and I. Paul was a flesh-and-blood man, with sinful tendencies that pulled at him constantly. This great Apostle was not created as some *superman* able to accomplish things that are unattainable for us.

You might not be aware of it but Paul was a recovered addict as well. He really was! Here was a man who was addicted to manmade religion before he came to know Christ. Paul, previously referred to as Saul in the scriptures, bowed down and worshipped the idol of religion before Christ saved him on the road to Damascus. Paul confessed that he was among the most religious:

Philippians 3:5-6 NKJV

"circumcised the eighth day, of the stock of Israel, of the tribe of Benjamin, a Hebrew of the Hebrews; concerning the law, a Pharisee; concerning zeal, persecuting the church; concerning the righteousness which is in the law, blameless."

Religion had become Paul's drug of choice and it controlled his life. He persecuted the church as a very religious man, but he was wrong. Following his salvation experience Paul became a giant of the Christian faith. You can read of Paul's salvation experience in Acts 9. God could now use him not only to write much of the New Testament, but also to plant several New Testament churches in different parts of the world. It is amazing what great things God did in and through this man's life once he stopped looking to his own power and simply trusted Christ instead.

You, too, will be amazed at what God will do in your life once you surrender your all to Him. God used Paul to write the Book of Romans which contains the most complete summary of Christian doctrine found in any one book in the Holy Bible. In the Book of Romans, you will find answers to questions such as: *How can I experience true freedom in my life? How does a person receive forgiveness and salvation from God? How is this forgiveness even possible? Who does God desire to save? What does God's salvation really mean for me in my own personal struggles?* The Holy Spirit, through Paul, teaches us the crucial answers to those soul stirring questions. This is where we must begin by placing first things first. What is your own personal response to the Gospel of Jesus Christ?

The Book of Romans lays out for us a road that we can follow to receive forgiveness and the power leading to real and lasting change. Today, as I was awakened in the very early morning hours, I was reminded of how God's power is so available to us, and yet so often hindered. Suddenly my electric fan turned off. Our air conditioner stopped. There was an eerie silence suddenly engulfing and filling our home. We had suffered a residential loss of electrical power. I would later learn that a tree had fallen on a nearby power line and knocked out our electricity for a brief time. Although I was aware that our source of electricity was disabled, I still found myself habitually flipping on light switches and adjusting the thermostat. Obviously, each time I received the same response-nothing happened!

The reason that I had failed so many times to walk away from the addictions that held my heart captive was because I was experiencing a power failure. It did not matter how many times I tried I did not have the power to make the needed changes last. I was flipping the switches, trying to change, but each time nothing happened. Like the electricity flowing back through the power lines once my power was restored, I needed power to flow through me. This power had to come from a greater source than within myself. I needed a greater power. I received that power when at the age of twenty-seven, I surrendered to Christ, giving Him my all. I began to look to Jesus for everything I needed. God instantly repaired what had hindered me from walking in victory. My sins are now forgiven and His Holy Spirit power has come to dwell within my mortal body forever. This became a blessed reality for me the moment I gave Christ full surrender. Oh, God is still repairing Mike Dixon, but now I have the power I need for that change to continue to be reality for me.

I ask you, "Do you really want to be set free? Do you really desire to stop hurting those who love you? Do you want the power to be the person God desires?" This doesn't come through willpower or the gaining of more knowledge, or through meditation, or through man's schemes and empty promises. There are no twelve steps or ten steps that will magically deliver you. Like me, you only need to take one step towards a Savior who is more than enough to meet your need. If you want this power to walk in victory I urge you to lay aside your doubts, stop making excuses, and open your heart to God.

Holy Spirit power is not given to everyone, but anyone can receive Him. I must make it clear that I am not talking about repeating a prayer or simply knowing in your mind information concerning who Jesus is. I am speaking of full surrender to God Who right now is drawing you through the power of His Spirit to Himself. This is where we must take first things first. Will you take this one step toward victory?

The Bible teaches that only those who believe in Jesus as their Lord receive the Holy Spirit.

1 John 4:15 (NKJV)
"Whoever confesses that Jesus is the Son of God, God abides in him, and he in God."

John 14:17 (NKJV)
"the Spirit of truth, whom the world cannot receive, because it neither sees Him
nor knows Him; but you know Him, for He dwells with you and will be in you."

So, as we begin, let us deal with first things first. What does it mean to believe in Jesus and to know God? You must understand these truths. Let us ask God right now through prayer to speak to our hearts as we examine His Word.

Please understand:

#1. We all have the same problem, we are sinners.

Romans 3:10-12 (NKJV)
"There is none righteous, no, not one; There is none who understands; There is none who seeks after God. They have all turned aside; They have together become unprofitable; There is none who does good, no, not one."

Romans 3:23 (NKJV)
"for all have sinned and fall short of the glory of God..."

God originally created everything in perfection. Adam and Eve, the first man and woman, were created in God's image. Then Satan slithered into that perfect sinless environment bringing with him temptation. Adam and Eve disobeyed God and as a result every person born through Adam's lineage has this germ of sin flowing through his veins. Every person born, with the exception of Jesus, was born through the line of Adam. There have been several scientific DNA studies conducted over the years that offer proof that all of mankind share a common ancestor.

We are all born with a soul, or inner man, that wants to be self-centered and self-consuming because of sin. Need an example? We have all witnessed, or even experienced, a small toddler in a department store's toy section throwing a fit because mommy told him he could not have the toy. That behavior was not learned, but was instilled within that child even before birth. The Apostle Paul put it this way:

Romans 7:15(NKJV)
"For what I am doing, I do not understand. For what I will to do, that I do not practice; but what I hate, that I do."

Doesn't Paul sound as if he were in the midst of an agonizing mental breakdown or suffering from bipolar disorder? No! What he is saying is simply, "I find it so easy to do wrong (sin) and so difficult to do right." To do just what comes naturally for us is to sin. Our natural man is prone to lead us in the wrong direction. We all have this problem because it is common to all of mankind.

There are many people who like to think of themselves as being good people. They would never refer to themselves as sinners since they have never committed any gross crimes and they try to treat others the way that they want to be treated. We are warned in scripture:

Romans 12:3 (NKJV)
"not to think of himself more highly than he ought to think, but to
think soberly, as God has dealt to each one a measure of faith."

We need to see ourselves the way that God sees us. Although most of us have never robbed a bank, murdered someone, nor committed some other heinous crime, we are still not good enough. The issues are within our hearts. Allow me to ask you, "Have you ever told a lie?" "Have you ever taken something that did not belong to you?" "Have you ever harbored lust or jealousy or hatred within your heart?" The answer, of course, would be a resounding "Yes! A million times over! Yes!" We are all guilty.

James 2:10 NKJV
"For whoever shall keep the whole law, and yet stumble in one point, he is guilty of all."

So, according to God, if you have committed one sin, then you are a sinner. If you have broken one of God's laws, then you are a law-breaker. There is a penalty for breaking the law. The old expression "Don't do the crime if you can't do the time" reminds us there is a price to pay.

#2. We all have a penalty which we owe because of sin, the penalty of spiritual death.

Romans 6:23 NKJV
"For the wages of sin is death, but the gift of God is eternal life in Christ Jesus our Lord."

Since we are all sinners by nature, we are all facing the same penalty for our sin which is death. When Scripture refers to death in this context, it refers to much more than physical death. This refers to a *spiritual* death. Just as physical death is the separation of a soul from the physical body, spiritual death is the separation of a soul from God forever.

The Bible tells us of a place which is prepared for the devil and his demons (Matthew 25:41). This place is referred to as Hades or Hell. It is a place of eternal torment (Matthew 25:46). Speaking of those who do not know God, the Bible says:

2 Thessalonians 1:9 (NKJV)
"These shall be punished with everlasting destruction from the
presence of the Lord and from the glory of His power."

Hell is a place where there is separation from God forever. This is what we all deserve because we are all sinners. We need mercy and grace and not justice. We do not want what we all deserve. We need forgiveness. God help us! God offers the solution for you.

#3. We all have someone who has willingly paid our sin debt.

Romans 5:8 (NKJV)
"But God demonstrates His own love toward us, in that
while we were still sinners, Christ died for us."

There was only one person who has ever lived who is capable of paying the sin debt that we all owe. His name is Jesus. What makes Jesus so special? Jesus was more than just a man. Jesus was God and man. Titus 2:13 teaches us that as we anticipate Christ's return to earth we are "looking for the blessed hope and glorious appearing of our great God and Savior Jesus Christ…" Upon seeing the resurrected Christ, Thomas cried out, "My Lord and my God!" (John 20:28). Jesus was born of a virgin (Matthew 1:18-23). Jesus lived a sinless life (1 Peter 2:22). Jesus died on the cross to pay your sin debt since He had no sin (Romans 5:8).

Why would Jesus die on a cross to pay for our sin?

John 3:16-17 (NKJV)
"For God so loved the world that He gave His only begotten Son, that whoever believes
in Him should not perish but have everlasting life. For God did not send His Son into
the world to condemn the world, but that the world through Him might be saved."

God loves you! God has already paid the price for your sin BUT you must willingly accept it through faith.

#4. We all have an invitation from God to be saved.

Romans 10:9 (NKJV)
"…if you confess with your mouth the Lord Jesus and believe in your
heart that God has raised Him from the dead, you will be saved."

That invitation is for everyone!

Revelation 22:17 (NKJV)
"And the Spirit and the bride say, "Come!" And let him who hears say, "Come!" And let him who thirsts come. Whoever desires, let him take the water of life freely."

2 Peter 3:9 (NKJV)
"The Lord is not slack concerning His promise, as some count slackness, but is longsuffering toward us, not willing that any should perish but that all should come to repentance."

Where must you begin in casting down these deceitful idols that bind you? You must be certain your sins are washed away and that you are God's child. You must be born again and filled with the Holy Spirit to have all you need for lasting change. The word *repentance* used in 2 Peter 3:9 means *to change*. We will look more closely at this word in week #14. Are you willing to change direction? Stop trying to run *from* God and turn *to* God instead. Receive His grace and mercy, His power and love, into your heart right now.

#5. Salvation through Jesus Christ brings us into a relationship of peace with God.

Romans 5:1 (NKJV)
"Therefore, having been justified by faith, we have peace with God through our Lord Jesus Christ."

Romans 8:1 (NKJV)
"There is therefore now no condemnation to those who are in Christ Jesus…"

Romans 8:38-39 (NKJV)
"For I am persuaded that neither death nor life, nor angels, nor principalities, nor powers, nor things present, nor things to come, nor height nor depth, nor any other created thing, shall be able to separate us from the love of God which is in Christ Jesus our Lord."

You can be saved today while the Holy Spirit is tugging upon your heart. Do you feel conviction? Is there a restlessness within your soul right now? Your sins can be forgiven and the chains can begin to fall off if you will look to Christ in simple faith believing. Go to God right now and confess to Him in prayer.

If you just prayed a prayer accepting Jesus as your Lord and Savior, I would love to pray for you. You can send me a note at my email address: mikelifeaddictionrecovery@gmail.com

PRAYER: *"Lord, right now I confess that I am a sinner. I understand that my sin will separate me from you forever. Right now, I cry out to you to save me. I place my faith in Jesus and His finished work on the cross and the empty tomb. I repent of my sin and turn to you right now. Take control of my life. I am yours. In Jesus' name. Amen."*

"First Things First"
Week #8 Assignment

1. Memorize **Romans 10:9-10: "··that if you confess with your mouth the Lord Jesus and believe in your heart that God has raised Him from the dead, you will be saved. For with the heart one believes unto righteousness, and with the mouth confession is made unto salvation."**

2. Describe your relationship with God:

3. Why did you describe your relationship with God the way you did?

Philippians 3:4-11 (ESV)

"though I myself have reason for confidence in the flesh also. If anyone else thinks he has reason for confidence in the flesh, I have more: ⁵ circumcised on the eighth day, of the people of Israel, of the tribe of Benjamin, a Hebrew of Hebrews; as to the law, a Pharisee; ⁶ as to zeal, a persecutor of the church; as to righteousness under the law, blameless. ⁷ But whatever gain I had, I counted as loss for the sake of Christ. ⁸ Indeed, I count everything as loss because of the surpassing worth of knowing Christ Jesus my Lord. For his sake I have suffered the loss of all things and count them as rubbish, in order that I may gain Christ ⁹ and be found in him, not having a righteousness of my own that comes from the law, but that which comes through faith in Christ, the righteousness from God that depends on faith— ¹⁰ that I may know him and the power of his resurrection, and may share his sufferings, becoming like him in his death, ¹¹ that by any means possible I may attain the resurrection from the dead."

4. Summarize Philippians 3:4-11 here:

The Poverty of Addiction
Week #9

I am so thankful for the life that Christ has granted me. I still have problems to deal with and troubles that come upon me, just as they do you, but now I know in my heart that I do not face them alone. The things I deal with now are not the same as things I use to have to deal with like hangovers, legal problems, court dates, and those sort of consequences from my former alcohol and drug use. That actually helps me today to stay focused when I remember what my life was like before. I never want to turn back to that life! It offers me nothing but pain and death. Let's consider "The Poverty of Addiction" in this lesson.

In the Bible the term "drunkenness" pictures all forms of substance abuse addictions. It is heart breaking whenever I hear of someone who has allowed addiction to take from them everything of value. I am so tired of hearing of the latest overdose death. My heart cries out to you today to realize how serious a life-style of addiction is and where it leads. The enemy's intent is to steal, kill, and destroy.

Proverbs 23:20-21 (ESV)
"Be not among drunkards or among gluttonous eaters of meat,
²¹ for the drunkard and the glutton will come to poverty,
and slumber will clothe them with rags."

At this point in the LIFE program I hope that you are beginning to realize the hope that you have for lasting change. You can come out of addiction! One tool that can help you in this endeavor is to simply remember, truly remember, what life was like when you were in the midst of active addiction. See it for what it really is!

Proverbs 23:29-35 (ESV)
"Who has woe? Who has sorrow? Who has strife? Who has complaining? Who has wounds
without cause? Who has redness of eyes?
³⁰ Those who tarry long over wine; those who go to try mixed wine.
³¹ Do not look at wine when it is red, when it sparkles in the cup and goes down smoothly. ³²
In the end it bites like a serpent and stings like an adder.
³³ Your eyes will see strange things, and your heart utter perverse things.
³⁴ You will be like one who lies down in the midst of the sea, like one who lies on

the top of a mast. [35] 'They struck me,' you will say, 'but I was not hurt; they beat me, but I did not feel it. When shall I awake? I must have another drink.'"

Write below the true effects of "drunkenness" or "addiction" based on verse 29 above:

DON'T FORGET WHAT YOUR LIFE WAS LIKE BEFORE YOU CAME TO CHRIST!

In what ways has your life of addiction left you poor?

Ephesians 2:1-3 ESV:
"And you were dead in the trespasses and sins [2] in which you once walked, following the course of this world, following the prince of the power of the air, the spirit that is now at work in the sons of disobedience— [3] among whom we all once lived in the passions of our flesh, carrying out the desires of the body and the mind, and were by nature children of wrath, like the rest of mankind."

It is stated clearly in Ephesians 2:1 that before salvation, "you were dead in trespasses and sin." You were simply "following the course of this world," and the passions and desires of the flesh. The battle is real my friend and the enemy is playing for keeps. His desire is to take from you everything that is good and godly, even your life if you allow him to.

Never forget God's goodness that has been extended towards you. Don't waste the chance that God is currently offering you to walk in a new life. Take a minute right now and instead of focusing on what you don't have, instead of complaining about where you are right now in life, rejoice that you are not where you once where! Don't forget where God has rescued you from!

Paul continues writing in **Ephesians 2** and he tells us what Christ has done on our behalf:

Ephesians 2:4-10 (ESV)
"But God, being rich in mercy, because of the great love with which he loved us, [5] even when we were dead in our trespasses, made us alive together with Christ—by grace you have been saved— [6] and raised us up with him and seated us with him in the heavenly

places in Christ Jesus, [7] so that in the coming ages he might show the immeasurable riches of his grace in kindness toward us in Christ Jesus. [8] For by grace you have been saved through faith. And this is not your own doing; it is the gift of God, [9] not a result of works, so that no one may boast. [10] For we are his workmanship, created in Christ Jesus for good works, which God prepared beforehand, that we should walk in them."

Write below what Christ has done for you:

PRAYER: "Dear God in Heaven, I know that addiction only leads to ruin. You desire good for me. I believe that with all my heart. Help me when I am tempted to see through the lies and to realize the true nature of sin. It never brings anything good. Give me wisdom to know the triggers and warning signs in my life. Lord, lead me not into temptation but lead me into victory. Whatever it takes. In Jesus' name, Amen."

"The Poverty of Addiction"
Week #9 assignment

#1. Begin a journal recording what your addiction really looks like especially noting all the negative consequences. See through the lies and see it for what it is. For example, the Bible tells us that "it leads to death" (Proverbs 2:18). Addiction is like "an ox going to slaughter." (Proverbs 7:22).

#2. When you are tempted to use, call someone to help you resist. First call on God in prayer and then reach out to someone who will pray for you and encourage you in your recovery. 1 Corinthians 10:13 promises that God will make a way of escape! Look for that escape!

Write 1 Corinthians 10:13 below:

#3. Attend a Bible believing church at least once this week for worship services. Take notes on the Pastor's message and jot down at least three truths that spoke to you.

#4. Think about and jot down some warning signs for you that have led to using in the past. What are some landmarks for you?

#5. Remember what God has done for you already! He will complete what He has started. Reach out to help someone else this week.

Facing the Truth; Admitting Your Sin
Week #10

John 14:6 ESV
"Jesus said to him, 'I am the way, the truth, and the life.
No one comes to the Father except through Me.'"

"Mirror, mirror, on the wall, who's the fairest of them all?" asked the wicked Queen gazing into her magical mirror in the fairytale of Snow White. The Queen could not bear the truth from the mirror's reply, that there was a maiden named Snow White much fairer than she. Jealousy and hatred raged within the witch's twisted heart as she pondered a plan to destroy Snow White. There are many people today who are just like that witch. They do not want to hear the truth, nor do they have any desire to face it. Yet, as they resist the truth, they become poisoned from within as a result of the lies they are embracing.

Jesus said in **John 8:32 NKJV, "You shall know the Truth and the Truth shall set you free."** Since the Truth will set you free it seems obvious what a lie will do. Lies lead us into bondage. The enemy of our soul desires to bring us into captivity. He accomplishes this by deceiving us with his lies. Just as Jesus called out His disciples to become fishers of men, Satan and his army are also fishing for men, women, and children. I envision demons sitting high above the earth with their fishing lines dropped down among us. Their hooks are carefully concealed within their baited deceptions and lies. What is their ultimate goal? They desire to steal, kill, and to destroy (John 10:10). Once we perceive the deceptive messages as truth, the enemy may then reel us in and we become hooked.

Jesus warns us concerning Satan's true nature in **John 8:43-44(NKJV), "Why do you not understand my speech? Because you are not able to listen to my word. You are of your father the devil, and the desires of your father you want to do. He was a murderer from the beginning, and does not stand in the truth, because there is no truth in him. When he speaks a lie, he speaks from his own resources, for he is a liar and the father of it."**

One of the devil's great lies is that we can find joy and life in what he offers us through the world's resources. Yet Jesus said of Himself in **John 14:6(NKJV), "Jesus said to him, 'I am the way, the truth, and the life. No one comes to the father except through Me.'"** When we believe that life can be found in anything or anyone other than God we are being deceived. Beware my friend! Do not take the bait!

Be certain that what you believe to be true is actually truth. Think about this; whatever you believe to be true, whether it is actually true or not, will affect your life. If you believe today's weather is going to be bitterly cold, you will dress accordingly. If you believe it might rain you may take along an umbrella. If you are visiting a friend and they have a barking dog that you believe will bite you, will that belief not affect your behavior? What you believe to be true affects your actions.

So many people are caught up in believing things that are not true at all. How many times have you told yourself, maybe under your breath, "This is impossible." "This is hopeless." "There is no way I can get through this problem." "Things will never change." This list of faulty messages sent from our sin cursed brains can reverberate through the hallways of our cognitive abilities for a lifetime.

I know that these messages, which echo in my mind, are not true because God tells me otherwise. In **Matthew 19:26(NKJV)** Jesus said **"with God all things are possible."** Nothing is impossible with God.

The Apostle wrote under the inspiration of the Holy Spirit in **Romans 15:13(NKJV), "Now may the God of hope fill you with all joy and peace in believing, that you may abound in hope by the power of the Holy Spirit."** God offers you hope to face any challenge in life. Paul victoriously declares in **Philippians 4:13(NKJV) "I can do all things through Christ who strengthens me."** It is truth that I need! Right action proceeds out of right thinking! The enemy's battlefield is within my mind. I need truth to counter his assaults. Where do I find truth that is reliable and worthy of my trust? God offers that truth in His Word. He is always faithful and always true. That is God's nature.

Do you really desire freedom? Does your heart long for the day that you can honestly say, "My addiction is in my past? I have been set free?" If this is your desire you must change your thinking. God offers you all that is needed for this life-changing and thought-transforming experience. Over and over again we are told from scripture to renew our minds. One of my personal favorites is found in:

> Testimony from a
> LIFE member:
>
> "LIFE Ministries showed me how I was conformed to this world. I was in bondage to Heroin and couldn't see a way out. LIFE Ministries never gave up on me. LIFE showed me a godly way out of my addictions. I now have years of sobriety behind me, thanks to God, Pastor Mike, and LIFE Ministries."
>
> Scott House, Whitakers, N.C.

Romans 12:2(NKJV)
"And do not be conformed to this world, but be transformed by the renewing of your mind, that you may prove what is that good and acceptable and perfect will of God."

Stop clinging to thoughts that are contrary to what God says and begin agreeing with His truth instead. Let's begin with the truth of who you are.

Outside of faith in Jesus you are lost and separated from God. This was discussed in the previous lessons. We are separated from God because we are all sinners (Romans 3:23). Jesus Christ can reconcile us to God as we are told in **1 Peter 3:18(NKJV), "For Christ also suffered once for sins, the just for the unjust, that He might bring us to God."** If you have not yet accepted Jesus into your life, I urge you to return to the first few lessons in this book and prayerfully read them again. You must *first* face the truth of who you are. Outside of Christ you are a lost sinner, separated from God and His truth, and headed for an eternity separated from God and His love.

My prayer for you is that you would come to saving faith in Christ. It is only in Christ that you can experience God's forgiveness and freedom. God's desire for you is not to simply help you feel better about yourself, but to bring you to conviction concerning your lost condition so you will turn to Him in saving faith.

We hear much discussion today concerning the topic of *self-esteem*. Experts teach that we should help our children feel good about who they are. In recent years, there have even been children's games developed in which there are no longer winners or losers for fear that losing a game might taint a child's self-image. What does the Bible say about this type of thinking?

Romans 12:3(NKJV)
"For I say, through the grace given to me, to everyone who is among you, not to think of himself more highly than he ought to think, but to think soberly, as God has dealt to each one a measure of faith."

Rather than feeling good about ourselves, we need the truth. The truth of who we are is discovered by seeing ourselves through God's perspective. How does God see you? Jesus tells us, as He told his disciples, **"You are my friends if you do whatever I command you. No longer do I call you servants, for a servant does not know what his master is doing; but I have called you friends, for all things that I heard from My Father I have made known to you." (John 15:14-15 NKJV).** If you are a Christian, you are a friend of God. Before you accepted Christ, scripture says you were an enemy of God (Colossians 1:21, Romans 5:10). We must be willing to face this truth in order to be saved.

Even following salvation, we continue to make mistakes and we often sin even though we have been forgiven. We all fall short. Often when I am faced with my own shortcomings and sin I feel unworthy of God's love. The Truth is that we are *all* unworthy. This is where God's grace steps in. You experience what you could never deserve, God's salvation, freedom, and blessings in your life. God loves you! Your sins are forgiven! You are of great value in His sight!

God desires for you to experience freedom from your addiction. God is for you in this endeavor. **"What then shall we say to these things? If God is for us, who can be against us? He who did not spare His own Son, but delivered Him up for us all, how shall He not with Him also freely give us all things?" (Romans 8:31-32 NKJV)**. Don't rely on *self* to find your *esteem*. Instead, look to God for your value and there you will find an incredible sense of worth. Face the truth of who you are. You are either an enemy of God or His friend. Jesus makes the difference.

Once you respond in faith to the Gospel of Christ you become a new person. **2 Corinthians 5:17(NKJV)** gives us this wonderful truth **"Therefore, if anyone is in Christ, he is a new creation; old things have passed away; behold, all things have become new."**

In Christ I know that I am:

- created in His image (Genesis 1:27).

- accepted by Christ (Romans 15:7).

- chosen by God (Ephesians 1:4).

- redeemed and forgiven (Ephesians 1:7).

- made righteous by Christ (2 Corinthians 5:21).

- a friend of God (John 15:15).

- complete, having all I need (2 Peter 1:2-4).

- free (John 8:36).

- indwelt by the Holy Spirit (Romans 8:9-11).

- loved by God (Romans 8:38-39).

Scripture teaches me even more about who I am in Christ. I must renew my mind with what God says. I need to see myself in the same manner in which God sees me. This truth will set me free from low self-worth, the feeling of worthlessness, and many other forms of mental and emotional bondage that the enemy would like to use to capture me.

We must also be willing to face the truth concerning our own sinful hearts if we are going to live a victorious Christian life. A key word in our society is *tolerance.* The world would like for Christians to soften their message. People prefer to call sin by so many other names, but fail to call sin what it is—sin. Society would rather talk about sin using terms such as weaknesses, shortcomings, affairs, mistakes and even disease and sickness. That is not the way the Bible refers to sin.

Scripture calls anything against God and His Word sin. I must begin to see my life through the lens of scripture. This is the truth that leads to freedom. In order to break free from the sinful habits that bind us we must first see them for what they really are, our sins. **1 John 1:9(NKJV)** tells *us* **"If we confess our sins, He is faithful and just to forgive us our sins and to cleanse us from all unrighteousness."** I would emphasize the possessive pronoun *our.* We must take responsibility for our own sin. Stop making excuses. Stop blaming others. Face the truth and admit your own sin. Stop referring to your addictive behavior as your *weakness,* your *crutch,* your *release.* Begin to see it and to call it what it is, sin.

You must also confess the true reality of where your addiction leads you. Realize that sin always brings destruction and pain. There is no doubt many people in your life who have been hurt as a result of your sin. It is usually those who are closest to us like our spouses, our children, and parents who are hurt the most. Some of them may have been hurt so many times that they no longer even desire to speak to you. You may be angry about their withdrawal from your life. Maybe you have told yourself, "They don't really care about me." Wait a minute! You must remember *whose* sin has caused this distance in your relationships. It is *your* sin that has created this mess. Take responsibility for your failures.

You must likewise seek the forgiveness of those you have hurt. Go to those people and confess your wrongs to them while asking them to forgive you. James 5:16 instructs us to confess our sins to one another. This confession is much more than a simple apology. You may indeed be sorry for the pain you have caused them in the past, but asking a person to forgive goes beyond the apology. Confessing your sin and asking a person's forgiveness gives them an opportunity to make a choice. They can choose to let go of the pain and bitterness through forgiveness or they can refuse to forgive. That choice will be theirs.

Do not expect too much too soon. No doubt your loved ones may respond much like some of mine did initially after God had changed me. They may be thinking "I have heard this before. I think I'll wait and see. They will have to prove to me that they have really changed." It may take some time to regain the trust of those you have wounded. Trust can be destroyed in a matter of seconds. It will take much longer for that trust to be restored. Be patient just as God is longsuffering toward us.

Face the truth about your addiction. Begin to see it for what it really is. It does not bring you happiness. It does not help you. It does not deliver what it promises to bring into your life. I have never met an alcoholic who planned to become a drunk when he took his first drink. I have never met a drug addict who ever desired to be at a place where he could not just stop whenever he wanted to stop.

How does this gradual process begin within a person's heart and mind? It is the deception of the enemy making promises that will only be broken in the end. Messages like: "This will feel good." "This will help you cope." "This will relax you." "You can stop any time you want." "You are in control." All those whispers of the enemy eventually are revealed as lies.

Maybe at this point you are wondering if you even have an addiction. How can you tell? Consider your honest answers to these questions:

- Does the habitual activity take the forefront in your thoughts several times each day?

- Have you tried to quit in the past only to fail?

- Have you turned down certain social opportunities simply because you would not be able to engage in your habitual behavior if you had accepted the invitation?

- Has your tolerance level increased so that you need more and more?

- Do you have secret stashes?

- Have you been denying that you have an addiction?

If you answered "yes" to any of the above questions there is a degree of addiction present in your life that must be dealt with biblically before it destroys you. God offers you all you need to break free from the bondage of addiction through the power of the Gospel of Christ. The first step as a born-again, Spirit-filled Christian, is to face your problem honestly. Confess the truth that your addiction is sin and you *must* deal with it.

PRAYER: *"Dear Heavenly Father, I confess that I need You in my life. You are holy and true. You are God. I admit that my life is not always reflective of You. Please forgive me for my sins. Help me to see my own faults through Your eyes. I stop making excuses for my sin. I stop blaming others for my sin. I confess that I have been guilty of worshipping idols. Please have mercy upon me, oh God. Help me to walk in Your power. I long to be set free from the idolatry. Do a great and mighty work in my heart and in my life. My longing is to live for You. In Jesus' name, Amen."*

"Facing the Truth; Admitting Your Sin"
Week #10 assignment

1. Check any of the thoughts that you have had concerning yourself:

___ I am a failure. (Philippians 4:13)

___ I have mental problems. (1 Corinthians 2:16)

___ I am hopeless. (Romans 15:13)

___ I am stupid. (Proverbs 2:6-7)

___ No one loves me. (John 15:9)

___ I am unworthy. (Colossians 1:14, 20)

___ My life is out of control. (Ephesians 2:10)

___ I am all alone in life. (Romans 8:38-39)

___ I am afraid. (Psalm 34:4)

___ I am unwanted. (Romans 8:16-17)

___ I am condemned. (Romans 8:1)

___ I am too messed up. (Hebrews 10:14)

___ I am already defeated. (Romans 8:37)

2. Now for each one of the items that you checked, lookup and read the scripture appearing next to it.

3. Begin writing a list of the negative consequences of your addictive behavior. This will help you see your addiction correctly.

4. During the next several weeks keep an ongoing journal in which you list the ways you have kept your secret addiction hidden from others. Include in this list any manner in which you have deceived others. Where there is addiction there is always a web of deceit.

5. Ask God to reveal to you how you have hurt others in your life because of your sinful behavior. Go to these individuals confessing your sin and asking them to forgive you.

Help! I've Been Snake Bitten!
Week #11

There are few people that really enjoy being around snakes. When I was growing up in eastern North Carolina back in the 70s there was a song that came out by Jim Stafford that went like this, "I don't like spiders and snakes and that ain't what it takes to love me…." That was my theme song back then! Hahaha….

Some people actually have an abnormal fear of snakes. This condition is referred to as Ophidiophobia. The word comes from the Greek words "ophis" (ὄφις) which refers to **snake**, and "phobia" (φοβία) meaning **fear**.

We will learn from our study this week that we have all been snake bitten from a spiritual perspective. This bite is lethal, meaning we will certainly die without a cure. Allow me to explain.

There is a very familiar verse found recorded in John 3:16:

John 3:16 (NKJV)
"For God so loved the world that He gave His only begotten Son, that whoever believes in Him should not perish but have everlasting life."

For many people this is one of the first Bible verses they ever memorized. It is very powerful in that it teaches us much about God.

According to the above verse, who does God love? _____.

His love motivated Him to give His _____.

If we will simply believe in Him, we gain what? _____.

That is a wonderful verse filled with such power and truth. If you do not already have it memorized, you should. God loves you! He has provided a way for you! God not only desires that you live with Him forever but He also desires that you walk in victory here and now. He has also provided everything you need for that to become a reality in your life!

It is always important when studying scripture that you consider the proper context. This means that you look at the verses surrounding the passage so you can understand how it fits into the surrounding message. Some of the contextual verses for John 3:16 are as follows:

John 3:14-15 (NKJV)

"And as Moses lifted up the serpent in the wilderness, even so must the Son of Man be lifted up, ¹⁵that whoever believes in Him should not perish but have eternal life."

We learn from verses 14 and 15 that before God speaks of His love for the world in sending His Son, a snake is mentioned. Jesus is referring to an event recorded in the Old Testament. This is where we learn of our own fatal snake bite. The account is printed below:

Numbers 21:4-9 (NKJV)

Then they journeyed from Mount Hor by the Way of the Red Sea, to go around the land of Edom; and the soul of the people became very discouraged on the way. ⁵ And the people spoke against God and against Moses: "Why have you brought us up out of Egypt to die in the wilderness? For *there is* no food and no water, and our soul loathes this worthless bread." ⁶ So the LORD sent fiery serpents among the people, and they bit the people; and many of the people of Israel died. ⁷ Therefore the people came to Moses, and said, "We have sinned, for we have spoken against the LORD and against you; pray to the LORD that He take away the serpents from us." So Moses prayed for the people. ⁸ Then the LORD said to Moses, "Make a fiery *serpent,* and set it on a pole; and it shall be that everyone who is bitten, when he looks at it, shall live." ⁹ So Moses made a bronze serpent, and put it on a pole; and so it was, if a serpent had bitten anyone, when he looked at the bronze serpent, he lived.

John 3 begins with a conversation Jesus had with a man named Nicodemus. Nicodemus was a very religious man who not only studied religion but he taught it. He came to Jesus asking what he could do to inherit eternal life and Jesus rocked his world when he told Nicodemus, "You must be born again." Jesus was referring to being born again spiritually, not physically. It is in this context that Jesus refers to the event in Numbers 21 with Moses and the serpent.

First notice, what were the people complaining about to Moses and to God in verse 5?

What did God do to make the people stop complaining?

Many of these people were dying because of these snake bites! Who sent the snakes?

This reminds us of how serious sin is! Sin brings God's judgement upon us. We must get rid of those things in our lives that are against God's plan and purpose for us. The people of Israel under Moses leadership were suffering under God's wrath because they were being disobedient and complaining against God's goodness for them. God had already done so much to bless these people by parting the Red Sea, protecting them, providing food from Heaven and water to drink. It was miracle after miracle that God had already performed to take care of them yet they still doubted.

Here's a truth you must grasp! You CAN trust God! You can trust God to take care of your past, present, and your future. God is always faithful! You may be going through a trial right now but instead of complaining and griping you must begin to praise God for His faithfulness. God is always good, without exception, even when you don't understand what He is up to. Trust Him. Praise Him. How easily and quickly we forget God's faithfulness towards us.

As the people were being bitten by these snakes, Moses went to God asking for His help. In response God told Moses to make a bronze serpent, place it on a pole, lift it high, and when people looked upon it they would be healed. There may have been many "cures" that people in the camp tried to offer those bitten but only one actually healed them and that was God's provision.

Here's the practical application:

The snake represents Jesus. Now, before you object by saying, "No, the snake represents Satan. He was the serpent in the Garden of Eden," think about this; When Jesus hung on the cross (another pole) He became sin for us.

2 Corinthians 5:21 (NKJV)
"For He made Him who knew no sin *to be* sin for us, that we
might become the righteousness of God in Him."

The serpent does represent everything evil. When Jesus hung on the cross He hung there because of everything evil. Who is guilty of sin? We all are! Every member of the human race has been bitten by the serpent of sin. We are all guilty and we will die in our sin unless there is a cure provided.

The cure for the Israelites was a bronze serpent raised on a pole. The cure for our sinfulness is Jesus, who became sin for us, hanging on the cross. According to Exodus 21:8 what did the people have to do in order to be healed from their snake bite? They simply had to _____ at it. Just look and live! Look in faith and be cured!

The world around us offers so many "cures" for what is wrong with us. We have so many 12 step programs, therapies, various philosophical approaches to dealing with addictions, that we often wonder which is correct? Many of these resources may help us overcome but without looking to God and receiving His answer to the problem of sin within us we will fall short in recovery.

I want to encourage you to take advantage of the resources that God has placed around you to aid you in living a clean, drug free, alcohol free, sober life. Stay involved in support systems. Allow people who love you to hold you accountable. Listen to your doctors, your counselor, your family and friends but most importantly LOOK TO GOD FOR HIS PROVISION!

Psalm 25:15 (NKJV)
"My eyes *are* ever toward the LORD, For He shall pluck my feet out of the net."

Isaiah 45:22 (NKJV)
"Look to Me, and be saved, All you ends of the earth! For I *am* God, and *there is* no other."

Hebrews 12:2 (NKJV)
"looking unto Jesus, the author and finisher of *our* faith, who for the
joy that was set before Him endured the cross, despising the shame,
and has sat down at the right hand of the throne of God."

What do the above three scripture passages say to you?

We must keep our focus! Many things may be helpful in our recovery but God's provision for you is vital if you are going to be who God desires you to be. Look in faith and live! Keep your eyes focused on Christ to live victoriously!

Write below what it means for you to live your life focused on God's provision, Jesus:

It is my earnest prayer for you that you will realize the fullness of God's love and provision in your life. When I lived my life as an addict there were many things I tried to do to be set free from drugs and alcohol. I did not enjoy bringing pain to those I loved and who loved me. I would try to overcome. I tried to quit. Many things were helpful in my recovery but the One who supplied me with the ultimate strength and power to overcome was God. When I looked to Him in faith, I received a greater power I had never known before. This power is yours today if you will look in faith and choose L.I.F.E.

PRAYER: *"I cry out to you Lord, for I know that I am a sinner. I understand that you became sin for me and because you died I now can live. I have decided to look in faith and live! Thank-you for the life you have granted me and for the deliverance you have provided. In Jesus' name, Amen."*

Examine Yourself
Week #12

One wonderful truth that the LIFE ministry desires to make abundantly clear is; DELIVERANCE IS POSSIBLE AND AVAILABLE TO YOU! You do not have to stay the way that you are. That is the good news of the Gospel. That message is also contrary to the message we hear coming from the world around us. Secular professionals tell us that "once an addict always an addict." This is the underlying message that is behind the phrase "recovering addict." While we strive to not condemn those around us who are trying to help others with addiction issues, we also need to proclaim truth as God supplies the answers we seek.

The Apostle Paul was writing to the Church at Corinth, writing to Christians, and this is what he said:

1 Corinthians 6:9-11 (NKJV)
"Do you not know that the unrighteous will not inherit the kingdom of God? Do not be deceived. Neither fornicators, nor idolaters, nor adulterers, nor homosexuals, nor sodomites, [10] nor thieves, nor covetous, nor drunkards, nor revilers, nor extortioners will inherit the kingdom of God. [11] And such were some of you. But you were washed, but you were sanctified, but you were justified in the name of the Lord Jesus and by the Spirit of our God."

The word found in verse 10 "drunkards" is representative of ALL substance abuse disorders including drugs and alcohol. Paul is not saying that these are the things that keep people out of Heaven because we know that we are saved by grace through faith as the passage below reminds us:

Ephesians 2:8-9 (NKJV)
"For by grace you have been saved through faith, and that not of yourselves; *it is* the gift of God, [9] not of works, lest anyone should boast."

What Paul is saying is that if we are Christians, saved by grace, empowered by the Holy Spirit, there will be fruits or evidence of that change in our lives. I do not want to remain in sin now that I am saved.

A little boy went over to a pastor's house, where the pastor was doing some carpentry in his garage. The boy simply stood there and watched him for quite a long time. The preacher wondered why this boy was watching him and was finally so curious that he stopped and said, "Son, are you trying to pick up some pointers on how to build something?" The little boy replied, "No, I am just waiting to hear what a preacher says when he hits his thumb with a hammer."

Listen, what comes out of your mouth in difficult times is a good indicator of what's in your heart. When you squeeze a lemon, you expect lemon juice. When a grape is squeezed, out flows grape juice. When you feel the pressure upon you what is it that comes out of your heart? If you are filled with the Spirit there should be evidence of that!

Galatians 5:22(NKJV)
"But the fruit of the Spirit is love, joy, peace, longsuffering, kindness, goodness, faithfulness, gentleness, self-control…"

Our lives should be characterized by these things. How about you? Are you producing fruit? Or is the opposite true? Instead of love, is there hatred, bitterness, or even prejudice in your life? Instead of compassion, is there harshness? Instead of joy, is there constant doom and gloom? Instead of peace, is there havoc? Instead of gentleness, is there anger? Instead of faith, is there endless worry? Instead of meekness, is there pride? Instead of self-control, are you out of control? If so, then either you don't know God at all or a recommitment to Christ would be in order.

In this assignment we will examine our hearts to find out what is lurking inside us. Are there areas of your life that you need to deal with before God and maybe even before others? Sin can hinder you from LIFE, living in freedom every day!

In the Book of Acts we read of the Apostle Paul's missionary journeys as the Gospel of Christ spread across the world to all people. The Apostle Paul witnessed the power of God everywhere he went. Sometimes the response towards him was violent and life threatening while at other times there were revivals that sprang up. Acts 19 records a time when Paul was ministering in the city of Ephesus. As a result of this time of preaching and teaching Christ, many of those who were involved in witchcraft and sorcery repented and turned from their evil. Remember that we have discussed repentance as a turning around.

Acts 19:18-20 (ESV)
"Also many of those who were now believers came, confessing and divulging their practices. [19]And a number of those who had practiced magic arts brought their books together and burned them in the sight of all. And they counted the value of them and found it came to fifty thousand pieces of silver. [20] So the word of the Lord continued to increase and prevail mightily."

There was a power that resulted in this action. **Verse 20 says "So the word of the Lord continued to increase and prevail mightily."** The power came after the people repented and turned from their sin. If we desire to walk in the power of God, and to live our lives as victorious Christians, we MUST cut off from our lives everything that is sinful. Burn those things that are causing you to fall into sin. Radically deal with those hindrances to your intimate walk with God.

Are you serious enough right now about your recovery that you will:

-Have a plan to succeed!

-Get rid of any stashes you might have!

-Pour out the alcohol!

-Destroy the idols!

-Sever those relationships that are causing you to stumble!

People who are living their lives contrary to the manner in which you desire to live yours should have no place in your circle right now. Don't think that you will remain clean if you hang out with users! Get serious about your recovery now! The place to begin is with faith in Christ. Following that decision, you must continually deal with any sin in your life. Get rid of it! As a Christian, purity before God comes before power from God. If you want to be able to live and operate in God's power in your life, stop quenching the Holy Spirit and begin to live in a manner that glorifies the Lord.

Let's examine ourselves.

Matthew 7:1-5 (ESV)
"Judge not, that you be not judged. [2] For with the judgment you pronounce you will be judged, and with the measure you use it will be measured to you. [3] Why do you see the speck that is in your brother's eye, but do not notice the log that is in your own eye? [4] Or how can you say to your brother, 'Let me take the speck out of your eye,' when there is the log in your own eye? [5] You hypocrite, first take the log out of your own eye, and then you will see clearly to take the speck out of your brother's eye."

You must deal with that log in your own eye! Ask yourself these questions. Be honest in your answers. There may be others questions that the Holy Spirit will bring to your mind as you work through these.

This activity will help you identify areas of your life that may need attention, repentance, and change. For those questions that really hit home for you write a brief answer.

1. Are you generally a negative person?

2. Are you physically abusive?

3. Are you an angry person?

4. Are you an ungodly role model?

5. Are you a perfectionist?

6. Are you unforgiving?

7. Do you usually insist on your way?

8. Are you prone to self-pity?

9. Does fear control you?

10. Does depression often weigh you down?

11. Are you disrespectful?

12. Are you dependent upon drugs or alcohol?

13. Are you sexually abusive?

14. Are you a controlling person?

15. Are you overly sensitive to criticism?

16. Do you often regret what you say?

17. Are you a good listener?

18. Are you involved in sexual sin including pornography?

19. Are you generous or do you tend to be selfish?

20. Are you a braggart, calling attention to yourself?

21. Are you hypocritical?

22. Do you often excuse sinful behavior in your life?

23. Are you legalistic?

24. Are you a people pleaser?

25. Do you encourage others?

26. Do you have a regular devotional time that you commune with God?

27. Are you involved in a Bible believing church?

28. Do you seek forgiveness when you wrong another?

29. Do you share love verbally?

30. Are you quick to forgive others?

31. Do you strive to love unconditionally?

32. Do you praise others for their successes or do they make you jealous?

33. Do you lack a sense of humor?

34. Do you avoid problems or deal with them?

35. Do you put others down by calling them names or gossiping?

36. Do you blame others for your troubles?

37. Are you sarcastic?

38. Do you really seek God's direction through prayer and Bible study?

39. Do you correct others in love?

40. Does your language honor God?

41. Are you a giver or a taker?

42. Do you struggle with your emotions on a regular basis?

43. Do you hide behind an image refusing to be real with others?

44. Are you difficult to get to know?

45. Are you flexible when it comes to daily disruptions in your plans or do these frustrate you?

46. Do you believe you are growing in your faith?

47. Are you greedy?

48. Are your feelings easily hurt?

49. Do you compare yourself to others?

50. Do you do what you say you will do? (integrity)

PRAYER: "Lord, it's difficult for me to truthfully examine my own heart. Help me be honest with you and with myself. Reveal to me any sin that remains within. Help me to change! In Jesus' name, Amen."

Bullseye Living
Week #13

---

1 Corinthians 10:31 (NKJV)
"Therefore, whether you eat or drink, or whatever you do, do all to the glory of God."

Why do you desire change in your life? This is the next area we must examine if you are going to be set free from the bondage that pulls at your heart. In the previous lessons we have discussed your relationship with God and how you can receive His salvation and power. I pray that you responded in faith and now you have assurance that your sins have been forgiven and God has come to dwell within your mortal body. You now have the power of God within you to change!

We have also discussed the need to face the truth concerning who you are and the sin in your life. You must be willing to admit and confess your sin. Call it what God calls it, sin. It is nothing good. Sin is destructive. Get it out of your life.

Our attention now turns to the reasons you desire change in your life. Upon careful consideration of your motivation you may need to adjust your aim. What are your goals in life--what is the bull's eye? Let's judiciously examine the answer to this question together.

I have spent countless hours sitting in the counseling room listening to counselees agonizing over their struggles and the initial perception of their problems. It is usually within the first session that I ask, "What is the number one thing that you desire out of life?" Overwhelmingly most people respond, "I just want to be happy." If that is the goal in an individual's life then that person will make decisions based upon what he/she believes will bring them the greatest degree of happiness. Is personal happiness the reason you desire to break free from your addictions? Is happiness your motivating desire in life?

Others respond to my question with "I just want to be successful." This can be a very relative determination since the definition of success can be very different from person to person. Some people stated their goals in life as, "I just want to be wealthy." Others said, "My only desire is that people respect me." Are those the worthy goals that should occupy the *bulls-eye* in living out our lives? What is it that you desire more than anything else? Give your answer some conscientious, heart-searching consideration. There is something that motivates you to live the way that you live.

What is the number one goal in your life that you long to obtain?

Now examine your response. This goal has become your focal point. It stands proudly at the epicenter of your existence. Everything you do is dictated by this goal. Those who live for wealth, when faced with choices, solemnly ask themselves "What will bring me the most riches?" All they want out of life is to be wealthy. Whatever we place in that bull's eye is what ultimately determines how we live out our lives. This desire, person, or thing becomes our god.

There are millions of people who live their lives controlled by false gods. Allow me to explain. God created us to worship. As God allowed the Apostle John to look into Heaven, John saw all creation worshipping as he wrote:

Revelation 4:11(NKJV)
"You are worthy, O Lord, to receive glory and honor and power; For You created all things, And by Your will they exist and were created."

The Old Testament prophet Isaiah recorded the words of God saying:

Isaiah 43:7 (NKJV)
"Everyone who is called by my name, Whom I have created for My glory; I have formed him, yes, I have made him."

We are created for God's glory!

The Psalmist proclaimed:

Ps. 100:2-3 (NKJV)
"Serve the Lord with gladness; Come before His presence with singing. Know that the Lord, He is God; It is He who has made us, and not we ourselves; We are His people and the sheep of His pasture."

We were created to serve the Lord with gladness.

The Apostle Paul clarifies our God-intended and God-given goal for life. Paul's words summarize the truth of scripture as it relates to our lives being fully devoted to God. Here is what we should be aiming for. This is what should always be at the center of our lives. This is the reason for which we live and breathe and were created. Here is our bulls-eye for living: **1 Corinthians 10:31(NKJV), "Therefore, whether you eat or drink, or whatever you do, do all to the glory of God."** Paul made it abundantly clear that whether I am eating, drinking, at work, at play, dealing with others, or simply dealing with myself, I am to bring glory to God. Any other goal becomes a false god, which the Bible calls an idol.

An idol is anything or anyone other than God that takes first place in your life. Even the atheist has a god. Whatever is in the number one slot in your priorities has become your god. It is at that altar that you worship. What is most important to you? To live a life simply acquiring as much wealth as possible is indeed a very shallow and ultimately worthless pursuit. I recall reading a fellow's bumper sticker recently which read, "Whoever dies with the most toys wins." That reflects a very self-centered and greedy attitude which will end in disappointment. When human life comes to its conclusion, it matters not how much stuff you possess.

The goal of personal happiness also reveals that self is seated on the throne in the sinner's heart. Most people live for what they want. They instinctively go where they desire to go. They live out their lives with the attitude, *"This is my life and I will live it the way I want to live it."* Note how many times *"I"* and *"my"* are used in that line of reasoning.

I am reminded of Lucifer's problem before he was cast out of Heaven. Scripture teaches that Satan was originally an angel in Heaven named Lucifer, which means *day star*. Because of Lucifer's desire to be God, he was cast out of Heaven to become the devil or Satan. The Bible reveals what was going on in Lucifer's heart during his rebellion.

Here is the biblical record:

Isaiah 14:12-14(NKJV)
"How you are fallen from heaven, O Lucifer, son of the morning! How you are cut down to the ground, You who weakened the nations! For you have said in your heart: 'I will ascend into heaven, I will exalt my throne above the stars of God; I will also sit on the mount of the congregation On the farthest sides of the north; I will ascend above the heights of the clouds, I will be like the Most High.'"

There are at least five times in Satan's heart talk that he uses the personal pronoun "I." Satan is not the only one who struggles with an "I" problem. Undoubtedly self is the greatest idol that mankind faces today.

Let's apply this truth to addiction recovery. Many people desire to break free because they feel they are losing their families. Maybe a spouse who has been hurt so many times is now expressing that they cannot go on living like this. It may have even reached a climatic point where you have been asked to move out of your home. Often it is at this point that many addicts begin to realize the severity of their problem for the first time. I can recall countless times waking up with a horrible and physically debilitating hangover. My head would be throbbing in pain. My throat would be dry and raw. My eyes would be burning while my entire body ached from the top of my head to the bottom of my feet. A drug-induced hangover is not a pleasant experience. It can be quite painful. Yet, as uncomfortable as it is, the addict continues his self-destructive pattern of living. How foolish. Yet scripture teaches us in **Proverbs 26:11(NKJV), "As a dog returns to his own vomit, So a fool repeats his folly."**

However, even more painful than the hangovers was the stark and disheartening realization of the pain I was causing those I cared for. Seeing the pain in my wife's face and the tears falling from her dark brown eyes, I always regretted my actions as a result of one of my binges. Melissa would plead with me to stop using the drugs and to stop going to the places I would frequently go. It was very common for me to leave home at six in the evening headed out to the bars. It would often be the next morning after sunrise that I would return home drunk and under the influence of whatever drug I could find the night before. It was in those moments when I was confronted with my wife's pain that I yearned for change with the greatest of longing. I wanted to change for her and even made promises that I would, only to fall right back into my old patterns time after time. There were a couple of truths that I did not yet understand.

First of all, I needed to surrender to God's love for me. As considered in the first chapter, my heart was sinful, fallen and leading me away from God. I needed what only God could offer me. I needed salvation and a power greater than my own in order to change.

My second problem was that my motivation for change was all wrong. I was attempting to reform myself for the wrong reasons. Some addicts want to quit their addictions because they see the mess that their life is in. They simply desire something better for themselves. Some want to change because they want to stop hurting those that they love. Some realize the need for change simply because their addiction is destroying their financial health or maybe even their physical health. These are not necessarily evil goals in themselves, but none is the one true goal for which we were created. My bulls-eye in living should be the same reason that I desire to break free from addictions. My aim in all I do must be to glorify God.

How do you discover what brings glory to God? Where can you find direction to help you live your life in such a manner that you hit that bulls-eye? God has given to us His guide, the Holy Bible, to teach us what brings glory to Him. He has also given to every believer the power of the Holy Spirit as we discussed in the first session. God has given me all that I need within the Word and the power of His Spirit to live my life in a manner that brings Him honor. Here's a powerful passage you should memorize that teaches this biblical truth:

2 Peter 1:2-4(NKJV)
"Grace and peace be multiplied to you in the knowledge of God and of Jesus our Lord, as His divine power has given to us ALL things that pertain to life and godliness, through the knowledge of Him who called us by glory and virtue, by which have been given to us exceedingly great and precious promises, that through these you may be partakers of the divine nature, having escaped the corruption that is in the world through lust."

You will notice that I have capitalized the word *ALL* in that passage. A seminary professor gave me a clear definition of that word. He said, "*All* means *all* and that is *all* that *all* means." That makes it pretty clear. God has promised to give to me all that I need for life through "the knowledge of Him" and "His divine power" which is given to me as I became a "partaker of His divine nature." Wow! I have the knowledge of God through the Word of God. I have "His divine power" through the presence of the Holy Spirit within me. That is all I need to live my life in a way which brings God glory and praise. So, how can you hit that bulls-eye? When you apply God's truth to your life in the power of God's Spirit, you will hit that bulls-eye head on.

As a teenager, and later as I entered my early twenties, I just wanted everyone to leave me alone and let me live my life the way I wanted to live it. I had placed myself on the throne of my life. I thought I knew best and no one could convince me otherwise. As a result, I was looking for what the world offered me as I attempted to fill a void deep within. I was searching for a joy for which my heart had always longed so intensely. I was like a thirsty man trying to satisfy his thirst by drinking mud. I was like a starving and dying man feasting on trash. Nothing I tried, quenched my thirst nor satisfied my hunger. I was just like those that the Prophet Jeremiah spoke of:

Jeremiah 2:13(NKJV)
"They have turned from the living water to their own wells."

The wells that I had turned to had all been dry and unsatisfying. I now understand that I was attempting to fill a God-shaped hole in my soul with all these other things. God created me to worship Him, to love Him, to serve Him. As long as I was living a life in contrast to the life for which I was created, I was sinking deeper and deeper into destruction and despair. I was living my life for a purpose for which I was not created. This is foolish. A carpenter in need of a hammer would never attempt to use a screw driver to drive a nail into a board. He would pound that nail with that screwdriver but with very little success. The carpenter needs a hammer for this task because that is the purpose for which this tool was invented. Once I accepted Christ into my life, I began to study His Word and I discovered that my heart had changed. I no longer desired to live in the manner in which I had been living. The Bible began to speak to me like never before. I began to discover on the pages of the Bible, truth that filled me up and flooded my life with great joy, peace, and purpose.

God's Word began to confront my idolatrous heart. My desire became simply to honor God with my life and to bring Him glory. I quickly understood that drug and alcohol abuse had no place in my life as a Christian. I wanted *God* to control me, and not some poisonous mind-altering substance. Paul wrote:

Ephesians 5:17-18(NKJV)
**"Therefore do not be unwise, but understand what the will of the Lord is. And do
not be drunk with wine, in which is dissipation; but be filled with the Spirit."**

God should be the One in control of your life. You are created to worship Him and Him alone. That is to be your bulls-eye. God warns us that to bring destruction to our bodies is to desecrate that which is holy. Paul writes in:

1 Corinthians 3:16-17(NKJV)
**"Do you not know that you are the temple of God and that the Spirit of
God dwells in you? If anyone defiles the temple of God, God will destroy
him. For the temple of God is holy, which temple you are."**

Idols always bring destruction!

Pay attention to Proverbs 23:29-35, a passage we looked at in lesson #9:

Proverbs 23:29-35 (NKJV)
"Who has woe? Who has sorrow? Who has contentions? Who has complaints? Who has

wounds without cause? Who has redness of eyes? Those who linger long at the wine. Those who go in search of mixed wine. Do not look on the wine when it is red, When it sparkles in the cup, When it swirls around smoothly; At the last it bites like a serpent, And stings like a viper. Your eyes will see strange things, And your heart will utter perverse things. Yes, you will be like one who lies down in the midst of the sea, Or like one who lies at the top of the mast, saying: "They have struck me, but I was not hurt; They have beaten me, but I did not feel it. When shall I awake, that I may seek another drink?"

This passage in the Book of Proverbs is the longest warning against substance abuse recorded in this book of wisdom. We are warned that substance abuse causes emotional problems (woe and sorrow), mental problems (hallucinations), social problems (contentions and complaints), and physical problems (wounds, redness of eyes). In the end it bites like a snake! Yet the addict is so addicted that he keeps coming back for more of the same. I am now a Christian and God lives within me. My body has become His temple. When I allow self-destructive habits to develop in my life, I am attacking what now belongs to God.

God warns His people as recorded **in Isaiah 48:11(NKJV), "I will not give my glory to another."** God will not share his honor and glory with idols. God declares to mankind in **Exodus 20:5(NKJV), "For I, the LORD your God, am a jealous God."** Life is about honoring Him. What are you aiming for?

Now that you understand more fully what God says should be your life's bulls-eye, does this truth affect your number one desire in life? If so, write below how a better understanding of 1 Cor. 10:31 has changed your goals.

PRAYER: *"Dear God, my Creator, Sustainer, and Lord. Your Word has taught me that I am created for the sole purpose of honoring and glorifying You. I confess that I have failed miserably so many times in the past. Right now I come before you in prayer committing myself to no longer simply live for me or the pleasures of this world. My heart's desire is to live for you. Help me apply Your living Word to my life in the power of your Holy Spirit that I can live victorious over sin. I pray that my motivations for change would honor you. I invite you to change my heart, my mind, my life in any manner that you desire. I belong to You. In Jesus' name, Amen."*

"Bullseye Living"
Week #13 assignment

1. Memorize 1 Corinthians 10:31.

1 Corinthians 10:31 (NKJV)
"Therefore, whether you eat or drink, or whatever you do, do all to the glory of God."

2. Write 1 Corinthians 10:31 in your own words:

3. What are some of the bullseyes that you have aimed for in the past?

4. What are you aiming for now?

5. Based upon your answer to the previous question, why do you desire to be free from addictions and to experience lasting change?

6. Read 2 Peter 1:2-4. What has God given us so that we can have ALL we need to live as God intends for us to live?

7. Read Isaiah 55:2. This passage says that people spend their money for things that are not _____ , meaning that they are preoccupied with things that they really don't need.

8. Read John 6:35. Complete this verse by filling in the blanks. *"And Jesus said to them, "I am the _____ of life. He who comes to Me shall never _____ , and he who believes in Me shall never _____ ."*

9. What does it mean to honor and glorify God?

A Change of Direction
Week #14

Acts 2:38 (NKJV)
"Then Peter said to them, 'Repent, and let every one of you be baptized in the name of Jesus Christ for the remission of sins; and you shall receive the gift of the Holy Spirit.'"

If your goal in life is anything other than to bring honor and glory to God, then your goal is faulty. If anything, or anyone else is at the center of your life, controlling your thoughts, and dictating your actions, then you are worshipping an idol. Jesus said:

Matthew 6:24 (NKJV)
"No one can serve two masters; for either he will hate the one and love the other, or else he will be loyal to the one and despise the other. You cannot serve God and mammon."

What is it that occupies the number one slot in your life? How do you spend your time, money and energy? Is honoring and glorifying God really your most valued goal in how you live your life?

We are commanded:

1 John 5:21 (NKJV)
"Little children, keep yourselves from idols. Amen."

God does not tell us these things for His benefit, or because He alone deserves our worship, but He tells us how to live life the way He created it to be lived. Since we are all created to worship, we will worship. If the person or thing we worship is not God, then we will worship at an idolatrous altar.

There must be a change of direction in your life. Instead of trying to move away from God you must now turn and run towards Him. How is this change of direction accomplished in our lives?

I remember when I first realized that God had called me to preach His Truth. I was about thirteen years old, very shy and somewhat withdrawn by nature. The very thought of standing before a group of people and speaking scared me to death. My response to this call was to run as hard and as fast as I could away from it. After all, my personal aspirations did not include becoming a preacher. That was the last thing that I felt I wanted to do with my life. I started running from God.

For the next fourteen years, I tried to find a sense of purpose and fulfillment in many different things, but to no avail. It was not until I surrendered to God at the age of twenty-seven that I discovered something I had never expected to find. God's will for my life was not a burden to bear but it became one of the greatest joys in my life. Once I surrendered to God's will I discovered that preaching was a great blessing in my life. Please note, I did not experience this transformation until I stopped trying to run from God and began running towards Him.

I needed a change of direction in order to understand that God's wonderful plan for me was not something that I should shun, but that it was a blessing I needed to embrace. Once I turned my heart towards God it was as though a light had been turned on in my mind. I began to understand things that I had never comprehended before. The scripture tells us in **2 Corinthians 3:16, "Nevertheless when one turns to the Lord, the veil is taken away."** As long as your heart is turned away from God, that veil covers your mind preventing you from understanding God's Word and will.

You can change! It does not matter how deep the addiction nor how strong the grip it seems to have upon your life. God is more than able to change you.

Paul, writing to the church at Corinth gives us these words of hope:

1 Corinthians 6:9-11 (NKJV)
"Do you not know that the unrighteous will not inherit the kingdom of God? Do not be deceived. Neither fornicators, nor idolaters, nor adulterers, nor homosexuals, nor sodomites, nor thieves, nor covetous, nor drunkards, nor revilers, nor extortioners will inherit the kingdom of God. And such WERE SOME OF YOU. But you were washed, but you were sanctified, but you were justified in the name of the Lord Jesus and by the Spirit of our God."

Paul says that there were some Christians at Corinth who were once caught up in habitual sexual sin, idolatry, stealing, and substance abuse (describe by the word drunkards). Paul says that people who show forth these evil works will not inherit the Kingdom of God. What does this mean? These habitual life sins are evidence of an unconverted, unchanged heart. If you have never been changed, then you have never been saved.

Paul writes that some at Corinth were once caught up in these addictions, but not any longer. Paul is saying "You use to be described by these addictions, but not anymore." Praise God! Freedom, healing, and a new life is possible in Christ.

Please hear what God is saying to us in this passage. Contrary to what many would like for us to believe today, addictions do not have to be the final word in your life. The belief that once an alcoholic, always an alcoholic is not what God says. It is contrary to biblical truth to believe that once you are an addict you will always be an addict. This is a lie that continues to hold many in bondage. The Bible promises that God never changes.

Hebrews 13:8 (NKJV)
"Jesus Christ is the same yesterday, today, and forevermore."

God set the Corinthians free from all these addictions. God is able to set you free, too. A change of direction is possible in your life. You can put down the cigarettes. You can stop drinking. Illegal drugs and the abuse of prescription drugs do not have to be a part of your present nor your future. The habitual pattern of lust that holds so many addicted to pornography can be lifted. There is hope offered to you through the power of the Gospel.

This change of direction does not begin with your outward movements. In an automobile there are many things that must happen underneath the hood before that car begins to actually turn around. Messages are sent to the various mechanical gears of the engine, transmission, and steering components through the instrument panel. Moments before that automobile begins to turn many other things are happening first.

In like manner, before your actions change, your thinking must change first. Here is one of my favorite verses on this subject:

Romans 12:2 (NKJV)
"And do not be conformed to this world, but be transformed by the renewing of your mind, that you may prove what is that good and acceptable and perfect will of God."

We are not to simply blend in with the world, but we are to stand out from the world as God's people. This difference begins in the mind. You must first change your thinking in order to change your direction. Instead of doting on your addictive behavior, you must grow to see it through God's eyes. Determine that you will despise sin as much as you have loved it in the past.

There is a Bible word for this changing of the mind. It is the word *repentance*. Repentance is not simply being sorry about what you have done. It is possible to be sorrowful and yet not be repentant. I have spoken with many people who have been sorry they got caught, but they were not willing to change through repentance. Paul wrote:

2 Corinthians 7:10 (NKJV)
"For godly sorrow produces repentance leading to salvation, not to
be regretted; but the sorrow of the world produces death."

The word *repentance* is translated from a Greek word that actually means "reversal."[1] A person does a one-hundred-eighty degree turn around when they truly repent. They reverse directions. Instead of always moving towards the idol of addiction, and away from God, they are now moving toward God.

I have always loved the story of the Sunday School teacher standing before her first- and second-grade class. The teacher was introducing her lesson on repentance and inquired of the class, "Does anyone know what repentance means?" One little boy in the back raised his hand. The teacher motioned for him to stand. As he stood to his feet he replied, "It's being sorry about your sin." The teacher responded that was not quite the answer she was looking for. Another little girl raised her hand. Upon recognition from the teacher she stood and answered confidently, "Repentance is being sorry enough about your sin to quit." That's it! A change is needed. A reversal in direction! There is a genuine change of mind and heart. This inward change leads to the change of direction that you seek in your life right now.

Do you see repentance in this part of Jessica's testimony? Why or why not?

Jessica Getsinger, a member of the LIFE program shares:

"I was sent to my first rehab, 'Holly Hills.' I was able to get clean from all the drugs that I had been doing. Honestly, I did whatever I could to get through it so I could return home. Once I was home, I could hardly wait to pick up some more pills, which I did and my addiction continued following only about one week clean after detox. When I came home, I went RIGHT back into the same things, with the same PEOPLE, into the same situations. All I wanted to do was get high. My addictive behavior continued to escalate."

---

1   James Strong, S.T.D., LL.D., *The Exhaustive Concordance of The Bible* (Peabody, MA: Hendrickson Publishers), #3341, p.47.

David gives us much insight into this matter through Psalm 51. Many scholars believe that this Psalm was written approximately one year after David's sin with Bathsheba that is recorded in 2 Samuel 11. Do you remember how David, a man after God's own heart, fell into sin? The scripture in 2 Samuel 11 records this event. King David was on the rooftop of his palace one evening. As he was walking upon the rooftop he noticed on the roof next door, a woman, Bathsheba, bathing. She was beautiful to look upon and as David's eyes gazed upon her beauty his heart was filled with lust. King David immediately sent his men to retrieve Bathsheba and to bring her to him. King David, knowing that this was a married woman, committed fornication with her. She soon discovered that she was carrying the king's baby. In an attempt to conceal his sin, the king began to scheme. He knew that Bathsheba's husband, Uriah, was a soldier in his army. In the next battle the king ordered Uriah to be sent to the frontline and then abandoned by his fellow soldiers. Uriah was killed and King David then took Bathsheba as his own wife. It seemed that his plan had worked and David thought he had gotten away with his sinful deeds. However, God knew exactly what he had done.

The final line in chapter 11 reads, ***"But the thing that David had done displeased the LORD."*** Sometime later God sent the prophet Nathan to confront King David concerning his sin. It was after this confrontation with Nathan that David's heart was broken and in repentance, David cried out:

Psalm 51:1-19 (NKJV)

"Have mercy upon me, O God, According to Your loving kindness; According to the multitude of your tender mercies, Blot out my transgressions. [2] Wash me thoroughly from my iniquity, And cleanse me from my sin. [3] For I acknowledge my transgressions, And my sin is always before me. [4] Against you, you only, have I sinned, And done this evil in your sight-- That you may be found just when you speak, And blameless when you judge. [5] Behold, I was brought forth in iniquity, And in sin my mother conceived me. [6] Behold, you desire truth in the inward parts, And in the hidden part you will make me to know wisdom. [7] Purge me with hyssop, and I shall be clean; Wash me, and I shall be whiter than snow. [8] Make me hear joy and gladness, That the bones you have broken may rejoice. [9] Hide your face from my sins, And blot out all my iniquities. [10] Create in me a clean heart, O God, And renew a steadfast spirit within me. [11] Do not cast me away from your presence, And do not take your Holy Spirit from me. [12] Restore to me the joy of your salvation, And uphold me by your generous Spirit. [13] Then I will teach transgressors your ways, And sinners shall be converted to you. [14] Deliver me from the guilt of bloodshed, O God, The God of my salvation, And my tongue shall sing aloud of your righteousness. [15] O Lord, open my lips, And my mouth shall show forth your praise. [16] For you do not desire sacrifice, or else I would give it; You do not delight in burnt offering. [17] The sacrifices of God are a broken spirit, A broken and a contrite

heart-- These, O God, You will not despise. ¹⁸ Do good in your good pleasure to Zion; Build the walls of Jerusalem. ¹⁹ Then you shall be pleased with the sacrifices of righteousness, with burnt offering and whole burnt offering; Then they shall offer bulls on your altar."

Can you hear the brokenness in David's heart? He is crying out to God not only for forgiveness, but also for change. David shows us some very important truths concerning biblical forgiveness. Let's consider these:

- **True repentance means you take ownership of your own sin.** Notice David states at least six times within the first four verses that he has sinned. David takes responsibility for his own personal failures. He is not blaming others nor is he pointing his finger at a dysfunctional childhood. No more excuses. You must be willing to confess and admit that your sin is your fault.

- **True repentance means you stop trying to cover up your sin and you begin dealing with it**. It is found in verses 5 and 6 that David confesses his own sinful nature. He confesses that God sees in the inner and hidden parts of us. You cannot hide anything from God. It is time to get real and to be honest with God. Pour your heart out to Him. He already knows everything about you anyway.

- **True repentance means you acknowledge that God is the One who can forgive your sin and heal your brokenness.** In verses 7-12 David seeks God's forgiveness. He also desires that God would renew his spirit and restore to him the joy of his salvation.

God can also do this for you. You may feel like you will never have joy again but God can restore your heart and spirit. Life *can* be better than it has ever been before through His power and grace. My life was at a point of certain ruin. My heart was empty. Then I surrendered to God's love. My heart is now full and there is a joy within me that cannot compare to anything this world can offer. What you are seeking can be found only in God. He is sufficient to meet your need. Turn to Him with all your heart. Rely upon His Truth and power to change you.

- **True repentance brings a genuine concern for others**. I know that this is true because of what God has delivered me from. I now have a special desire to help others who are now where I once was. That *can* be you. David said in verse 13 that he wanted to *"teach transgressors"* God's ways. David desired to see sinners be converted. Once you respond to God's offer of salvation in Christ and repent of your sins, your heart is motivated to help others experience what you now have. Oh, that the entire world would know the joy and the peace that Christ brings to a heart surrendered to Him! I am so thankful for the change in my life.

True Biblical repentance invites the change into your life that brings the joy and the hope you seek. Rufus H. McDaniel describes this so well in the words of his famous hymn written in 1924, "Since Jesus Came into My Heart."

What a wonderful change in my life has been wrought

Since Jesus came into my heart!

I have light in my soul for which long I had sought,

Since Jesus came into my heart!

Refrain

Since Jesus came into my heart,

Since Jesus came into my heart,

Floods of joy o'er my soul

Like the sea billows roll,

Since Jesus came into my heart.

I have ceased from my wandering and going astray,

Since Jesus came into my heart!

And my sins, which were many, are all washed away,

Since Jesus came into my heart!

Refrain

I'm possessed of a hope that is steadfast and sure,

Since Jesus came into my heart!

And no dark clouds of doubt now my pathway obscure,

Since Jesus came into my heart!

Refrain

There's a light in the valley of death now for me,

Since Jesus came into my heart!

And the gates of the City beyond I can see,

Since Jesus came into my heart!

"A Change of Direction"
Week #14 assignment

1. What does the term "repentance" mean?

2. In Luke 13:5 Jesus told the people that if they did not repent they would _____ .

3. Who was to blame for King David's sin with Bathsheba?

4. Who is to blame for your sin?

5. According to Romans 2:4 God's kindness should lead you to what?

6. Describe some ways that you have tried to change in the past but failed:

7. Read Psalm 51. How does David's prayer recorded in Psalm 51 relate to you?

8. Are there certain areas of this Psalm that you have experienced? If so, what?

9. Read Acts 5:31. Is repentance something that you do or is it something that you receive?

10. According to 2 Peter 2:9 who is it that God desires to come to repentance?

Addictions; Dead and Buried
Week #15

Romans 6:6(NKJV)
"Knowing this, that our old man was crucified with *Him,* that the body of sin might be done away with, that we should no longer be slaves of sin."

I trust that the work we have completed thus far has been a great blessing to you. We have talked about how we all need a greater power for change than what we find within ourselves. God offers the power you seek and need. We have also discussed how we must face the truth. Jesus Himself said as recorded in John 8:32 that we would know the truth and the Truth would set us free. God offers that truth. JESUS IS TRUTH! When we begin to see ourselves the way that God sees us we are a huge step closer to freedom. How does God see you? Are you one of His children, born again by grace through faith, or are you lost outside of Christ.

It is also the truth concerning our sinful habits that we must see in reality. Every addiction is intertwined with lies from the enemy. We have all heard these whispered to our hearts; "No one will ever know." "No one will find out." "It's your life." "This isn't hurting anyone." "Go ahead. It will be fun." There is of course the familiar lie which leads into addiction, "You can stop whenever you want." Then comes the day you realize that quitting seems impossible. The addiction seems to have taken control of your mind, your behavior, and your life. Facing the truth concerning your addiction requires that you identify all these lies for what they really are.

We must also begin to see God truthfully. Your perception of God makes a big difference in how you live and what you believe. Our source for knowing God is the Word of God. God reveals Himself through the pages of scripture. The Bible reveals a God who is all powerful and at the same time who is all loving. A God who is a perfect, righteous judge yet He continually extends His grace. A God who needs no one or nothing yet He yearns so greatly to have you near Him that he became like you, a human, and walked where you walk. Oh, yes, my friend God did even more than that. God died for you and in your place to pay a debt you could not pay.

What is the greatest sacrifice that a person can make? Jesus said as recorded in **John 15:13, "Greater love has no one than this, than to lay down one's life for his friends."** For a person to willingly sacrifice their life to protect another life is the ultimate sacrifice and the greatest expression of love. We often refer to such a person as a "hero." Yet the hero of all heroes is our Lord Jesus Christ. He did not only lay His life down for us but He was perfect in every way, innocent on every level, and blameless of any wrong. There is no other person who has ever lived that we can say that of. What would motivate the perfect Son of God to willingly lay down His life for you? **"For God so loved the world that He gave His only begotten Son, that whoever believes in Him should not perish but have everlasting life." (John 3:16).** Indeed, it was God's love that brought this sacrificial death for you. Jesus died in your place!

Why was such a price for sin demanded? God is a holy and righteous God and any rebellion, any wrong, anything that is not holy or righteous must be dealt with. There is a price for sin that must be paid to satisfy the righteousness of a holy God. That sacrifice is Jesus. **"For He made Him who knew no sin *to be* sin for us, that we might become the righteousness of God in Him." (2 Corinthians 5:21).**

Those who have been exposed to the Gospel, and believe, would agree that Jesus died for our sins. But that is not all that His death brings to us, although that is a wonderful truth. Jesus not only died for you but He also died AS YOU. Jesus died not simply to pay a debt that you owed and that you could not pay, but He died in your place! He died not only to offer life in the sweet by and by but He died to give life in the not-so-sweet here and now. The power of Christ's crucifixion changes us now. A.W. Tozer writes, "The cross will cut into our lives where it hurts worst, sparing neither us or our carefully cultivated reputations. It will defeat us and bring our selfish lives to an end."[2] There is a tremendous blessing in the present through Christ's death in the past.

This is where freedom from past behaviors and addictions can be realized once we understand this truth. There is great power in Christ's death on the cross to free you from bondage. We will examine this eternal truth closer in a moment. First let's turn our attention to the biblical record of Christ's death upon the cross.

As we read the biblical record recorded in Matthew 27 we find so many different reactions surrounding the death of Christ on the cross. These various reactions proceed from a faulty understanding of who Jesus was and what His death really meant. The people mentioned in the Bible surrounding the death of Christ did not comprehend what was actually taking place right there before their eyes. Let's begin with the reaction of Pilate, the Roman Governor.

Matthew 27:15-26 (ESV)

Now at the feast the governor was accustomed to release for the crowd any one prisoner whom they wanted. [16] And they had then a notorious prisoner called Barabbas. [17] So when they had gathered, Pilate said to them, "Whom do you want me to release for you: Barabbas,

---

2   A.W. Tozer, The Radical Cross, Camp Hill, Pennsylvania: WingSpread Publishers, 2009), p.5.

or Jesus who is called Christ?" ¹⁸ For he knew that it was out of envy that they had delivered him up. ¹⁹ Besides, while he was sitting on the judgment seat, his wife sent word to him, "Have nothing to do with that righteous man, for I have suffered much because of him today in a dream." ²⁰ Now the chief priests and the elders persuaded the crowd to ask for Barabbas and destroy Jesus. ²¹ The governor again said to them, "Which of the two do you want me to release for you?" And they said, "Barabbas." ²² Pilate said to them, "Then what shall I do with Jesus who is called Christ?" They all said, "Let him be crucified!" ²³ And he said, "Why, what evil has he done?" But they shouted all the more, "Let him be crucified!" ²⁴ So when Pilate saw that he was gaining nothing, but rather that a riot was beginning, he took water and washed his hands before the crowd, saying, "I am innocent of this man's blood; see to it yourselves." ²⁵ And all the people answered, "His blood be on us and on our children!" ²⁶ Then he released for them Barabbas, and having scourged Jesus, delivered him to be crucified.

We see clearly here the attitude of indecision. Jesus appeared before the Roman Governor Pilate. Pilate could find no fault in Jesus. Pilate's wife even warned him **"Have nothing to do with that righteous man." (Matthew 17:19).** I am telling you my friend it is impossible for anyone to have nothing to do with Jesus. It is true that you have only two choices concerning Jesus and indecision is not one of them. You will either receive Jesus as your Lord and Savior or you will reject Him. It is not possible to remain neutral concerning Christ.

This public politician, Pilate, wanted to please the people and left the fate of Christ to popular opinion. When the people shouted, "Crucify Him," Pilate washed his hands and said, "I am innocent of the blood of this just person." It was at that moment, Pilate being under conviction, his heart stirred, his conscience bothered, that he should have accepted Jesus for who He was. Instead Pilate felt He could just sit on the fence and not decide either way. In not accepting Jesus, Pilate rejected Jesus.

Listen, if you desire lasting change in your life turn your heart toward God for He has the power you need. There is no riding the fence in this matter. You will either be for Jesus or against Him. It is my sincere prayer that through these studies you will be listening to God as He speaks to you. In my personal journey in recovery I discovered that once I accepted who Jesus was, and what he had accomplished for me on the cross and the empty tomb, my life began to dramatically change. He is more than able to do the same for you. There is really no indecision when it comes to faith in Christ, either you choose to trust Jesus or you don't.

I also see the attitude of careless indifference around the cross in the soldiers who crucified Jesus.

Matthew 27:27-31 (ESV)

"Then the soldiers of the governor took Jesus into the governor's headquarters, and they gathered the whole battalion before him.
28 And they stripped him and put a scarlet robe on him,
29 and twisting together a crown of thorns, they put it on his head and put a reed in his right hand. And kneeling before him, they mocked him, saying, 'Hail, King of the Jews!'
30 And they spit on him and took the reed and struck him on the head.
31 And when they had mocked him, they stripped him of the robe and put his own clothes on him and led him away to crucify him."

These professional executioners hurriedly slammed Jesus down upon those timbers, driving the spikes in His wrists and into His feet, lifting Him up suspended between Heaven and earth. Once their job was completed these hardened men sat down at the foot of the cross. It was there that they played a game while Jesus hung there in agony dying there in our place.

Matthew 27:35-37 (ESV)

"And when they had crucified him, they divided his garments among them by casting lots. 36 Then they sat down and kept watch over him there. 37 And over his head they put the charge against him, which read, 'This is Jesus, the King of the Jews.'"

The attitude of these men is amazing to me. How could these men be so complacent and unaffected by what was taking place before them? There hanging before them was a man who had been beaten almost to the point of death. These soldiers witnessed the back of Jesus ripped open by the cruel soldier's lashings. They saw the blood slowly fill His eyes. They heard His agonizing groans from the cross as he hung there in intense pain and suffering. What a careless attitude they demonstrated!

Yet there are many people today who fail to recognize that Jesus was dying there in their place. They would rather play the games offered by this sin cursed world than to look in faith to the greatest sacrifice ever offered.

What was it about these soldiers that caused them to be so blind to what was happening in the death of Jesus? Their hearts had become so hardened and calloused that they were no longer convicted or even bothered by what was taking place. I would imagine that the first time they had to execute a man that it bothered them tremendously. I am sure that they lost much sleep over those first few executions. Maybe they even experienced nightmares where they heard the echoing cries of those prisoners dying! Now as they came to Jesus they had grown so accustomed to executing men that it didn't seem to bother them in the least.

This is the nature of sin and addiction. The first few times you engage in the activity your conscience is bothered and guilt ridden. Once you continue on this idolatrous path you fail to realize just what is happening to you as you sink deeper and deeper into a state of hardness and carelessness. I urge you to receive the death of Jesus for you, and as you, with all seriousness and careful consideration. Stop playing the games the world offers you while Jesus is extending His forgiveness. Don't have a careless attitude as we consider Calvary's cross. Don't be complacent and indifferent towards this truth.

I also see the attitude of unbelief present before the cross of Christ. Notice the reaction of those who were simply passing by that day.

Matthew 27:39-44 (ESV)
"And those who passed by derided him, wagging their heads ⁴⁰ and saying, 'You who
would destroy the temple and rebuild it in three days, save yourself! If you are the Son
of God, come down from the cross.' ⁴¹ So also the chief priests, with the scribes and
elders, mocked him, saying, ⁴² 'He saved others; he cannot save himself. He is the King
of Israel; let him come down now from the cross, and we will believe in him. ⁴³ He trusts
in God; let God deliver him now, if he desires him. For he said, "I am the Son of God."'
⁴⁴ And the robbers who were crucified with him also reviled him in the same way."

Here we find the attitude of unbelief. These people failed to see who Jesus was and they refused to believe in what He had come to accomplish. Jesus dying there on the cross was much more than just being a good example for us. Jesus did not die on that cross just to illustrate for us how we should deal with our enemies as He prayed, "Father forgive them." Jesus was not simply giving us a clear model to follow, to encourage us to stand for our convictions no matter what. No, please don't miss what Jesus' death means for you! Do not read this with carelessness in your heart. Don't skim over these words thinking you don't have to decide concerning the death of Jesus. Look to that cross where Jesus died and believe today that He died there paying your sin debt but he also died there in your place! The Apostle John declared this truth:

1 John 2:2 (NKJV)
"And He Himself is the propitiation for our sins, and not for
ourselves only but also for the whole world."

1 John 4:10 (NKJV)
**"In this is love, not that we loved God, but that He loved us and
sent His Son to be the propitiation for our sins."**

There is a rich word that John used in both of those verses that may seem foreign to you. It is the word "propitiation." The English word "propitiation" in both of those verses is translated from a Greek word meaning "becoming our substitute." This is where true freedom from addiction can be realized. Jesus not only died to pay for my sins but he also died as me, in my place, as "the propitiation," and as my substitute.

This means that as I look in faith to Christ, my past addictions and past behaviors, and everything that was part of my old person has died.

Galatians 2:20(NKJV)
**"I have been crucified with Christ; it is no longer I who live, but Christ
lives in me; and the *life* which I now live in the flesh I live by faith in
the Son of God, who loved me and gave Himself for me."**

I have served as a pastor since 1991. During those many years I have stood by the bedside of individuals as they have breathed their last breath and slipped off into eternity. I have stood in the midst of grieving families in funeral home chapels where a casket stood with an open lid. One thing I know is true of those who have died, they are lifeless. I see no movements. I hear no sounds. There are absolutely no signs of activity from someone who has died. Since Christ died as our substitute on the cross we can claim the promise that our old man is dead. We are free from the life that we once lived. Paul wrote in **Romans 6:6-7(NKJV), "knowing this, that our old man was crucified with *Him,* that the body of sin might be done away with, that we should no longer be slaves of sin. For he who has died has been freed from sin."** The old man is dead!

You may ask, "If my old man is dead then why am I still tempted to live in the deadness of the past?" The influence of the old man is still present within me but it cannot make me do anything. That person I use to be no longer has any power over my life when I accept Christ's death in my place. The person I use to be is not who I am any longer.

So why do so many born again believers still allow the chains of their past lives to bind them? They are not recognizing the full impact of Christ's death in their place. **2 Corinthians 5:21(NKJV)** tells us **"For He made Him who knew no sin *to be* sin for us, that we might become the righteousness of God in Him."** Jesus became sin for you! Your lust, your sinful habits, your greed, your addictions were all nailed to the cross. **Colossians 3:5(NKJV), "Therefore put to death your members which are on the earth: fornication, uncleanness, passion, evil desire, and covetousness, which is idolatry."** All those sinful habits and ways of living have died and were buried in a tomb. They can have no more power over your life today in Christ unless you allow them to.

Following the death of Jesus on the cross two of Jesus followers came and took possession of His body making certain there was a proper burial. The dead body of Jesus was placed in a grave. This is where your past needs to be laid to rest. This should be a time of beginning again in your life. You are now a new creature in Christ Jesus and old things have passed away. It is time to stand on the truth that Jesus died in your place and was buried in your place. Don't allow the influence of the person you were to take control of your new life now.

This also means that you must put any bitterness and unforgiveness that is within your heart to rest as well. We have all been hurt by others. We have all been sinned against. Sin always bring with it pain and destruction. As a born-again believer in Jesus Christ you no longer have to live in the pain from your past. That pain has been put to death as well.

I will never forget just a few years ago standing with a few members of my family in a field beneath a small tree as we laid to rest the cremated remains of my uncle who has sinned against me as a child. This was the man who had seemed to have the greatest ungodly influence upon my life. This was the person who introduced me to drugs, alcohol, and sexual immorality. This was the uncle that had sexually molested me over a period of years as I was only a young boy. My family had invited me to pray at this small gathering around the grave. I sought God's grace to help me as I sought to minister to those present that day. I had told no one of my uncle's abuse towards me with the exception of my precious wife who stood by my side. I bowed my head and prayed asking God to help us each one to forgive this man for any hurt he had caused us or pain he had inflicted upon our lives. That was a moment of tremendous release for me. I believe that I had forgiven him long before his funeral but I had not laid the pain to rest until that day as we laid his ashes in the earth. As I stood there gazing at that spot of freshly turned soil, where this man's human remains now laid covered under the earth, I realized for the first time in my life the power of God's healing grace.

For so many years I had felt that I was so unworthy of anything good in my life. The sin which I had experienced in my childhood only made me feel as though I alone was the problem. I now understand that all these feelings, the guilt, and the shame were part of the enemy's plot to destroy me and to thwart God's victorious purpose for my life in ministry.

Even today the enemy of our souls fights against our witness in every deviate manner in which he can. I know today that God's grace not only saves a hell deserving sinner but God's grace is so amazing that it also heals the sinful heart. I remain a sinner, yet saved by grace, still undeserving of anything good or godly. Oh, but His grace rescues me, restores me, sustains me, and keeps me. His grace heals the wounded heart.

What does the death of Christ mean for you? He died for you but he also died as you. You don't have to remain the person you have always been. That old person who was addicted to drugs, alcohol, greed, lust, or whatever has been your idol has been laid to rest. Let go of the bitterness in your heart. Look to the God who loves you and offers you healing through His Spirit and through His Word.

Would you look to the cross of Christ and claim God's truth? You can move beyond your past.

Philippians 3:13(NKJV)
"Brethren, I do not count myself to have apprehended; but one thing *I do,* forgetting those things which are behind and reaching forward to those things which are ahead."

There is a new life, a new destiny, which awaits you in Christ Jesus!

PRAYER: "Thank-you God for dying on the cross for me and as me. Thank-you for loving me so much that you became my substitute as you endured the wrath of God against my sin. My heart is burdened that such a price had to be paid. However, my heart rejoices that such a price was paid for me. I am eternally grateful. My desire is to bury my sinful past in the sands of yesterday. They are not who I am now. The old man has died. Thank-you Lord for You have placed my past under the Blood and I am now forgiven. Create in me a new heart, a clean heart. I am not the person that I was. I give you praise for the change that has begun in me. In Jesus' name, Amen."

"Addictions; Dead and Buried"
Week #15 assignment

#1. As you think about Jesus dying on the cross what does that mean in overcoming your addictions?

#2. Scripture teaches that there were two people crucified with Jesus, one on each side of Him. Read the response of one of these criminals toward Jesus that day:

Luke 23:40-43(NKJV):
"But the other, answering, rebuked him, saying, 'Do you not even fear God, seeing you are under the same condemnation? [41] And we indeed justly, for we receive the due reward of our deeds; but this Man has done nothing wrong.' [42] Then he said to Jesus, 'Lord, remember me when You come into Your kingdom.' [43] And Jesus said to him, 'Assuredly, I say to you, today you will be with Me in Paradise.'"

According to Luke 23:40-43 there was another attitude towards the death of Jesus. It was not one of carelessness, indecision or unbelief. Can you identify what this positive attitude was?

#3. Thinking back on the old you, the person you were before Christ, what are some habits, thought processes, attitudes, or actions you need to lay to rest?

#4. Everyone is a sinner (Romans 3:23). We all grew up in a sinful world. As a result of that we are all hurt because of sin, our own and the sins of those around us. Is there anyone you need to forgive from your past? Identify any pain or bitterness that is present within your heart. Write out a brief description of the manner in which you were sinned against.

#5. Go to God in prayer seeking His forgiveness for your sins. Also ask God to help you forgive just like he has forgiven you. Choose right now to forgive anyone who has sinned against you in the past. If possible, go to that person and tell them you forgive them. Now mark a big X across your answer to #4 above. You have forgiven this offense and the offender. Let it go. Put it to rest.

#6. Memorize Colossians 3:12-13.

Colossians 3:12-13 (NKJV)
"Therefore, as *the* elect of God, holy and beloved, put on tender mercies, kindness, humility, meekness, longsuffering; [13] bearing with one another, and forgiving one another, if anyone has a complaint against another; even as Christ forgave you, so you also *must do.*"

#7. Who have you hurt in the past? Who have you sinned against? List their names below:

#8. Go to those listed above. Admit to them that you have sinned against them. Ask them to forgive you.

Arise to Walk in Newness of Life
Week #16

Romans 6:1-4 (NKJV)
"What shall we say then? Shall we continue in sin that grace may abound? Certainly not! How shall we who died to sin live any longer in it? Or do you not know that as many of us as were baptized into Christ Jesus were baptized into His death? Therefore we were buried with Him through baptism into death, that just as Christ was raised from the dead by the glory of the Father, even so we also should walk in newness of life."

Thank God for His Gospel! Praise Him for making a way for us to begin again! Our God is a God of another chance. Long ago I use to preach "God is the God of second chances." Over the years that sermon has evolved into *"God is the God of another chance."* He offers that new beginning to you, a chance to begin again.

The power of the Gospel does not simply apply to life beyond the grave but it also is relevant to life this side of Heaven. I love the promise that Jesus made as recorded in **John 10:10; "The thief does not come except to steal, and to kill, and to destroy. I have come that they may have life, and that they may have it more abundantly."** I have shared that verse countless times in the counseling room with men who were struggling or to couples in a difficult place in their marriages. I would ask, "What do you think that word abundant means?" It is translated from the Greek word "perissos" which means "exceedingly, very highly, beyond measure, more, superfluous."[3]

Jesus does not simply offer you just enough to get by but He offers you more than enough. Jesus is not simply referring to quantity of life, life forever, but He also refers to the quality of life He offers. This life is not limited to the future but is graciously extended to you in the present. The words of Jesus as recorded in **Revelation 21:5** ring true, **"Behold I make all things new."** Jesus offers life to you right where you are! It is a new beginning He offers right now. Wow!

In our previous chapter we examined the truth of propitiation, meaning that Jesus died in our place and as our substitute. However, He did not remain in that cold, dead, lifeless tomb. Jesus is not in the grave today. He lives! He lives! It was on the third day according to the Scriptures that Jesus came forth victorious over

---

3   James Strong, S.T.D., LL.D., The Exhaustive Concordance of The Bible (Peabody, MA: Hendrickson Publishers), #4053, p.57.

death, Hell, and the grave. In the same manner in which he died in our place, as us, He also arose from the dead for us and as our substitute. His resurrection offers new life for me right where I am.

Listen to Paul's words as the Holy Spirit gave him this text:

Romans 6:8-11(NKJV)
"Now if we died with Christ, we believe that we shall also live with Him, knowing that Christ, having been raised from the dead, dies no more. Death no longer has dominion over Him. For *the death* **that He died, He died to sin once for all; but** *the life* **that He lives, He lives to God. Likewise you also, reckon yourselves to be dead indeed to sin, but alive to God in Christ Jesus our Lord."**

Pay close attention to the last sentence; **"Likewise you also, reckon yourselves to be dead indeed to sin, but alive to God in Christ Jesus our Lord."** Paul is not speaking in southern lingo when he wrote "reckon yourselves." Paul is saying that we should conclude, or count on the truth, that we are dead in Christ but also alive in Him.

This all occurs through the miraculous power of the Gospel of Christ. Just to remind us of the context in which this new life can take place. **"For by grace you have been saved through faith, and that not of yourselves;** *it is* **the gift of God." (Ephesians 2:8).**

Grace is God giving you what you do not deserve and cannot earn. No one deserves to be forgiven. Many years ago I heard someone define "grace" using an acrostic type of approach; "God's Redemption At Christ's Expense." I recently asked a group of inmates who were doing this study, "What do you desire, justice or grace?" The overwhelming answer was "both."

Oh my friend, we don't want justice. If we received what we deserve Hell would be our eternal home. The story is told of a woman who was leaving the beauty parlor after having her hair done. "I hope I did you justice," the hairdresser shouted as the woman opened the door to exit. The woman immediately turned and responded, "Justice? I don't want justice. I want grace!" If we received what we deserved (justice) we would all be in trouble. **Romans 6:23** reminds us that **"The wages of sin is death."** God's grace is the means whereby we receive salvation. It is also only by God's grace that we can live this abundant life that Christ said He had come to offer. Let's examine a bit closer what the resurrection life of Christ really means for us in overcoming addictions.

When Christ arose from the dead according to the scriptures He arose in your place. The old you, before you came to know Jesus, who was bound to drugs, alcohol, and all types of immorality, is now put to death. You are not the person that you use to be. I am also thankful that I am not what I am going to be either. God is currently conforming me into the image of Jesus through a process called sanctification. I am currently being sanctified or transformed into Christ's image.

Jesus used the term "born again" when speaking with Nicodemus as recorded in John 3. Nicodemus came asking Jesus questions pertaining to the new life that Jesus offers. Our Lord informed this Jewish leader that he needed to be born again spiritually, not physically. We are physically born into this world but that birth does not make us children of God. We all have the sin problem that all humanity shares. Jesus told Nicodemus, **"Most assuredly I say to you, unless one is born again, he cannot see the Kingdom of God."** **(John 3:3).** The expression is true; **"If you have been born only once you will die twice. If you have been born twice you will only die once."**

Jesus continued in His conversation with Nicodemus and said, **"Most assuredly, I say to you, unless one is born of water** (*physical birth*) **and the Spirit** (*spiritual birth*), **he cannot enter the Kingdom of heaven."** **(John 3:5).** We have all been born physically but we need to also be born of the Spirit. This is reference to the Holy Spirit of God. The same Spirit which embodied Jesus is the same Spirit who embodies you now as a believer. You have a power you did not have before, resurrection power to walk in newness of life. You were resurrected the moment you trusted in Christ.

That is wonderfully good news for us as we strive to overcome temptation. We can be victorious. How do I know this is true? I see this truth revealed at the empty tomb of Jesus. It is an awesome power that can raise a dead man. In fact, it is death which is the final enemy mentioned in 1 Corinthians 15. As born-again believers, that same Spirit, with that same power, lives within us! Jesus promised His followers just before he left this earth to return to Heaven:

Acts 1:7-8 (NKJV)
"But you shall receive power when the Holy Spirit has come upon you; and you shall be witnesses to Me in Jerusalem, and in all Judea and Samaria, and to the end of the earth."

The Apostle Paul writing to the church at Corinth wrote **1 Corinthians 3:16-17, "Do you not know that you are the temple of God and *that* the Spirit of God dwells in you?"**

Think about this magnificent truth a moment. Ponder the implications for you my friend. The Holy Spirit of God lives in you. That is real power! If the Holy Spirit of God could raise a dead man to new life He can certainly give you all you need to break free from your addictions. Renew your mind with that truth.

Walk in that truth. When you feel weak and discouraged; stand upon that truth. When the enemy begins to fill your mind with doubts remember this divine power you possess within.

In light of this great truth, how should we then live? I return to the Apostle Paul's words in **Romans 6:1-2, "What shall we say then? Shall we continue in sin that grace may abound?"** Paul has been discussing the truth that we are saved by grace through faith. In the previous chapter, Romans 5, and verse 2 Paul said, **"into this grace in which we stand."** He goes on in Romans 6:15 and discusses **"the free gift"** and **"the gift by the grace of the one Man, Jesus Christ."** It is within that context that Paul's asks the question, "Since it is all about God's grace then we can just live in sin, right?" Paul's answer to that is recorded in the next verse, **"Certainly not! How shall we who died to sin live any longer in it?" (Romans 6:2).** In verse 4 Paul writes that we should **"walk in newness of life."**

I sometimes hear people who really don't understand God's wonderful life changing grace ask the question, "Do you mean that since we are saved by grace that we can live any way that we want to live?" My answer to that is "absolutely yes!" Now, before you stop reading and say "I don't agree with Pastor Mike" hear me out. As a Christian I am able to live as I want. The key is to remember that I no longer want the same things I use to want. I do not want to go to the same places I use to go. I do not want to engage in the activities I once engaged in. I don't want to return to the life I lived before I met Christ. God has given to me a brand new "wanter." So yes, I can live as I want now that I have been born again. I no longer want the things I use to want.

That means there is going to be a clear and evident change seen in my life by others as well. Just as an apple tree bears apples, our lives should show forth fruits which are in agreement with our profession that we are saved. Jesus spoke of this as recorded in **Matthew 7:17-20, "Even so, every good tree bears good fruit, but a bad tree bears bad fruit. A good tree cannot bear bad fruit, nor *can* a bad tree bear good fruit. Every tree that does not bear good fruit is cut down and thrown into the fire. Therefore by their fruits you will know them."** What are the fruits which a Christian should bear? In Galatians 5:22-23 they are referred to as "the fruit of the Spirit." **"But the fruit of the Spirit is love, joy, peace, longsuffering, kindness, goodness, faithfulness, gentleness, self-control. Against such there is no law." (Galatians 5:22-23).** These are the evidences of a person who has been born again because these are present within the new man in the Person and power of the Holy Spirit.

Is it always easy for me as a born-again Christian to continually bear the fruit of the Spirit? No, sometimes it is very difficult but it is nonetheless always possible. I still have the influence left behind by the old man who was crucified. I must choose on a daily basis to allow the Holy Spirit to control me instead of the influence of the old person I was before Christ.

The Apostle Paul knew this struggle all too well:

Romans 7:15-24 (NKJV)

"For what I am doing, I do not understand. For what I will to do, that I do not practice; but what I hate, that I do. If, then, I do what I will not to do, I agree with the law that *it is* good. But now, *it is* no longer I who do it, but sin that dwells in me. For I know that in me (that is, in my flesh) nothing good dwells; for to will is present with me, but *how* to perform what is good I do not find. For the good that I will *to do,* I do not do; but the evil I will not *to do,* that I practice. Now if I do what I will not *to do,* it is no longer I who do it, but sin that dwells in me. I find then a law, that evil is present with me, the one who wills to do good. For I delight in the law of God according to the inward man. But I see another law in my members, warring against the law of my mind, and bringing me into captivity to the law of sin which is in my members. O wretched man that I am! Who will deliver me from this body of death?"

What in the world is wrong with Paul? What is he talking about?

Paul is referring to the battle within every born-again believer. We have the Spirit of God within but we also have the influence of the old person remaining. These two are polar opposites. Paul says that he finds it difficult at times to do the things that he knows he should be doing and so easy at times to do the wrong.

Did you notice Paul's conclusion? **"O wretched man that I am!"** Paul understood that he is not everything he should be. I'm thankful that God is still working on me as well. Like Paul, I am not always everything I should be but I am so much more of what God desires me to be today than I ever was before. Paul gives us the answer to this dilemma. Paul asked in **verse 24, "Who will deliver me from this body of death?"** The answer is found in the very next verse, **"I thank God-through Jesus Christ our Lord!"** My hope is found in Him. Jesus offers me the power to change and live my life for Him.

It is not always easy, and at times I fail, but I am striving to live my life to glorify my Lord. As I live with that goal, the fruits produced from my life will be consistent with my new birth.

There is a promise that God offers to us that can help you in this struggle to overcome temptation. This promise has helped me many times to overcome the tempter, Satan. It is found in **1 Corinthians 10:13, "No temptation has overtaken you except such as is common to man; but God *is* faithful, who will not allow you to be tempted beyond what you are able, but with the temptation will also make the way of escape, that you may be able to bear *it.*"** That is a promise from God who always keeps His Word. **"God** *is* not a man, that He should lie." (**Numbers 23:19**). You can count on what God says every single time. It is against God's very nature not to be true to His promises.

The promise recorded in 1 Corinthians 10:13 offers us great strength and assurance. First of all, it reminds us that when we are tempted we are not the only one facing this temptation." **"No temptation has overtaken you except such as is common to man…"** Don't allow the enemy to convince you that you are the only one being attacked with this temptation. Don't begin to think that something is wrong with you that is not wrong with others. We all have the same problem and it is nothing new. King Solomon declared in **Ecclesiastes 1:9, "There is nothing new under the sun."** Find comfort in knowing that others have struggled with these temptations before you. Our enemy may have different tools to use in his attack, for example the internet, but the temptations are the same. The struggles you face are not unique to only you. Others have, and do, and will struggle in the same manner.

Also find great strength in knowing that Jesus too was tempted just as you are yet He overcame. The writer of Hebrews declares, **"For we do not have a High Priest who cannot sympathize with our weaknesses, but was in all *points* tempted as *we are, yet* without sin" (Hebrews 4:15).** Our Lord knows your struggles and walks with you through each one of them.

The promise of 1 Corinthians 10:13 also assures us that God is ALWAYS faithful. He will never allow the temptation to be so great in our lives that we cannot overcome it. God will either give you the strength you need to bear it or He will open a way of escape.

Sometimes the best thing to do is to run. I think of young Joseph and how his brothers sold him into slavery thinking they were getting rid of him. God however had other plans. It was by God's providence that Joseph became a leader in Egypt. Joseph endured many trials before God raised him up as a great leader in Egypt. One such trial is recorded in Genesis 39:

Genesis 39:1-23 (NKJV)
¹ **Now Joseph had been taken down to Egypt. And Potiphar, an officer of Pharaoh, captain of the guard, an Egyptian, bought him from the Ishmaelites who had taken him down there.**
² **The Lord was with Joseph, and he was a successful man; and he was in the house of his master the Egyptian. ³ And his master saw that the Lord *was* with him and that the Lord made all he did to prosper in his hand. ⁴ So Joseph found favor in his sight, and served him. Then he made him overseer of his house, and all *that* he had he put under his authority. ⁵ So it was, from the time *that* he had made him overseer of his house and all that he had, that the Lord blessed the Egyptian's house for Joseph's sake; and the blessing of the Lord was on all**

that he had in the house and in the field. ⁶ Thus he left all that he had in Joseph's hand, and he did not know what he had except for the bread which he ate. Now Joseph was handsome in form and appearance. ⁷ And it came to pass after these things that his master's wife cast longing eyes on Joseph, and she said, "Lie with me." ⁸ But he refused and said to his master's wife, "Look, my master does not know what *is* with me in the house, and he has committed all that he has to my hand. ⁹ *There is* no one greater in this house than I, nor has he kept back anything from me but you, because you *are* his wife. How then can I do this great wickedness, and sin against God?" ¹⁰ So it was, as she spoke to Joseph day by day, that he did not heed her, to lie with her *or* to be with her. ¹¹ But it happened about this time, when Joseph went into the house to do his work, and none of the men of the house *was* inside, ¹² that she caught him by his garment, saying, "Lie with me." But he left his garment in her hand, and fled and ran outside. ¹³ And so it was, when she saw that he had left his garment in her hand and fled outside, ¹⁴ that she called to the men of her house and spoke to them, saying, "See, he has brought in to us a Hebrew to mock us. He came in to me to lie with me, and I cried out with a loud voice. ¹⁵ And it happened, when he heard that I lifted my voice and cried out, that he left his garment with me, and fled and went outside." ¹⁶ So she kept his garment with her until his master came home. ¹⁷ Then she spoke to him with words like these, saying, "The Hebrew servant whom you brought to us came in to me to mock me; ¹⁸ so it happened, as I lifted my voice and cried out, that he left his garment with me and fled outside." ¹⁹ So it was, when his master heard the words which his wife spoke to him, saying, "Your servant did to me after this manner," that his anger was aroused. ²⁰ Then Joseph's master took him and put him into the prison, a place where the king's prisoners *were* confined. And he was there in the prison. ²¹ But the Lord was with Joseph and showed him mercy, and He gave him favor in the sight of the keeper of the prison. ²² And the keeper of the prison committed to Joseph's hand all the prisoners who *were* in the prison; whatever they did there, it was his doing. ²³ The keeper of the prison did not look into anything *that was* under *Joseph's* authority, because the Lord was with him; and whatever he did, the Lord made *it* prosper.

What an interesting account we find recorded here. Joseph had been placed under the authority of Potiphar who was the highest ranking guard under the King of Egypt. Joseph found himself facing temptation. Potiphar's wife attempted to seduce young Joseph one day while her husband was away. The Bible tells us that Joseph left her presence as quickly as he could. He ran and escaped this temptation leaving his coat in the seductress' hands. God made a way of escape for Joseph to be the godly man he was called to be. Even in the end after Joseph was falsely accused, condemned, and imprisoned God faithfully provided for him and blessed him.

There are a few things I want you to notice in this encounter that Joseph experienced with Potiphar's wife. Please understand that it is God's people to whom the enemy comes against. Joseph was a believer! It is the believer that the devil so fiercely wages war against.

The reason the devil could not defeat Joseph is the same reason that he can't defeat you unless you allow him to. You are under no obligation to allow the enemy to run all over you! You can rise above your circumstances! To key is revealed to us in **verse 2, "For God was with him…"** My friend, you can walk in newness of life when you remember that you do not walk alone. You can actually count it a compliment if you are tempted because that simply means you must be a threat to the enemy. This temptation came against Joseph not because he was guilty of wrong doing. This temptation came upon him because he was doing exactly what God wanted him to do. His life was bearing fruit for Christ. He had become a threat to the devil. Does your life present any threat to our enemy? Does the devil laugh at you or does he tremble?

I also want you to see how the enemy enters into our situations attempting to lure us away. All this began for Joseph with a simple suggestion. Do you see that? It is recorded in **verse 7** as Potiphar's wife gave Joseph her invitation, **"Lie with me. Come to bed with me."** She was very suggestive in her indecent proposal.

The enemy comes against us in the same manner. First of all, there is a simple suggestion. Joseph could have made excuses and given into the temptation as well. Have you ever thought about that? Joseph could have reasoned within himself and rationalized this whole encounter by saying, "Well, I have served the Lord all these years and look where it has gotten me." That is not what Joseph did. He would not give into the temptation. Why did Joseph stand so firm on his convictions? He knew that it was wrong to do what this woman was asking him to do. There is a good reason to do right because it is the right thing to do! It is as simple as that.

There is much that we can learn about overcoming temptation from the young man named Joseph. Notice how Joseph resisted this temptation. He left his garment and ran probably as fast as he could run. There is a time to stand but there is also a time to flee. Make up your mind now, before the temptation ever comes your way. Decide right now that you are going to resist it no matter what. Go ahead and make up your mind that you are not going to return to your old way of life. The addictions are over. Make the choice now to move ahead in your new walk with God.

I heard a story many years ago about an older gentleman who had loved sports all his life. He loved to attend ballgames and cheer his favorite teams on to victory. In high school and college he actually played on the football team. This man was involved in a terrible farming accident one day in which he lost his right arm at the elbow. Depression and despondency begin to settle into his heart. He felt like life would never be enjoyable again. He became so discouraged that he even stopped attending ballgames. He was devastated. One day a friend convinced him to go out and play some handball with him for exercise. This man with the one arm discovered that he was pretty good at this sport. He began playing handball on a regular basis and before long he became very competitive at playing this sport. He even began to play in tournaments and won many of those even over men much younger than he. People were amazed at how well this one arm man could play handball. People were fascinated by his story and determination. Well, the newspaper came to interview this man and the reporter asked him, "How did you do it?" The older man responded, "Decisions." The reporter of course was not satisfied with that simple response so she asked him, "What do you mean by decisions?" He answered, "Well, it's simple, when the ball comes at my opponent he has to immediately decide whether he is going to hit that ball with his right hand or his left hand. When the ball is swirling towards me I have already made my decision." That is what we must do. Decide right now to overcome and even flee if needed.

God will give you all you need to be the godly person He desires you to be. God did it for Joseph and God will do it for you. Claim that promise of 1 Corinthians 10:13.

Living out the Christian life is not about turning over a new leaf. This is not about trying harder or self-reformation. This is not like making a New Year's resolution that you are going to be a better person. This living out the resurrection life is not even about religion or religious ordinances.

I remember when I was 12 years old walking the aisle of East Tenth Street Church of Christ in Washington, North Carolina. I remember coming forward in that service because my friend Andy had recently taken the same step. I don't remember what happened next but I know I was baptized and added to the membership of that local congregation. I really thought that walking the isle in a church service and being baptized made me a Christian. I had head knowledge but inside I remained unchanged. I had gained a little religion but my heart was untouched and my soul was just as lost as it ever was. I soon became disappointed with my so-called salvation experience. Nothing had really changed within me. I ended up drifting away from the church.

My life began to take a downward turn into the world of drugs and alcohol. It was not until later in life that the Holy Spirit revealed to me from God's Word that what I needed was not some religious ordinance. What I needed was Jesus and His resurrection life in me. Once I surrendered to Him and determined in my heart to live for Him I was able to walk away from my past and into a future so bright and so hopeful that words fail me in describing its beauty.

Temptations still come against me. However, I know in Christ I have all I need to resist and to be the man God has called me to be. I choose to worship only Him. My life has been clean from alcohol and drug abuse now for over 30 years but I know I must remain diligent against temptation.

For a period of about 12 months following my salvation decision at the age of 27 there were some very strong temptations trying to pull me back into the life I had been delivered from. It was during those moments of intense temptation that I simply stood on the promise of 1 Corinthians 10:13 and drew as close to God as I could through prayer, bible study, and active participation in a Bible believing church. At the end of that twelve-month period of time I realized that I was now walking in freedom from my past in a new resurrection life that God had granted me through His grace. I began to realize that the pull of the old addictions had begun to quickly fade into the vast shadows of yesterday. Those former self-destructive patterns of life were losing their grip on me! I begin to realize the power of His resurrection life within me. Today I am no longer an alcoholic. Today I am no longer a drug addict. Today I have been delivered and healed. I have been empowered by God's presence in my life. This resurrection life can be yours today.

PRAYER: "I know Dear God that I am now a new creation. You have not simply remodeled my old nature but you have granted unto me a new nature. I have Your resurrection life in me. When the enemy comes against me to steal, kill, and destroy I can be victorious over his schemes because of You. You have granted me all I need to live a victorious Christian life. That is my desire. I never want to return to the life that you have delivered me from. Your life is now my life. In Jesus' name, Amen."

"Arise to Walk in Newness of Life"
Week #16 assignment

#1. Memorize 1 Corinthians 10:13. Once you have it memorized write it out below:

#2. Write in your own words what 1 Corinthians 10:13 means to you.

#3. A city without a wall is wide open for the enemy to overtake it. Read Proverbs 25:28. What are some very practical things that you can do that will act as bricks in the wall to protect you from temptation? (For example changing the places you go or the people you associate with). List these on the wall below.

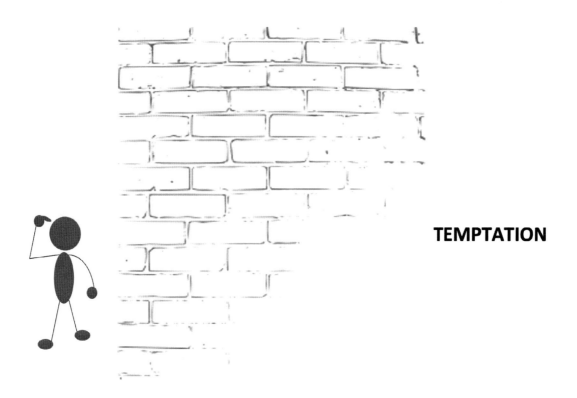

TEMPTATION

Proverbs 25:28 (ESV)
"A man without self-control is like a city broken into and left without walls."

#4. Read Ephesians 4:22-24. This passage is a "change passage." It speaks of "putting off" and "putting on." List below under the appropriate heading what you need to "put off" and then what it is you should "put on" in its place.

PUT OFF: PUT ON:

_____   _____
_____   _____
_____   _____
_____   _____
_____   _____
_____   _____
_____   _____
_____   _____
_____   _____
_____   _____
_____   _____

#5. You need to restructure your life! Think of the times when you are tempted the greatest, for example, a certain time of the day or night? Maybe in certain situations like especially on payday? When you are discouraged? Etc..... Identify those times below:

#6. What can you change (restructure) in your life to protect you in the times/situations that you identified above? For example, places you use to frequent or people you use to fellowship with. Think about your answers to #3.

#7. Return to those you have wronged in the past. If you have stolen from others attempt to make it right by returning or repaying what you have stolen. Just as Zacchaeus responded following his life changing encounter with Jesus, **Luke 19:8, "Then Zacchaeus stood and said to the Lord, 'Look, Lord, I give** half of my goods to the poor; and if I have taken anything from anyone by false accusation, I restore fourfold.'"

The Bible says, **"If he gives back what he took in pledge for a loan, returns what he has stolen, follows the decrees that give life, and does no evil, he will surely live; he will not die. None of the sins he has committed will be remembered against him. He has done what is just and right; he will surely live."** (Ezekiel 33:15-16).

The Struggle Within
Week #17

We have studied during the past few weeks how we must begin calling our struggles what God calls them-sin. It is time to begin taking responsibility for our own sinful choices and decisions. It is no one's fault but my own if I yield to temptation and fall into sin. We must also remember that the results of sin are always damaging and harmful. It is the enemy that has come to steal, kill, and to destroy (John 10:10). Once we come to Christ, and place our faith in Him, we have been forgiven but the real struggle is just beginning.

Prior to coming to Christ, we are simply living life for ourselves, in the flesh. Now that we are looking to God for our deliverance, and our bullseye in living is to glorify God (1 Cor. 10:31), there is a conflict within us. There is now a pulling to do what is right in God's sight and yet we are so easily pulled away into that which is sinful.

In a previous lesson we discussed biblical repentance. This means a turning away from the manner in which we once lived and a turning toward the new life that Christ offers. This repentance must be continual as we make daily conscious decisions to continue to glorify God with our lives. As we do this, all along yielding to God's power in our lives, God changes us.

Romans 8:29 (NKJV)
"For whom He foreknew, He also predestined *to be* conformed to the image of His Son…"

God is making us more like Jesus!

2 Corinthians 5:17 (NKJV)
**"Therefore, if anyone *is* in Christ, *he is* a new creation; old things
have passed away; behold, all things have become new."**

Did you get that last part, **"…all things have become new?"** Let's get real here! There are many things about me as a Christian that just don't seem to be new. There are parts about me, like my thinking, that still desires to return to the old manner of life before I trusted Jesus. What is up with that? Let's consider this issue in light of where we have been thus far.

Christ has given us new life! We are not only declared to be righteous but He has made us righteous. The old man is dead and buried. There is now a new person within me! Yet there are many times in my life when I want to shout out, "If the old man is dead and buried why is the dead still haunting me?" Why is it that I continue to struggle in my walk with the Lord? This week we are going to study the reality of "The Struggle Within" and how we deal with this struggle. You can overcome!

As you read Romans 7:14-25 listen for the struggle that the Apostle Paul experienced. Remember that this was the man that God chose to write at least half of the New Testament. Paul was probably the greatest missionary who ever lived. A great man of God and yet he knew the same struggle we face.

Romans 7:14-25 (ESV)

"For we know that the law is spiritual, but I am of the flesh, sold under sin. ¹⁵ For I do not understand my own actions. For I do not do what I want, but I do the very thing I hate. ¹⁶ Now if I do what I do not want, I agree with the law, that it is good. ¹⁷ So now it is no longer I who do it, but sin that dwells within me. ¹⁸ For I know that nothing good dwells in me, that is, in my flesh. For I have the desire to do what is right, but not the ability to carry it out. ¹⁹ For I do not do the good I want, but the evil I do not want is what I keep on doing. ²⁰ Now if I do what I do not want, it is no longer I who do it, but sin that dwells within me. ²¹ So I find it to be a law that when I want to do right, evil lies close at hand. ²² For I delight in the law of God, in my inner being, ²³ but I see in my members another law waging war against the law of my mind and making me captive to the law of sin that dwells in my members. ²⁴ Wretched man that I am! Who will deliver me from this body of death? ²⁵ Thanks be to God through Jesus Christ our Lord! So then, I myself serve the law of God with my mind, but with my flesh I serve the law of sin."

It seems at first read that Paul is in an impossible dilemma. He wants to do what is right and godly but he finds this great desire still remaining within him to do the opposite. We often read a passage like that and we immediately begin to think it's referring to the constant struggle between doing what is right and doing what is wrong. The struggle goes much deeper than that! The word "doing" is not at the root of the struggle. At the root of the turmoil is not me "doing right" or me "doing wrong." It is not about "doing" but it is about "being."

Our Lord Jesus said as recorded in **John 5:24 (NKJV), "Truly, truly, I say to you, whoever hears my word and believes him who sent me has eternal life. He does not come into judgment, but has passed from death to life."** Have you heard the Gospel and responded in faith? Have you trusted Jesus Christ? If you have then Jesus says you have passed from death unto life. You have been changed! This change is not dependent on how you feel or what you do. This change is so because Jesus says it is so. The authority is God's Word and not your experience. Although we may fail at times we remain what God says is true about us. Listen, get this settled now; What God says is truth regardless of anything else.

Let's consider the very next chapter in Romans as Paul continues this teaching. Read below these verses from Romans 8:

Romans 8:1-11 (ESV)
"There is therefore now no condemnation for those who are in Christ Jesus. ² For the law of the Spirit of life has set you free in Christ Jesus from the law of sin and death. ³ For God has done what the law, weakened by the flesh, could not do. By sending his own Son in the likeness of sinful flesh and for sin, he condemned sin in the flesh, ⁴ in order that the righteous requirement of the law might be fulfilled in us, who walk not according to the flesh but according to the Spirit. ⁵ For those who live according to the flesh set their minds on the things of the flesh, but those who live according to the Spirit set their minds on the things of the Spirit. ⁶ For to set the mind on the flesh is death, but to set the mind on the Spirit is life and peace. ⁷ For the mind that is set on the flesh is hostile to God, for it does not submit to God's law; indeed, it cannot. ⁸ Those who are in the flesh cannot please God.⁹ You, however, are not in the flesh but in the Spirit, if in fact the Spirit of God dwells in you. Anyone who does not have the Spirit of Christ does not belong to him. ¹⁰ But if Christ is in you, although the body is dead because of sin, the Spirit is life because of righteousness. ¹¹ If the Spirit of him who raised Jesus from the dead dwells in you, he who raised Christ Jesus from the dead will also give life to your mortal bodies through his Spirit who dwells in you."

#1. According to Romans 8:1-2 why are we not under condemnation now?

#2. According to verse 3 what is it that makes the law of God weak in us?

#3. It is in verse 4 that we find the real struggle within. The struggle is not about "doing" but rather it is about "being." We must not simply walk (live) in the flesh but we must walk (live) in the Spirit. That means simply living out who I am in Christ. According to 2 Corinthians 5:17, I am a new creation. In verse 5 we are told to set our _____ on the things of the Spirit.

#4. We cannot please God if we are simply "in the flesh" according to verse 8. We must be "in the Spirit," which is a reference to the Holy Spirit, if we are to win the struggle within. According to verse 9 who has the Holy Spirit? _____

John 6:63 (NKJV)
"It is the Spirit who gives life; the flesh profits nothing. The words that I speak to you are spirit, and *they* are life."

#5. According to John 6:63 (above) what does the Spirit of God give? _____.

John 14:17 (NKJV)
"the Spirit of truth, whom the world cannot receive, because it neither sees Him nor knows Him; but you know Him, for He dwells with you and will be in you."

#6. According to John 14:17 (above) where does the Holy Spirit live? _____.

As Christians we are not simply declared to be righteous, but we are made righteous by the Holy Spirit who lives within! Yes, we all struggle but we have been given all we need to be victorious in the righteousness that Christ provides for us. Read the text below and see if you can identify what God has given us so that we can live victoriously over our struggles:

2 Peter 1:2-4 (NKJV)
"Grace and peace be multiplied to you in the knowledge of God and of Jesus our Lord, ³ as His divine power has given to us all things that pertain to life and godliness, through the knowledge of Him who called us by glory and virtue, ⁴ by which have been given to us exceedingly great and precious promises, that through these you may be partakers of the divine nature, having escaped the corruption that is in the world through lust."

#7. There are 3 things promised in those verses that God has given to us that provide ALL we need to be godly:

_____.

_____.

_____.

#8. How have you tried to live your life your way, in your own power?

#9. What were the results from living life your way?

#10. Write a thank-you note below to The Holy Spirit, expressing your gratitude for all that He has done, is doing, and will do in your life:

PRAYER: "Lord, as I come to the end of this lesson I can clearly identify with the struggle within. Everyday of my life I experience this struggle between good and evil. I want to live a holy and righteous life but so many times I fail to do the right thing. This struggle simply reminds me of how dependent I am upon you. Lord, I confess that I need you in my life. I will fail without your presence and your power. Have your way in my life. In Jesus' name, Amen."

Anger Part 1 "The Heart"
Week #18

The common goal in counseling is always the same, change. The counselor, or group leader, desires to promote some type of change in those who are listening. In biblical counseling the goal is to promote godly thinking and biblical behavior. We are all in need of that type of change. None of us have perfectly arrived yet, have we? However, we certainly should be making progress in our Christian walk. Can you look back over your life and honestly say, "I am much closer to what I should be today than I have ever been before." I know that we are not always what we should be, but we should be more like Christ today than we have ever been before.

Change, however, doesn't come easy for most. Often the old manner of thinking and living doesn't want to adjust to the new truth we are striving to apply. The result is oftentimes ANGER. We become angry with ourselves when we fail and disappoint everyone. We get angry at others when they continually attempt to hold us accountable and we shout from within, "Get off my back! Let me breathe! Will you ever trust me again?" In those times you must remember that the reason others struggle to trust you is because of your past history. Maybe you haven't as of yet proven yourself to be trustworthy. Be determined more than ever before to show everyone that you are not the person you use to be! Trust will return once you prove yourself to be trustworthy.

Many other situations in life can invoke anger within us as well. We often get angry when things don't go the way we would like for them to. When we feel threatened in some way, whether that pertains to our physical well-being, or even our plans and dreams being threatened, we often attempt to regain control by expressing anger.

I should clarify at the beginning that all anger is not sinful. There is a type of anger that is righteous and godly, even needed in our world. We even see Jesus in the Gospels getting angry at times. Read the biblical account below:

Mark 3:1-6 (ESV)
"Again he *(Jesus)* entered the synagogue, and a man was there with a withered hand.
² And they watched Jesus, to see whether he would heal him on the Sabbath, so that they might accuse him. ³ And he said to the man with the withered hand, 'Come here.' ⁴ And he said to them, 'Is it lawful on the Sabbath to do good or to do harm,

to save life or to kill?' But they were silent. ⁵ And he *(Jesus)* **looked around at them with anger, grieved at their hardness of heart, and said to the man, 'Stretch out your hand.' He stretched it out, and his hand was restored. ⁶ The Pharisees went out and immediately held counsel with the Herodians against him, how to destroy him."**

What was it that angered Jesus?

Jesus, who was without sin, became angry at the unrighteousness that He saw within the religious leaders of His day. So, there is such a thing as good anger, or righteous anger. The anger we often experience however, is another kind of anger, which is sinful. We have all heard the horrible stories of mass murders, road rage, and violent encounters in our society that occurred in anger. Horrible things are done in sinful rage.

The first thing I want to say about anger is that anger is a choice. You are choosing to become angry and you are choosing how you will express that anger. It's very easy for us to develop unhealthy habits which seem to become automatic responses. Have you ever known a chain smoker? They are lighting up another cigarette immediately after they have just extinguished one. I knew a man like that once, before he died of cancer. I remember one day confronting him with his chain-smoking habit. I said, "You just put a cigarette out! Why are you lighting another one?" This man looked at me and did not realize he had just put one cigarette out and was immediately preparing to smoke another. This had become almost "second nature" to him and he was doing it without really thinking about it. We can likewise develop emotional responses which become habitual in our lives. We can become so accustomed to responding or acting in a certain manner that it seems to be our automatic response.

I have heard people who have struggled with anger issues tell me, "It's just an automatic response I have to want to hit something." This has become the manner in which this person has expressed their anger for so long now he doesn't even think about his response before he lets it fly. Much like a volcano getting ready to blow, some people seem to always be just one rumble away from exploding in rage. What is "it" within you that wants to rise up and explode?

Well, first of all, anger is not an "it" but rather it is an emotional and moral response that you are experiencing because you feel threatened in some way. Anger is not something inside that you must release (like venting). Anger is a choice that originates within your heart and mind.

Let's do an activity to illustrate this truth. List below the names of individuals that you are most likely to express anger towards:

_____

_____

_____

Secondly, I want you to list the names of a few people with whom you would NEVER lose your temper with. These may include parents, police officers, your probation officer, your employer, pastor, etc....List these below:

_____

_____

_____

Thirdly, allow me to ask you a question; If your anger is totally out of your control, how can you choose to control it around a certain group of people more so than around others? The answer is that you choose to. For example, if you were angry at your spouse and in the midst of a terrible fight, and a police officer showed up at your door, how would you respond to him? Would your anger be displayed towards him as it was towards your spouse? You would respond, "Of course not!" You CAN control your anger.

Look up the following passages and write out in your own words what they mean to you:

Proverbs 22:24-25

Proverbs 29:22

Galatians 5:19-21

Have you really tried everything in dealing with your anger? Have you come to God and sought His aid and instruction? If not, then you have not tried everything. God's way is the way to victory! Through His Spirit you can overcome according to Galatians 5:22-25.

Take time now to prayerfully complete the "Anger Inventory." If there are other areas which the Holy Spirit reveals to you where you are displaying anger add those on the back of the following assignment.

PRAYER: *"Dear God in Heaven, I confess that many times I know that anger gets the upper hand in my life. I allow anger to fill my heart when I become self-centered and focused upon this world more than I am focused upon you. Please forgive me. Cleanse my heart Oh Lord! I do not want to be filled with anger but I desire to be filled with your presence. Help me to overcome my emotions. Take control of my heart. In Jesus' name, Amen."*

Anger Part 1 "The Heart"
Week #18 assignment

INVENTORY ASSIGNMENT"

The first step in dealing with and overcoming your anger issues is to identify the many different faces of anger. The following inventory can help you identify those areas in your life. Check the statements that apply to you.

___ I am impatient more than I would like to be.

___ I admit that I focus on negative thoughts much of the time.

___ When someone upsets me I tend to withdraw, get silent, and lack a desire to interact.

___ I often feel stressed and tense when facing demanding situations.

___ I become annoyed whenever I feel like I am not valued or listened to.

___ I often feel frustrated when I see others who seem to have fewer struggles than I.

___ I can become obsessive whenever I am facing an important event in which I have an active part in.

___ I sometimes go out of my way to avoid people I do not like.

___ Whenever I am expressing my opinion to someone who doesn't agree with me, my tone becomes louder.

___ I detest being around people who act like they never make mistakes.

___ When someone wrongs me, I never forget.

___ I get so discouraged at times that I almost quit.

___ Sarcasm is a trait I use in expressing humor.

___ I struggle with depression and discouragement.

___ I often get loud in my tone when trying to prove a point.

___ I can become insensitive sometimes when I am in a role of authority.

___ I can sometimes have a "I don't care" attitude towards others.

___ I sometimes blame others for my problems.

___ I can be quite aggressive.

Anger Part 2 "The Inner Man"
Week #19

Thus far we have discussed the truth that anger is a choice we make. You are making choices inside to become upset, bitter, and angry about things going on around you. This is clearly revealed in the fact that you are able to stay calm around certain people while you tend to express anger before another group of people. These are choices that are being made. If anger can be controlled in the presence of one group, then it can be controlled before another. We have defined anger as "An emotional response to a perceived threat." Whenever we feel threatened we attempt to control the situation with angry responses.

Last week I introduced the idea that anger is an issue of the heart. Our actions, words, and behavior do not simply come out of thin air. Our outward expressions, including our emotional responses, come from within us. The key to dealing with anger, as is true of any emotional response, is to get down deep to where it originates which is within our hearts.

When the Bible refers to the heart it is not referring to that organ within your chest that is constantly pumping blood. When the Bible refers to the heart of man it is talking about the center of who you are. The things that you value as most important in life are in your heart. One of the clearest examples of this in the Bible has to do with the way of salvation as recorded in **Romans 10:9 (NKJV), "that if you confess with your mouth the Lord Jesus and believe in your heart that God has raised Him from the dead, you will be saved."** When you place your faith in Christ He becomes a priority in your life. You no longer want to live life your way but you seek to live your life His way. He is in your heart, as well as His teachings, His Word and His plan for your life.

As Jesus walked this earth, God in human flesh, He cast out demons, healed the sick, and blessed those who were hurting. There were some, like the Pharisees, who accused Jesus of doing these good things in the power of the devil. Read our Lord's strong response to those accusers and pay attention to what He says about the source of their evil words:

Matthew 12:34-35 (NKJV)
"Brood of vipers! How can you, being evil, speak good things? For out of the abundance of the heart the mouth speaks. A good man out of the good treasure of his heart brings forth good things, and an evil man out of the evil treasure brings forth evil things."

Jesus said that it was out of the abundance of the _____ that they spoke the words that they spoke. See, when Jesus referred to the heart He is including your thought processes but more than that, He is also including the real you and what it is that makes you who you are. This includes your priorities, your belief system, and everything that is most valuable in your life. Many times people will speak a curse word when they are in a difficult spot and they may say, "Opps, where did that come from? That slipped." No, that didn't slip. I know exactly where it came from. It proceeded from the heart. If there is trash coming forth then there is trash within. Deal with it! Get rid of it!

King David, following his sin of adultery and even murder, cried out to God in brokenness as recorded in **Psalm 51:10 (NKJV), "Create in me a clean heart, O God, And renew a steadfast spirit within me."** King David understood that his sin of adultery originated in his heart before it ever became manifested in his behavior. So, what is going on in our heart when we choose to respond in anger?

Galatians 5:16-21(NKJV):
"I say then: Walk in the Spirit, and you shall not fulfill the lust of the flesh.
[17] For the flesh lusts against the Spirit, and the Spirit against the flesh; and these are contrary to one another, so that you do not do the things that you wish. [18] But if you are led by the Spirit, you are not under the law. [19] Now the works of the flesh are evident, which are: adultery, fornication, uncleanness, lewdness, [20] idolatry, sorcery, hatred, contentions, jealousies, <u>outbursts of wrath,</u> selfish ambitions, dissensions, heresies, [21] envy, murders, drunkenness, revelries, and the like; of which I tell you beforehand, just as I also told _you_ in time past, that those who practice such things will not inherit the kingdom of God."

It is clear from verse 20, within several words used, that anger is something that can go against the Holy Spirit and what He desires to achieve in our lives. I believe that unrighteous anger comes from a heart that is self-focused and not God focused. Again, go back to our definition of anger, "An emotional response to a perceived threat." Notice, I said unrighteous anger, because some anger can be good. If you awaken in the middle of the night and someone is attempting to break into your home, you should become angry. If someone is harming another who is helpless you should become angry. Our problem is that we often become angry because it is our plans, our dreams, our ego, our pride, etc. that is threatened so we attempt to gain control. Think about what you are thinking about when anger begins to rise up within you. Are you thinking as you should? If not, change your thinking.

This is not an exhaustive list, but I believe the statements listed below may sound familiar to you. These are often trigger messages in the heart that lead to anger:

"I don't deserve this."

"My time is valuable."

"I deserve to be happy."

"I have a right to lose my cool because people around me are so stupid!"

"My opinions are better than anyone else's."

"I deserve the best in life."

"I can speak my mind because what I have to say needs to be heard."

"I'm more important than those around me."

"I will be successful no matter what I have to do to achieve it."

"It's okay to compromise what is right to get ahead."

"I am in control of my life."

"I am the way I am. I can't change."

"I'm just a chip off the old block."

See if you can write some others below:

The way we think is corrupted. **Proverbs 14:12(NKJV), "There is a way *that seems* right to a man, But its end *is* the way of death."** We must ask God to forgive us and to help us change our thinking. We must become more God-centered than we are self-centered. Instead of thinking "I am in control" I must begin to believe "God is in control." Instead of telling myself "I deserve better" I must understand "I deserve worse." (Rom 6:23). I don't want what I deserve! I thank God for His grace. So when someone wrongs me instead of thinking "I deserve better treatment than this" I remember God's grace and what I really deserve is much worse. This helps me to forgive the offense.

Forgiveness is key to overcoming anger. Forgive yourself. Forgive others. Receive and accept God's forgiveness and offer that same forgiveness to those around you. We will discuss this further next time.

PRAYER: "Lord, I know that I need help with my inner man. Sometimes I am such a mess inside. You know me better than I even know myself. Help me to forgive those who have wronged me. Help me to renew my mind with what is true. I know that when my inner man is focused upon my desires, my dreams, my plans and there is an interruption to those plans I do not always respond in the manner that I should. Have mercy upon me. Thank-you for your patience as you continue to transform who I am. In Jesus' name, Amen."

Anger Part 2 "The Inner Man"
Week #19 assignment

Expectations Worksheet

Think of at least three expectations that you usually have of yourself or of others, when not met will cause you to become irritated and angry. Beside the expectation write YES if you feel this expectation is being met. Write NO if you feel it is not being met.

1. _____ _____

2. _____ _____

3. _____ _____

God created us to need Him and to need each other. We were never intended to be totally independent creatures. We all have needs. It is at those times when we feel that our needs are not being met that we can become angry. I have listed below a few needs that are common to us all. Beside the need I want you to write the name of the person whom you believe is responsible for meeting this particular need in your life. (Yourself, Spouse, Friend, Parent, Others, etc…)

1. To be loved _____

2. To be safe _____

3. To feel wanted _____

4. To feel of value _____

5. To be fulfilled _____

6. To be happy _____

7. To be understood _____

We often become angry when we feel that our "rights" are being threatened. We often think thoughts like "I don't deserve this" or "Who does he think he is talking to me like this?" There is a list of "rights" below. Circle those that you feel are NOT being honored.

1. The right to be treated fairly

2. The right to be happy

3. The right to be heard

4. The right to be understood

5. The right to be obeyed

6. The right to be respected

7. The right to be appreciated

Can you think of any other "needs" or "rights" that people often focus upon?

Romans 8:28-29 (NKJV)
"And we know that all things work together for good to those who love God, to those who are the called according to His purpose. ²⁹ For whom He foreknew, He also predestined to be conformed to the image of His Son, that He might be the firstborn among many brethren."

1. Choose today to surrender your unmet needs and expectations to God, trusting that He is working these out for your good.

2. Make the choice right now to forgive those who have neglected and hurt you.

3. Surrender your rights to God.

4. Begin to journal your thoughts. What are you thinking when you begin to become angry?

Philippians 2:5-8 (NKJV)

"Let this mind be in you which was also in Christ Jesus,
[6] who, being in the form of God, did not consider it robbery to be equal with God, [7] but made Himself of no reputation, taking the form of a bondservant, *and* coming in the likeness of men. [8] And being found in appearance as a man, He humbled Himself and became obedient to *the point of* death, even the death of the cross."

Forgiveness;The Key to Overcoming
Week #20

For the past few weeks we have been discussing anger from a biblical perspective. We have noted that anger is actually a choice that we are making. Anger may seem like an automatic response for you but that is only because you have developed a habit of becoming angry and expressing that emotion in a certain way. As is true with all habitual behavior, it becomes a pattern of life. Patterns and habits, addictions, can be broken. We have also discussed the definition, "Anger is an emotional response to a perceived threat." Whenever truth is threatened we should become angry. This would include times when others are devalued or mistreated, when sin inflicts pain on humanity, or anger over evil. This anger can actually be beneficial if we allow that emotion to create passion within us to correct a wrong or to protect what is good and godly. Our problem however is usually related to sinful anger which is more than likely self-centered. We should live our lives God centered and not self-centered. We have also discussed that at the root of our anger issues, as is true with all emotional responses, there are beliefs that we are holding true within that become the source for our emotional responses. If you believe that you are the master of your domain, that you are in full control of your life, you will be frustrated most of the time. So, we must renew our minds and understand that God is the one in control.

This week we are looking at the key to overcoming anger; Forgiveness. Have you ever been hurt by another? Have you ever disappointed yourself? Have you ever made a foolish decision that you wish you could go back and make differently? WE ALL HAVE! We live in a fallen world, full of fallen people, within a body, mind, and heart that is imperfect. Stuff is going to happen! Sin is going to be an ever-present issue as long as we live this life. The modern psychiatric world talks a lot about "dysfunction." Did you know that dysfunction is a relatively modern term? It is within the past 50 years that this word has been used to describe something or someone who is not functioning correctly. Many use their dysfunctional past to excuse their current behaviors. The Bible calls this sin. We are all affected by sin. We sin (Romans 3:23) and we are also sinned against because we live in a sinful world.

Sin always brings with it pain. It steals, kills, and destroys everything that is dear to us. Sin is that pulling within to live our lives, and to think, in a manner which God never intended or desired for us.

Let's discuss how we can overcome this pain. You may ask, "Why is this such a big deal?" If you do not deal with the pain inflicted on you because of sin, that pain will progress into bitterness, a critical spirit, hardness of heart, and the ultimate joy-killer. You cannot live out the abundant life that Christ offers you if you hold unforgiveness in your heart.

There is much that we can learn about forgiveness, as well as unforgiveness, from the parable of The Prodigal Son:

Luke 15:11-32 (NKJV)

[11] Then He said: "A certain man had two sons. [12] And the younger of them said to *his* father, 'Father, give me the portion of goods that falls *to me.'* So he divided to them *his* livelihood. [13] And not many days after, the younger son gathered all together, journeyed to a far country, and there wasted his possessions with prodigal living. [14] But when he had spent all, there arose a severe famine in that land, and he began to be in want. [15] Then he went and joined himself to a citizen of that country, and he sent him into his fields to feed swine. [16] And he would gladly have filled his stomach with the pods that the swine ate, and no one gave him *anything.* [17] But when he came to himself, he said, 'How many of my father's hired servants have bread enough and to spare, and I perish with hunger! [18] I will arise and go to my father, and will say to him, "Father, I have sinned against heaven and before you, [19] and I am no longer worthy to be called your son. Make me like one of your hired servants." ' [20] And he arose and came to his father. But when he was still a great way off, his father saw him and had compassion, and ran and fell on his neck and kissed him. [21] And the son said to him, 'Father, I have sinned against heaven and in your sight, and am no longer worthy to be called your son.' [22] But the father said to his servants, 'Bring out the best robe and put *it* on him, and put a ring on his hand and sandals on *his* feet. [23] And bring the fatted calf here and kill *it,* and let us eat and be merry; [24] for this my son was dead and is alive again; he was lost and is found.' And they began to be merry. [25] Now his older son was in the field. And as he came and drew near to the house, he heard music and dancing. [26] So he called one of the servants and asked what these things meant. [27] And he said to him, 'Your brother has come, and because he has received him safe and sound, your father has killed the fatted calf.' [28] But he was angry and would not go in. Therefore his father came out and pleaded with him. [29] So he answered and said to *his* father, 'Lo, these many years I have been serving you; I never transgressed your commandment at any time; and yet you never gave me a young goat, that I might make merry with my friends. [30] But as soon as this son of yours came, who has devoured your livelihood with harlots, you killed the fatted calf for him.' [31] And he said to him, 'Son, you are always with me, and all that I have is yours. [32] It was right that we should make merry and be glad, for your brother was dead and is alive again, and was lost and is found.'"

The father in this parable represents our Heavenly Father. The 2 sons represent us. Often in ancient days a father would advance to his children their portion of their inheritance before he died. This practice helped to relieve the aging father of the responsibility of managing his entire estate himself. In this parable we are given this example of a father who gave his two sons their inheritance. One of the sons stays home and continues serving his father on his estate. The youngest son received his inheritance and went out and wasted it all on worldly living.

Who had actually earned what the younger son had received?

God grants to us what we do not deserve and what we have not earned. How about another chance to live life? How about a new beginning? That is what our Heavenly Father offers us!

I also want you to note that when the younger son left home to live his life his own way, the father did not go running after him. This is so hard for a parent. Often our first response is to bail that son or daughter out of the mess they have gotten themselves into. If your mother or father has refused to bail you out, if they have not seemed eager to get you out of trouble, that response does not mean they do not love you. That response in fact demonstrates that they do love you. They love you enough to allow the lesson you must learn to sink in. God loves us! We know without a doubt this is true. If you want evidence, look to the cross. The father in the parable did not chase after the son but he is described in verse 20 as waiting and watching. I believe he was also praying for his son's return. When the father saw the son coming toward the house verse 20 tells us that he ran to meet his boy. This is the only place in the Bible where God is pictured as running. God is not running from anything but rather He is running toward someone. Who is it that God is so eager to run to, to wrap His arms around, to kiss and welcome back home? It's the undeserving, rebellious son who has broken his father's heart but has now returned home. I want you to know that it doesn't matter what you have done, God still loves you. He is waiting with open arms to receive you home. God is ready and willing and desiring to forgive and restore you.

Once the son returned home the father hosted a huge party including a feast because his son who was lost was now found. Remember that this was the son who previously was in the pigpen contemplating eating the husks that were fed to the pigs. Listen, the food the world offers you will never satisfy. You must come to your Father's table, approach His presence in faith, and feast on His provision. God's person in Jesus Christ and God's Word revealed in the Holy Bible is the truth your inner person hungers for. God's forgiveness is amazing!

Did you know that it is this same kind of forgiveness that we are to offer others and to receive ourselves?

Colossians 3:12-13 (NKJV)

"Therefore, as *the* elect of God, holy and beloved, put on tender mercies, kindness, humility, meekness, longsuffering; [13] bearing with one another, and <u>forgiving one another,</u> if anyone has a complaint against another; even as Christ forgave you, so you also *must do.*"

We must choose to forgive ourselves and others the way that Christ has forgiven us!

HOW DO I BEGIN THIS JOURNEY OF FORGIVENESS?
Colossians 3:12-13

#1. Confess your hurt and pain to God. Be real with God. Tell Him how you are feeling and how you are struggling. God can handle it!

#2. Ask God for forgiveness because unforgiveness is a sin. 1 John 1:9

#3. Make the choice now to forgive the way that God forgives.

As you do, make these promises:

A. I will no longer think about this offence in a negative manner. When it returns to my mind I will consciously recall that I have chosen to forgive this sin because I have been forgiven so much. It will not hinder my relationship with God, myself, or with others.

B. Commit now to never use this offense against the other person or even against yourself. God says that it is gone.

C. Make a promise now that you will not talk about this to others in a hurtful manner. Settle it right now.

#4. Give thanks for God's forgiveness and grace. Worship Him.

Psalm 103:8-12 (NKJV)
"The LORD *is* merciful and gracious, Slow to anger, and abounding in mercy.
⁹ He will not always strive *with us,* Nor will He keep *His anger* forever.
¹⁰ He has not dealt with us according to our sins, Nor punished us according to our iniquities.
¹¹ For as the heavens are high above the earth, *So* great is His mercy toward those who fear Him; ¹² As far as the east is from the west, *So* far has He removed our transgressions from us."

PRAYER: *"My Heavenly Father, thank-you for your forgiveness extended towards me. Please help me to forgive those around me. I know that unforgiveness is a sin and that it will hinder me from living the life you desire for me. I repent of this bitter spirit of unforgiveness. Lord God, I desire to reflect your nature in my life. Mold me into the image of Jesus. I want to be like Him. In Jesus' name, Amen."*

"Forgiveness-The Key to Overcoming"
Week #20 assignment

Read each statement. Then under each one explain what is wrong with believing the statement:

#1. I will forgive when I feel like it.

#2. If I ignore it, the problem will go away.

#3. If I forgive this person, I will look weak.

#4. I'm letting that person off the hook if I forgive.

#5. I want revenge!

#6. I have to forgive myself before I can forgive others.

#7. I'm waiting for him/her to come to me first and ask for forgiveness.

Can you think of other excuses?

Ready for Battle; Equipped to Win!
Week #21

The battle is real! You have stepped out from your past life and former conduct. You are looking to God and His Word for guidance and power to change. You have begun to surround yourself with a support group. You are working through the assignments as you renew your mind. I commend you and encourage you in all these things. However, I must also warn you as well because the enemy is real and the battle fierce. Our flesh, the devil and his demons, and this fallen world do not want you to succeed.

This week we are considering a special armor that God has provided that will equip us to fight and win the battle over the temptation to sin. Each piece of this armor is important to our well-being. Read the passage below and recognize the warfare:

Ephesians 6:10-18 (NKJV)

"Finally, my brethren, be strong in the Lord and in the power of His might. [11] Put on the whole armor of God, that you may be able to stand against the wiles of the devil. [12] For we do not wrestle against flesh and blood, but against principalities, against powers, against the rulers of the darkness of this age, against spiritual *hosts* of wickedness in the heavenly *places*. [13] Therefore take up the whole armor of God, that you may be able to withstand in the evil day, and having done all, to stand. [14] Stand therefore, having girded your waist with truth, having put on the breastplate of righteousness, [15] and having shod your feet with the preparation of the gospel of peace; [16] above all, taking the shield of faith with which you will be able to quench all the fiery darts of the wicked one. [17] And take the helmet of salvation, and the sword of the Spirit, which is the word of God; [18] praying always with all prayer and supplication in the Spirit, being watchful to this end with all perseverance and supplication for all the saints...."

Notice the phrase **"Be strong in the Lord and in the power of His might."** The victory over temptation will only be realized as you rely upon a power and a strength that is greater than your own. What are some ways that you have relied on your own strength in the past only to fail?

Every command of God, every requirement that God issues to us, should drive us back to Christ and His sufficiency. It is about grace. I am reminded that I don't have what it takes. It is not about my own efforts, my own inner strength, or my schemes and plans. It is all about Christ. This realization causes me to cry out, "Lord, I need You!" It is then that I can stand strong in this battle.

Verse 11 reminds me that it is not good enough for me to have part of this armor on, but I must **"put on the WHOLE armor of God."** If one piece is missing then I am leaving a kink, a gap, that the enemy can deliver a devastating blow. Let's consider what each piece of this armor is and how we can be certain we have on the whole armor.

Paul begins in verse 14 with **"truth."** If you know very little of God's truth then you are in a dangerous position indeed. In biblical times the men wore these long flowing robes with a belt at the waist. When a man was preparing to go into battle he would tuck the bottom of the robe under his belt so he would not trip on the hem of his garment and fall. It is truth that keeps you from tripping and falling! Jesus said as recorded in John 8:32 that the truth will set us free. Just as that belt on the soldier would free him up for battle, God's truth frees us up from sin so that we can fight unhindered by the enemy.

The second piece of this armor is **"the breastplate of righteousness."** It is not enough to simply know the truth (the belt) but we must apply that truth to our lives. The result is right living! How are you doing at applying God's truth to your life? Do not be lazy in this endeavor because the stakes are high. List here areas in your life where you need to improve at applying God's truth to your life:

The third piece of armor are the shoes, **"shod your feet with the preparation of the gospel of peace."** This is saying that we should be prepared to share the Gospel. Get ready to run with it! A good defense is a good offense. When we go out and share our faith we are pushing back the forces of evil in the world.

In verse 16 we find the fourth piece of our armor, **"the shield of faith."** We need a shield! In the times in which this was written, soldiers would have these huge wooden shields that were about the size of a door, sometimes 4 feet tall. They would soak these shields in water. As they would approach the enemy in combat they would come alongside one another bumping their shields together, forming a wall. As the enemy would shoot these fiery arrows they would stick in these shields and immediately be extinguished. Faith means that we are believing God. There is also power and strength when we believe together!

What promises of God do you need to believe right now in order to have victory?

Take your Bible and look up these verses and read them:

1 Cor. 10:13   Deut. 20:4   1 John 1:9

Can you think of some other promises of God that we must believe in order to be victorious?

Next we must have our head protected with **"the helmet of salvation."** Too many Christians are what I call "spiritual streakers" because this is the only piece of the armor that they have bothered to put on. They are saved and that's about it. This study is useless unless a person has accepted God's gift of salvation. Can you think of excuses people give for not accepting Christ?

The Word of God is our **sword.** Note something very important about this sword; It is not your sword but it is the sword of the Spirit. I can't fight this battle in my might. The Holy Spirit's power is the greatest power in all the world. If you are a Christian you have the Holy Spirit living within you. That power is right there inside your mortal body. You must however yield to this power and allow Him to work through you. You need to get you out of the way and make sure God is controlling your mind, soul, and spirit.

All of this must be put on **prayerfully**, knowing we are dependent upon God. Prayer is communicating with God. We speak to Him in prayer. God speaks to us through His Word. When was the last time you spent time just talking and listening to God?

Take time right now to consider the "Spiritual Warfare Prayer" points on the next page. Use these points along with the scripture verses provided to express your heart felt prayer to God.

SPIRITUAL WARFARE PRAYER

Points to remember:

1. Every born-again child of God has been given a promise of victory over Satan.

Isaiah 54:17 (ESV)
"no weapon that is fashioned against you shall succeed, and you shall refute every tongue that rises against you in judgment. This is the heritage of the servants of the LORD and their vindication from me, declares the LORD."

Luke 10:19 (ESV)
"Behold, I have given you authority to tread on serpents and scorpions, and over all the power of the enemy, and nothing shall hurt you."

James 4:7 (ESV)
"Submit yourselves therefore to God. Resist the devil, and he will flee from you."

John 4:4 (ESV)
"Little children, you are from God and have overcome them, for he who is in you is greater than he who is in the world."

2. Recognize who your enemy is. It's not your dealer or supplier. It's not your probation officer. It's not the police. It's Satan and his host of demons as well as your own sin nature.

Ephesians 6:11 (ESV)
"Put on the whole armor of God, that you may be able to stand against the schemes of the devil."

2 Corinthians 2:11 (ESV)
"so that we would not be outwitted by Satan; for we are not ignorant of his designs."

3. It is your responsibility to prepare for battle, to "put on the whole armor of God" (Ephesians 6:11), and to "stand against the evil one" (vv. 11-14) – these are active verbs. But the battle belongs to God and the victory is found through Christ. We must simply walk in the victory!

Deuteronomy 20:1 (ESV)

"When you go out to war against your enemies, and see horses and chariots and an army larger than your own, you shall not be afraid of them, for the LORD your God is with you, who brought you up out of the land of Egypt."

2 Chronicles 20:15 (ESV)

"And he said, 'Listen, all Judah and inhabitants of Jerusalem and King Jehoshaphat: Thus says the LORD to you, "Do not be afraid and do not be dismayed at this great horde, for the battle is not yours but God's."'"

PRAYER: *"Lord God, I know the spiritual battle is real! I experience the attacks everyday as I strive to live my life for you. Thank-you for providing this special armor that I may be equipped to fight against the attacks of the wicked one. I know that it is my responsibility to receive this armor, to wear it, and to allow you, Lord God, to flow through me in your power and presence. I believe that I have more than enough to be victorious in this warfare. I am claiming the victory, expecting the victory, and I am praising you for the victory. In Jesus' name, Amen."*

"Ready for Battle: Equipped to Win"
Week #21 assignment

#1. Use the points from the previous "Spiritual Warfare Prayer" to write your personal prayer to God:

#2. As you consider each individual piece of this spiritual armor, which do you feel is the weakest in your own life?

#3. What will you do right now to begin strengthening that weak piece?

#4. Which piece of the spiritual armor do you believe is MOST important to you? Why?

Sweet Victory
Week #22

Romans 6:12-14 (NKJV)
"Therefore do not let sin reign in your mortal body, that you should obey it in its lusts. And do not present your members as instruments of unrighteousness to sin, but present yourselves to God as being alive from the dead, and your members as instruments of righteousness to God. For sin shall not have dominion over you, for you are not under law but under grace."

You do not have to live under your circumstances any longer. You can rise above the problems and struggles of your past. You no longer have to live your life as a victim. You can now live a life that is victorious over those things which have held you captive. This is not always easy, but it is always possible for those who have placed their faith in Jesus as their Lord and Savior. You are now a Spirit-empowered child of the King! You now have royal blood flowing through your veins. Live out who you are in Christ Jesus.

First of all, listen to what God says about you. This message of truth from your Creator may be in direct contrast with what others are saying about you. In fact, what God says about you may not be what you have been saying is true about yourself. I ask you, "Whose evaluation of your identity is more trustworthy? Is it God's, others, or your own?" I think you get my point. We can always trust God's Word to be perfectly trustworthy and reliable. His Word is indeed the *truth* that is able to set us free. What does God say about who you are now? Please open your heart and listen to God speak to you through Ephesians 1:

God says that He has chosen you!

Ephesians 1:4 (NKJV)
"… just as He chose us in Him before the foundation of the world, that we should be holy and without blame before Him in love…"

To ponder this eternal truth that you are chosen by God should fill your heart with humility and amazement. Looking back on my childhood, I remember myself as a rather awkward adolescent struggling with acne and a poor evaluation of myself. I always wanted to fit in with those who were the most popular, but always felt that I never could.

In junior high school I was always one of the last ones chosen during physical education when the captains chose their teams. Sometimes I felt as if the two team captains were going to actually fight over which team was going to be burdened with me! Now I know that I am chosen by God Himself. Wow! The Creator of all the world, chose me! The One who one day so long ago gazed down into nothingness and purposed in Himself to form the earth and to fling the stars into the Milky Way, chose me. The One who is omniscient, omnipotent, and omnipresent picked me! I am of great eternal value.

God says that He has adopted you!

Ephesians 1:5 (NKJV)
"having predestined us to adoption as sons by Jesus Christ to
Himself, according to the good pleasure of His will…"

It was part of God's plan from the very beginning to save you and to bring you unto Himself. This concept of adoption spoken of here does not refer to our salvation as much as it does to the benefits of our salvation. We are saved by being born into God's family. This new birth, or regeneration, begins the moment a person believes in Christ as their personal Lord and Savior. Certainly, we were all born babies, correct? People do not enter into this world as toddlers, or teenagers, or adults. Just as we are born as infants physically we are also born as "babes in Christ" spiritually the moment Christ saves us. Paul wrote to the people in Corinth addressing their many problems:

1 Corinthians 3:1 (NKJV)
"And I, brethren, could not speak to you as to spiritual
people but as to carnal, as to babes in Christ."

According to ancient Roman law, and it is basically still true today, a baby could not claim his or her inheritance until he or she became of adult age. So, what has God done for you? He has brought you into His family through regeneration and justification. This is the act whereby you are born again. However, at the same time God also adopted you as an adult spiritual son or daughter, who can immediately begin accessing his/her inheritance and benefits as His child. Immediately upon salvation, God extended to you love, joy, peace, longsuffering, kindness, goodness, faithfulness, gentleness, and the power to exercise self-control (Galatians 5:22-23). Who are you? You are a born again, adopted, blood-bought, redeemed, empowered, eternally rich and currently blessed child of God. That's not self-esteem but that is God esteem!

God says that you are accepted!

Ephesians 1:6 (NKJV)
"to the praise of the glory of His grace, by which He has made us accepted in the Beloved."

You are not accepted because you are good enough, but you are accepted because of God's grace. When God looks upon your soul, He no longer sees the ugliness of your sin. God now sees Jesus and His imputed righteousness. You are covered from head to toe with Jesus. Now as God looks upon you, He no longer sees your unrighteousness, but He sees only Christ's righteousness which makes you acceptable to Him.

God says that you are redeemed and forgiven!

Ephesians 1:7 (NKJV)
" … In Him we have redemption through His blood, the forgiveness of sins, according to the riches of His grace."

The word *redemption* means "to ransom in full."[4] Your sin debt has been paid in full. In Paul's day, this word would be used to describe someone purchasing a slave and then simply releasing that slave to be free.[5] Your debt has been paid in full and you are now forgiven. You can choose to no longer listen to the lies from the enemy telling you that you are guilty, unworthy, unloved, and unforgiven. You know it is only through Jesus' blood and by His grace that you are redeemed and forgiven.

God says that you have been sealed!

Ephesians 1:13 (NKJV)
"In Him you also trusted, after you heard the word of truth, the gospel of your salvation; in whom also, having believed, you were sealed with the Holy Spirit of promise…"

This truth brings certainty to your salvation experience. You are secure in Christ and in God's family. This is a finished transaction.[6] In ancient days there were several uses for a seal:

A seal would confirm something as being genuine.

A seal would identify personal property.

---

4   James Strong, S.T.D., LL.D., The Exhaustive Concordance of The Bible (Peabody, MA: Hendrickson Publishers), #629, p.14.
5   Warren W. Wiersbe, The Bible Expositional Commentary (BE Series), New Testament, Volume 2, (Database @ 2007 WORDsearch Corp.), p.11.
6   Ibid., p.12.

A seal was used to make something secure.[7]

All three of these uses can be applied to your life as a born-again, adopted, child of God. First of all, this seal makes you a genuine Christian. God is the One who does the sealing.

Secondly, you now belong to God and Him alone. This means that you are not to worship other gods. You are not to allow anyone or anything else to control you. You belong exclusively to Him. You are His property.

Thirdly, this seal guarantees your full salvation. You are secure in Christ and now nothing nor anyone can ever change that. Ephesians 4:30 reminds us that we are sealed *"for the day of redemption."* That will be the day of full redemption when you stand justified, sanctified, and gloried in the presence of God. In the meantime, you can trust God to transform your life into His image. He is going to finish what He has begun in you.

Philippians 1:6 (NKJV)
"being confident of this very thing, that He who has begun a good
work in you will complete it until the day of Jesus Christ."

The truth of God sets you free to be who you are in Christ. You no longer live as a victim, enslaved by your past mistakes and controlled by your natural man, but now you can walk in victory. This victory was not realized in my life through some man-made twelve-step program. I actually took only one step. That one step was the step I took many years ago when I surrendered to the Holy Spirit's prompting and invited Jesus to be my Lord and my Savior. That was the day of my deliverance and salvation. That was also the beginning of a new life. Each day I live, I must choose to be victorious over my past and over the temptation that comes upon me.

It is a daily choice I make to live as a victor and not a victim. What choice have you made? Will you choose to live the same empty and destructive lifestyle that you have lived in your past? Or will you choose life today? Stop living as a victim and live in the victory Christ offers.

This struggle to live in victory takes place upon the battlefield of your mind. You must think about yourself as God now sees you. What does that mean? The Bible teaches in **Proverbs 23:7, "For as he thinks in his heart, so is he."** If you listen to the lies of Satan you will always struggle. Your thoughts concerning yourself will be extremely negative and degrading. The result will be a life lived in defeat. Do not be a

---

7   Charles Hodge, A Commentary on Ephesians, (database@2004 WORDsearch Corp., Ephesians 1:13.

victim. Remember who you are, my friend. You have been chosen, adopted, accepted, redeemed, forgiven, and sealed. You are saved and secure in God's family. The truth concerning all born-again and adopted believers is that we are children of the King who immediately have access to everything we need from our Father Who is in Heaven.

I want to share with you one of my favorite promises in God's Word. It is within these words that I am promised by God to have all that I need to live this victorious Christian life.

2 Peter 1:2-4 (NKJV)
"Grace and peace be multiplied to you in the knowledge of God and of Jesus our Lord, as His divine power has given to us all things that pertain to life and godliness, through the knowledge of Him who called us by glory and virtue, by which have been given to us exceedingly great and precious promises, that through these you may be partakers of the divine nature, having escaped the corruption that is in the world through lust."

You can experience grace and peace when you rely upon God's resources for your life. There are two sources of power and strength revealed to us in this passage.

First of all, **"His divine power"** speaks of the Holy Spirit. **Romans 8:9** says **"But you are not in the flesh but in the Spirit, if indeed the Spirit of God dwells in you. Now if anyone does not have the Spirit of Christ, he is not His."** I am saved and adopted into God's family thus I know I have the Holy Spirit of God. Then Peter writes in **2 Peter 1:3 "through the knowledge of Him who called us."** Where do I find this knowledge about God? I learn about God through the pages of the Bible.

The Bible is also the same place I will find **"exceeding great and precious promises."** God is telling us that with these two resources from God, His Spirit and His Word, we have **"all things that pertain to life and godliness."** The life referred to here is spiritual life. I can live in abundance (John 10:10) and walk in victory as I apply the Word of God in the power of God's Spirit to my life. There are no VALID excuses for a believer who lives a defeated and sin-ridden life.

Prayer: *"Dear wonderful Heavenly Father, Giver of every good and perfect gift, my heart worships You. You and You alone have given me the victory over sin. Sin no longer has a hold on my life. I accept the truth of Who You say that I am. Help me to put off the lies that I have believed for so long. I desire to renew my mind with Your truth. Help me to understand the truth about the world around me, and who I am through Your eyes. It is Your truth that sets me free. I desire to always live in Your freedom. Thank-you, my God. In Jesus' name, Amen."*

Sweet Victory
Week #22 assignment

1. From week #16, write out 1 Corinthians 10:13 here:

2. Read Philippians 4:8. What do you think? This verse tells us how we should be thinking. Write out the key words given in this verse concerning the type of things you are to be thinking. *Whatsoever things are:*

3. How can I apply Philippians 4:8 to my thoughts concerning who I am in Christ and living out the victorious Christian life?

4. Read Ephesians 6:10-18. List the different parts of the Armor of God:

   a.

   b.

   c.

   d.

   e.

   f.

   g.

5. 1 Corinthians 15:57, *"But thanks be to God, who gives us the victory through our Lord Jesus Christ."* What is it that you need victory over?

6. Who do you say that you are? Place a check beside each statement below that you believe is true about you. Then read the corresponding scripture beside that statement and write below that statement what God says about you.

_____ I can't break the power of sin. (Romans 6:6, 11, 17-18)

_____ Nobody really loves me. (John 15:9; Ephesians 2:4, 5:1-2)

_____ I don't have enough faith. (Romans 10:17; Hebrews 12:2)

_____ I don't have what it takes to live right. (Philippians 4:19)

_____ I am hopeless. (Hebrews 6:19; Romans 15:13)

_____ I am a failure. (2 Corinthians 3:5-6)

_____ I am going crazy. (1 Corinthians 2:16)

_____ I am afraid. (1 John 4:18; 2 Timothy 1:7)

_____ I'm not strong enough. (Romans 8:9-11; Ephesians 1:19)

_____ I'm condemned. (Romans 8:1; Colossians 1:22)

_____ I am guilty. (Hebrews 10:10; Colossians)

"The LIFE program has been such an inspiration. I was bound and chained to addiction for five years. I felt there was no hope for recovery. I attempted to quit many times but I always failed. Jesus has broken the shackles of addiction and LIFE Ministries has been my guide. LIFE has taught me how to repent, to forgive, and to live life the way that God intended. The shame and lies of addiction are no more!" 1 Corinthians 6:9-11

Jim Brie, LIFE member

Understanding and Defeating Temptation
Week #23

This week's study deals with an issue we can ALL relate to-**temptation!** We are all tempted to do what we shouldn't be doing. Just remember that being tempted is not a sin. It is when we yield to the temptation that we fall into sin. Jesus understands our struggle even better than we do.

Hebrews 4:15 (NKJV)

"For we do not have a High Priest who cannot sympathize with our weaknesses, but was in all *points* tempted as *we are, yet* without sin."

Jesus faced temptations yet He never sinned. The Biblical record of Jesus' temptation and how He overcame can teach us a great deal.

Luke 4:1-15 (ESV)

[1] And Jesus, full of the Holy Spirit, returned from the Jordan and was led by the Spirit in the wilderness [2] for forty days, being tempted by the devil. And he ate nothing during those days. And when they were ended, he was hungry. [3] The devil said to him, "If you are the Son of God, command this stone to become bread." [4] And Jesus answered him, "It is written, 'Man shall not live by bread alone.'" [5] And the devil took him up and showed him all the kingdoms of the world in a moment of time, [6] and said to him, "To you I will give all this authority and their glory, for it has been delivered to me, and I give it to whom I will. [7] If you, then, will worship me, it will all be yours." [8] And Jesus answered him, "It is written, "'You shall worship the Lord your God, and him only shall you serve.'" [9] And he took him to Jerusalem and set him on the pinnacle of the temple and said to him, "If you are the Son of God, throw yourself down from here, [10] for it is written, "'He will command his angels concerning you, to guard you,' [11] and "'On their hands they will bear you up, lest you strike your foot against a stone.'" [12] And Jesus answered him, "It is said, 'You shall not put the Lord your God to the test.'" [13] And when the devil had ended every temptation, he departed from him until an opportune time. [14] And Jesus returned in the power of the Spirit to Galilee, and a report about him went out through all the surrounding country. [15] And he taught in their synagogues, being glorified by all.

The biblical account of the temptation of Jesus happened immediately following an extreme mountain-top experience for Jesus. Jesus had just been baptized by John the Baptist in the Jordan River. Matthew 4 records how God spoke from Heaven as Jesus came up out of that water, "This is my Beloved Son, in whom I am well pleased." The Bible records for us how the heavens opened up and the Holy Spirit descended in the form of a dove. That was an awesome experience in the life of Christ. However, immediately following that adrenaline rushing event He is faced with probably one of His lowest emotional times prior to His crucifixion.

I remember years ago counseling a couple who were struggling in their marriage. The husband and wife both had positions of ministry within their church. The husband had recently attended a men's conference out of town. It was a "Promise Keepers" conference held in Raleigh, N.C. The husband began to confess how he had such an awesome time at the conference. He drew closer to God, met new friends, and really believed he was stronger in his commitment to his wife and family when it was over. However, before he even arrived back home he had fallen into sin. He had stopped off at a strip club before returning home. Once he did arrive home his wife later found the parking stub in his pocket, confronted him, and now he was sitting before me.

The enemy seems to attack us not only when we are down and discouraged but even when we are just coming out of a victorious period in our life. What does this mean? We must always be on guard against temptation. We can never safely let our guard down.

Can you think of a time in your life when you failed miserably following a great period of success?

A common word that we hear often is "relapse." A relapse can occur when we yield to temptation.

In the previous passage of scripture from Luke 4, "What did Jesus do each time He was tempted?"

The Psalmist wrote in Psalm 119:

Psalm 119:9-12 (ESV)
"How can a young man keep his way pure? By guarding it according to your word.
[10] With my whole heart I seek you; let me not wander from your commandments!
[11] I have stored up your word in my heart, that I might not sin against you.
[12] Blessed are you, O LORD; teach me your statutes!"

There is power to overcome temptation found recorded in God's Word. What really matters is what God says! It is not what I say, how I feel, what others say, or even what so called experts tell me that really matters. I need a word from God. This is how you can overcome those "relapses" in life. Know what God says and when the enemy tempts you, stand firm on God's truth. Don't give an inch!

Read and study the passages below from 1 Corinthians 10. Following this personal time of study journal your personal thoughts at the end.

1 Corinthians 10:12-13 (ESV)

"Therefore let anyone who thinks that he stands take heed lest he fall. ¹³ No temptation has overtaken you that is not common to man. God is faithful, and he will not let you be tempted beyond your ability, but with the temptation he will also provide the way of escape, that you may be able to endure it."

1 Corinthians 10:23-33 (ESV)

²³ "All things are lawful," but not all things are helpful. "All things are lawful," but not all things build up. ²⁴ Let no one seek his own good, but the good of his neighbor. ²⁵ Eat whatever is sold in the meat market without raising any question on the ground of conscience. ²⁶ For "the earth is the Lord's, and the fullness thereof." ²⁷ If one of the unbelievers invites you to dinner and you are disposed to go, eat whatever is set before you without raising any question on the ground of conscience. ²⁸ But if someone says to you, "This has been offered in sacrifice," then do not eat it, for the sake of the one who informed you, and for the sake of conscience— ²⁹ I do not mean your conscience, but his. For why should my liberty be determined by someone else's conscience? ³⁰ If I partake with thankfulness, why am I denounced because of that for which I give thanks? ³¹ So, whether you eat or drink, or whatever you do, do all to the glory of God. ³² Give no offense to Jews or to Greeks or to the church of God, ³³ just as I try to please everyone in everything I do, not seeking my own advantage, but that of many, that they may be saved.

Ten Truths about Temptation from 1 Corinthians 10

#1. If you think you are strong enough not to fall, be careful that you don't. verse 12

#2. Your temptation is not unique. verse 13

#3. God will not allow you to be tempted beyond what you can bear. verse 13

#4. God will provide a way out for you to withstand the test. verse 13

#5. Just because you can do something, doesn't mean you should. verse 23

#6. Focus on the welfare of others, not yourself. verse 24

#7. Don't allow your spiritual freedom to violate the conscience of others. verse 27

#8. Do everything, including what you put into your body, for the glory of God. verse 31

#9. Don't be a stumbling block to others. verse 32

#10. Seek the good of others so that they will be saved. verse 33

PRAYER: "My Father, who art in Heaven, lead me not into temptation. Please protect me from the evil one. I understand that if I let my guard down I can fall into sin. Give me strength, discernment and wisdom so that I will not be deceived. Thank-you Lord. In Jesus' name. Amen."

"Understanding and Defeating Temptation"
Week #23 assignment

#1. Just as Jesus faced temptation, so will you. Be prepared now so when it comes you will be ready. List below a few of your favorite verses which give you strength when you are tempted:

#2. When you remember that Jesus faced temptation, just as you do, how does that help you overcome?

#3. If you have not already done so, memorize 1 Corinthians 10:13. This is a passage, a promise from God, that can help you overcome temptation.

#4. In the previous passage found recorded in 1 Corinthians 10:23-33 Paul writes that just because we can legally do something doesn't mean that we should do it. What are some things that you should consider before you engage in some activity that is legal and that you are free to do?

Walking in Obedience
Week #24

God's way is the best way! I hope that you already know this is true. God created us and He knows better than anyone the purpose for which we were created. God desires that we worship Him. In fact, I would go as far as to say that this is the ultimate aim of mankind, to worship God. This endeavor even trumps evangelism. When you think about it, evangelism is simply helping others correct a worship disorder. The lost nations are not worshipping God, for whom they were created to worship, because they don't know God. Evangelistic outreach is the attempt to help them know God so that they may worship Him.

What is worship? Worship means to ascribe worth, to honor, and to have reverence. When we worship God we are acknowledging who He is and that He is of eternal worth and value. He is God! Jesus said about the hypocritical Pharisees of His day, **"This people honor me with their lips, but their heart is far from me; in vain do they worship me, teaching as doctrines the commandments of men." Matthew 15:8-9 (ESV).** Worship is much more than simply the words we speak. Worship originates in our hearts and affects what we do. Indeed, it is what goes on in the heart that proceeds forth in our speech and actions. Make sure your heart is right first and the outward responses will be in agreement!

Obedience is an indicator of your worship. If you really honor God and reverence Him, you will seek to obey His Word. Did you realize that obedience to God always precedes God's blessings upon you? Everyone wants a blessing but there seems to be few who really desire to walk in obedience. You will not experience one without the other friend.

Psalm 37:4 (ESV)
"Delight yourself in the LORD, and he will give you the desires of your heart."

You see, God's will must become your will, and His plans, your plans. His purpose must become your purpose. As a young man I tried to run from God's will for my life. I knew by the age of 13 that God had called me to preach. I knew within my heart that this was the calling that God had placed upon my life. That calling was not what I wanted so I began my futile attempt to run from this calling. I lived my life in disobedience and almost destroyed myself in the process. Do you know what was so amazing? When I surrendered to Christ and accepted the call to preach, I found one of the greatest joys in my life is to simply do what God has called me to do. Obedience is a great joy, not a burden.

If you are a parent, allow me to ask you a question; "Do you require your child to do things simply for your benefit or for their own good?" "Don't touch that hot pan!" "Don't get near the street!" "Don't run with a sucker in your mouth?" (Didn't your parents ever tell you that?). All of these commands were for our benefit.

God tells us how to live because God knows better than anyone, including us, how our lives were created to be lived. Those "thou shalt not" passages in the Bible are not there to hinder you but to bless you. OBEDIENCE COMES BEFORE BLESSING!

Think about the fact that every decision we make has consequences. The place where you decide to live; the person you decide to marry; the profession you enter into; the diet you maintain; these all have consequences. The "small decision" to add salt to my French fries even has consequences (higher blood pressure, sodium levels change in my bloodstream, thirst increases, etc…). Every choice you make will have a consequence. Think about this as you are faced with a decision to make. What will the outcome be?

Some decisions have eternal consequences. Let's consider the story of Lot.

Genesis 13:5-18 (ESV)

And Lot, who went with Abram, also had flocks and herds and tents, ⁶ so that the land could not support both of them dwelling together; for their possessions were so great that they could not dwell together, ⁷ and there was strife between the herdsmen of Abram's livestock and the herdsmen of Lot's livestock. At that time the Canaanites and the Perizzites were dwelling in the land. ⁸ Then Abram said to Lot, "Let there be no strife between you and me, and between your herdsmen and my herdsmen, for we are kinsmen. ⁹ Is not the whole land before you? Separate yourself from me. If you take the left hand, then I will go to the right, or if you take the right hand, then I will go to the left." ¹⁰ And Lot lifted up his eyes and saw that the Jordan Valley was well watered everywhere like the garden of the LORD, like the land of Egypt, in the direction of Zoar. (This was before the LORD destroyed Sodom and Gomorrah.) ¹¹ So Lot chose for himself all the Jordan Valley, and Lot journeyed east. Thus they separated from each other. ¹² Abram settled in the land of Canaan, while Lot settled among the cities of the valley and moved his tent as far as Sodom. ¹³ Now the men of Sodom were wicked, great sinners against the LORD. ¹⁴ The LORD said to Abram, after Lot had separated from him, "Lift up your eyes and look from the place where you are, northward and southward and eastward and westward, ¹⁵ for all the land that you see I will give to you and to your offspring forever. ¹⁶ I will make your offspring as the dust of the earth, so that if one can count the dust of the earth,

your offspring also can be counted. ¹⁷ Arise, walk through the length and the breadth of the land, for I will give it to you." ¹⁸ So Abram moved his tent and came and settled by the oaks of Mamre, which are at Hebron, and there he built an altar to the LORD.

What is this story about? Abram and his nephew Lot have travelled to the land of Promise because God has led them. Once there they find that there is not enough grazing land for all their animals. Uncle Abram, desiring to keep the peace, offers his nephew first choice of the grazing land. Abram states that he will be content to simply take what is left. Lot chose the fertile lush land of Jordan. This choice was the beginning of Lot's downfall. Lot began to compromise in his relationship with God because the area he chose was near the wicked city of Sodom. He gave the enemy a foothold. We see his progression downward in Genesis:

In Genesis 13:10 Lot LOOKED toward Sodom.

In Genesis 13:12 Lot MOVED near Sodom

In Genesis 14:12 Lot is LIVING in Sodom

In Genesis 19:1 Lot is SITTING at the gate of Sodom, meaning he holds a position now in the city's governing body.

What were the consequences for Lot's decisions?

He lost his wife. He barely escaped with his life from God's judgement. We then find him drunk, hiding in a cave and guilty of incest with his daughters. The offspring from that incestuous relationship would become Israel's greatest two enemies, the Ammorites and the Moabites. It all began with Lot's choice to live near Sodom.

Think about choices you are faced with right now. What will be the consequences for the choices you make?

When Lot began to drift away from God he got drunk and made even more foolish choices. This is the danger of becoming controlled by something or someone other than God. Maybe Lot was trying to forget his previous foolishness but by becoming a drunkard he only made his situation worse. Can you relate? Write out briefly below of a situation in your life when you made unwise choices and then trying to forget about those, you only made your situation worse:

Since obedience to God invites God's blessings upon your life, what will disobedience to God invite?

Job 22:21-26 (ESV)

"Agree with God, and be at peace; thereby good will come to you. [22] Receive instruction from his mouth, and lay up his words in your heart. [23] If you return to the Almighty you will be built up; if you remove injustice far from your tents, [24] if you lay gold in the dust, and gold of Ophir among the stones of the torrent-bed, [25] then the Almighty will be your gold and your precious silver.
[26] For then you will delight yourself in the Almighty and lift up your face to God."

What do you think it means to agree with God?

The enemy set Lot up for failure when Lot began to look to the most pleasing grazing land that was just outside the wicked city of Sodom. It mattered not to Lot what was going to keep him God-focused. He was simply looking out for himself, not considering if his decisions were going to bring God glory or not.

Matthew 6:33 (ESV)

"But seek first the kingdom of God and his righteousness, and all these things will be added to you."

Write Matthew 6:33 in your own words:

Write in the center of the bullseye below what you should be aiming to accomplish in every decision you make based upon 1 Cor. 10:31:

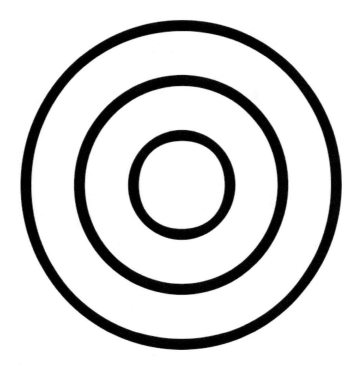

Seeing through Eyes of Faith
Week #25

The story is told of a father and his eight-year old son who were busy working together in the yard. The father, wanting to teach his son a valuable lesson, instructed him to use every resource at his disposal to load some heavy lumber into the back of his truck. The father knew that his boy would not be able to accomplish this task on his own, but was hoping the boy would turn to him for help. After several minutes of attempting to move the lumber by himself, the son approached his father, "Dad, I am sorry but I am not able to move this wood all by myself." The father asked, "Are you using all the resources at your disposal?" The son replied, "Yes father." The dad responded, "No, you haven't son since you have not asked for my help."

Addictions can seem like an enemy that we do not have the power to overcome. Sometimes the chains which bind us feel unbreakable and far too heavy for us to render apart on our own. Yet we are not utilizing all the resources at our disposal if we are not calling upon our Father for His help.

In this lesson we will consider the importance of looking past our human resources, what we see with our human eyes, to see and realize the resources we have that are invisible. Once you realize these unseen resources you will know that victory is possible in your life.

The text below deals with a time in Israel's history when Syria's armies were fighting against them. Syria kept attempting to ambush the Israelites but God was revealing to the prophet Elisha every plot that the King of Syria was planning. Following several unsuccessful attempts to trap Israel, the King of Syria began to wonder if there was a spy among his people. There was no spy. God had been instructing Elisha concerning every move Israel needed to make to stay safe. Once the Syrian King understood that it was Elisha who was warning Israel of each and every move his armies made, the King surrounded Elisha's dwelling with the intentions of getting Elisha out of his way once and for all. The Syrian armies had Elisha surrounded. Elisha's servant looking out at all the horses and chariots and soldiers that surrounded them exclaimed that all hope of escape was gone. Elisha prayed that his servant would see past their human resources and realize the resources made available to them by the Father in Heaven.

Read what happened:

2 Kings 6:8-17 (NKJV)

Now the king of Syria was making war against Israel and he consulted with his servants, saying, "My camp *will be* in such and such a place." ⁹And the man of God sent to the king of Israel, saying, "Beware that you do not pass this place, for the Syrians are coming down there." ¹⁰Then the king of Israel sent *someone* to the place of which the man of God had told him. Thus he warned him, and he was watchful there, not just once or twice. ¹¹Therefore the heart of the king of Syria was greatly troubled by this thing; and he called his servants and said to them, "Will you not show me which of us *is* for the king of Israel?" ¹²And one of his servants said, "None, my lord, O king; but Elisha, the prophet who *is* in Israel, tells the king of Israel the words that you speak in your bedroom." ¹³So he said, "Go and see where he *is,* that I may send and get him." And it was told him, saying, "Surely *he is* in Dothan." ¹⁴Therefore he sent horses and chariots and a great army there, and they came by night and surrounded the city. ¹⁵And when the servant of the man of God arose early and went out, there was an army, surrounding the city with horses and chariots. And his servant said to him, "Alas, my master! What shall we do?" ¹⁶So he answered, "Do not fear, for those who *are* with us *are* more than those who *are* w them." ¹⁷And Elisha prayed and said, "LORD, I pray, open his eyes that he may see." Then the LORD opened the eyes of the young man, and he saw. And behold, the mountain *was* full of horses and chariots of fire all around Elisha.

This passage is a beautiful illustration of the truth we find recorded in the New Testament:

2 Corinthians 10:3-4 (NKJV)

"For though we walk in the flesh, we do not war according to the flesh. ⁴For the weapons of our warfare *are* not carnal (not human) but mighty in God for pulling down strongholds."

The Holy Spirit, through the Apostle Paul, is telling us that we cannot fight this battle in our own strength and win. This is a supernatural battle which requires supernatural weapons. We have studied Ephesians 6 in a past lesson where we are told to "Put on the whole armor of God that we might be able to stand against the schemes of the devil." Yes, the enemy is real but so are the weapons that our God has provided for us.

Notice in Verses 9 and 10 the title given to Elisha: "the man of _____" You and I should strive to be that type of person! First, get serious about your walk with God. Get out of your life anything that does not look, act, or sound like Jesus. Have such a reputation that others would refer to you as "a man/

woman of God." This means that not only do you believe in God but you have also been to the cross in faith and trusted Christ as your personal Savior. This title also belongs to a person who has made God a priority in their life. Does that describe you? God is looking for some full-time Christians who are passionate about living for Him. Did you realize that this type of relationship with God will affect the places you go and the people you hang with?

Elisha kept warning the Israelites, "Don't go over there. It's a trap. The enemy will ambush you there." God keeps warning us through His Word and through Christians around us, like the leaders of your recovery group, to stay away from that place. Don't hang with your old friends. These are warnings to keep you safe.

List below some places that God has already warned you not to go if you are to remain clean:

Elisha's servant looked around and saw the enemy surrounding them and he cried out, "What can we do? All hope is lost!" Maybe you feel this way today. Maybe you are surrounded with grief, financial stress, trouble, and temptation. You cry out, "Pastor Mike, what on earth can I do?" You can't do anything BUT God can do everything. Decide right now to look through eyes of faith and not through eyes of fear.

FEAR FOCUSES ON SEEN REALITIES.

FAITH FOCUSES ON UNSEEN REALITIES.

FEAR ONLY FOCUSES ON RESOURCES IN THE NATURAL WORLD.

FAITH FOCUSES ON RESOURCES IN THE SUPERNATURAL WORLD.

FEAR FOCUSES ON ME, MY ABILITY AND MY STRENGTHS.

FAITH FOCUSES ON GOD.

You see, when Elisha's servant looked around at the enemy he forgot all the deliverances in the past that God had already provided. Such great miracles like the parting of the Red Sea so that His people could walk across on dry land. Elisha told him in verse 16, "**Do not fear, for those who *are* with us *are* more than those who *are* with them.**" Get focused on God!

Can you think of any times in your life that God has seen you through and given you victories?

Fear will not dwell in the same heart where there is faith! Remember God's faithfulness to you in the past. He has not changed! Choose right now to believe He will come through for you. There are angels all around you! The Holy Spirit lives within you as a believer! You have your support group to pray for you! The Word of God to direct you!

Romans 8:31 (NKJV)
"What then shall we say to these things? If God *is* for us, who *can be* against us?"

What does that verse mean to you?

1 John 4:4 (NKJV)
"You are of God, little children, and have overcome them, because
He who is in you is greater than he who is in the world."

What does that verse tell you?

BIG God; little problems.
Little god; BIG Problems.

It is my prayer that you begin to see and realize what God is offering you for permanent and lasting change in your life. I am so tired of seeing people die and fall by the way side, one after another, while God is offering them all they need to be victorious in the struggle. Focus on the God of the Bible my friends! BIG God; little problems. Little god; BIG Problems. Here's what I mean; Focus on God instead of your struggles. The God of the Bible far exceeds and over powers any trouble we have. When we realize who God is, our problems don't seem that big in comparison.

I want you to search your Bible and write down words which describe God:

No More Excuses
Week #26

In 1981 the southern gospel quartet known as "The Kingsmen" released a song entitled, "Excuses." It became a very popular song in Christian circles because people so readily identified with the lyrics:

Excuses, excuses, you'll hear them every day.
And the Devil he'll supply them, if the church you stay away.
When people come to know the Lord, the Devil always loses
So to keep them folks away from church, he offers them excuses.

In the summer it's too hot. And, in the winter, it's too cold.
In the spring time when the weather's just right, you find some place else to go.
Well, it's up to the mountains or down to the beach or to visit some old friend.
Or, to just stay home and kinda relax and hope that some of the kin folks will start dropping in.

Well, the church benches are too hard. And, that choir sings way too loud.
Boy, you know how nervous you get when you're sitting in a great big crowd.
The doctor told you, "Now, you better watch them crowds. They'll set you back."
But, you go to that old ball game because you say "it helps you to relax."
Well, a headache Sunday morning and a backache Sunday night.
But by worktime Monday morning, you're feeling quite alright.

While one of the children has a cold, "Pneumonia, do you suppose?"
Why the whole family had to stay home, just to blow that poor kid's nose.
Excuses, excuses, you'll hear them every day.
And the Devil he'll supply them if the church you stay away.
When people come to know the Lord, the Devil always loses
So to keep them folks away from church, he offers them excuses.

Written by Jim Kimerely and William Topley

Let's talk about excuses this week as we think about our recovery. It's time for NO MORE EXCUSES. Excuses keep many people from doing what they need to do and getting to where they need to get.

First, what does it mean to give an excuse? When someone offers an excuse, they are simply attempting to justify a mistake, a failure, or they use the excuse to try and lighten the load of guilt or punishment related to their actions.

In the Bible, we see how God promises victory for all those who trust in Him. This victory is based on God's faithfulness and His ability to relate to, comfort, and rescue all who call upon Him. Therefore, if we come to God, there are no excuses for our sin. If God has promised recovery, then there is no good excuse for not recovering. I say this not to "guilt" you but to encourage you.

Let's consider a biblical example. In the context of 1 Samuel 13, Saul is King over Israel. Saul was the first king of Israel (approximately 1,000 BC). Israel is faced with their enemy, the Philistines, and King Saul and the people became worried. Instead of trusting God and being obedient to God, Saul took matters into his own hands. King Saul decided to do things his way instead of God's way.

1 Samuel 13:5-14 (NKJV)

5 Then the Philistines gathered together to fight with Israel, thirty thousand chariots and six thousand horsemen, and people as the sand which *is* on the seashore in multitude. And they came up and encamped in Michmash, to the east of Beth Aven. 6 When the men of Israel saw that they were in danger (for the people were distressed), then the people hid in caves, in thickets, in rocks, in holes, and in pits. 7 And *some of* the Hebrews crossed over the Jordan to the land of Gad and Gilead. As for Saul, he *was* still in Gilgal, and all the people followed him trembling. 8 Then he waited seven days, according to the time set by Samuel. But Samuel did not come to Gilgal; and the people were scattered from him. 9 So Saul said, "Bring a burnt offering and peace offerings here to me." And he offered the burnt offering. 10 Now it happened, as soon as he had finished presenting the burnt offering, that Samuel came; and Saul went out to meet him, that he might greet him. 11 And Samuel said, "What have you done?" And Saul said, "When I saw that the people were scattered from me, and *that* you did not come within the days appointed, and *that* the Philistines gathered together at Michmash, 12 then I said, 'The Philistines will now come down on me at Gilgal, and I have not made supplication to the LORD.' Therefore I felt compelled, and offered a burnt offering." 13 And Samuel said to Saul, "You have done foolishly. You have not kept the commandment of the

LORD your God, which He commanded you. For now the LORD would have established your kingdom over Israel forever. ¹⁴ But now your kingdom shall not continue. The LORD has sought for Himself a man after His own heart, and the LORD has commanded him *to be* commander over His people, because you have not kept what the LORD commanded you."

As King Saul faced the Philistines he disobeyed God by offering a sacrifice that only the prophet Samuel was qualified to offer. The offering of the sacrifice was exclusively reserved for the prophet according to God. When the prophet Samuel showed up and realized what Saul had done he asked King Saul, "What have you done?" (verse 11). The king proceeded to give excuses for why he had disobeyed God.

1. Summarize Saul's three excuses? See 1 Samuel 13:11-12.

A.

B.

C.

2. What are some excuses that people in recovery usually make for using again?

When King Saul saw that his people were scattered he became afraid. This is called the "fear of man." It was this fear of man that motivated the King to disobey God. The fear of man is when we fail to trust God in the midst of a crisis because we fear rejection or disapproval from other people. Simply stated, it is putting the opinions of others before the Truth of God. Let's look at what God's Word says about the fear of man.

3. Write out Proverbs 29:25:

4. Write out Proverbs 3:25-26:

5. Write out Psalm 34:4:

When Samuel, the prophet, didn't arrive in the time frame that Saul expected, he became impatient, which led to taking matters into his own hands.

6. Write out Psalm 27:14:

We must learn to follow God's plan regardless of the consequences. Obedience to God must be first. Trust Him instead of fearing man. Samuel knew this was true as he proclaimed in 1 Samuel 15:22:

1 Samuel 15:22 (ESV)
"And Samuel said, 'Has the LORD as great delight in burnt offerings
and sacrifices, as in obeying the voice of the LORD? Behold, to obey
is better than sacrifice, and to listen than the fat of rams.'"

Saul had plenty of excuses for his disobedience but Samuel zeroed in on the real issue:

"You have not kept the commandment of the Lord your God" (1 Samuel 13:13). Like Saul, we often gloss over our mistakes and sins, trying to justify our actions because of our "special" circumstances. Our excuses, however, are nothing more than disobedience. God knows our true motives. He forgives, restores, and blesses only when we are honest about our sins. By trying to hide his sins behind excuses, Saul lost his kingship. When we rely on God's faithfulness and depend upon God's strength, we won't have to excuse our behavior.

PRAYER: "Dear Creator, Master, Sustainer, and Lord, I confess that I sometimes make excuses for my sinful actions. I don't want to be an excuse maker, but I desire to be a disciple maker. I want to be used by you to reach those around me. I know that I cannot show others the way out of bondage and sin while I am still trapped by it myself. There are no valid excuses for me to not be who you desire me to be. Help me to claim your promises instead of making excuses. In Jesus' name. Thank-you Lord. Amen."

SNAP! CRACKLE! POP!
Week #27

I have always been fascinated with anything that lights up without batteries or electricity. In recent years I have enjoyed building four feet stars out of vintage tobacco sticks, covering them with 400 solar lights and selling them to earn a little Christmas cash. I had one of those solar powered stars mounted in a tree in my yard for years. It's pretty cool to me when I think about capturing energy from the sun and harnessing that energy to radiate power within a lightbulb. What is even more awesome is that there is an eternal power within us as Christians, that never needs recharging, and it is a power that is unmatched by this world.

> *"It's okay to be broken; God is able to put the pieces back together better than before with His transforming touch."*
>
> *Pastor Michael Dixon*

John 8:12 (ESV)

"Again, Jesus spoke to them, saying, 'I am the light of the world. Whoever follows me will not walk in darkness, but will have the light of life.'"

In the above verse Jesus describes Himself as _____.

John 1:5 (ESV)
"The light shines in the darkness, and the darkness has not overcome it."

Think about when you light a candle. That light overcomes the darkness. The darkness cannot put the flame out.

Matthew 5:16 (ESV)
"In the same way, let your light shine before others, so that they may see your good works and give glory to your Father who is in heaven."

Here is our bullseye of 1 Cor. 10:31 yet again in the Bible. We are created to bring honor and glory to God. We do this by letting our light shine through our good works. We are not saved by our works but if we are saved there will be good works. As Christians, sinners saved by grace and recovering from addiction, we are to shine for Christ! How do you think your light is being displayed to the world?

Circle one:

- It's not

- Sometimes it dimly flickers

- It is just a nightlight

- It's as bright as a flashlight

- Man, It's like the sun! I'm lighting up my world for Christ!!!!

Sometimes our problem is that there is a lot of stuff that is blocking our Jesus light from shining through. The Bible calls that stuff "sin." In order to get the sin out of the way so our light can be seen, God must break those obstructions and get them out of the way.

SNAP! CRACKLE! POP! SNAP! CRACKLE! POP!

Psalm 51:17 (ESV)
"The sacrifices of God are a broken spirit; a broken and
contrite heart, O God, you will not despise."

Do you feel broken? Crushed? Bewildered? My friend, those are not bad things in the hands of Almighty God! God really can't use you until you reach this place of brokenness. It's like a glow stick that you can purchase at the Dollar Tree store. It doesn't begin to glow until you break it. In that one defining moment, when you snap it and shake it, that enchanting soft light begins to radiate through its clear shell of plastic.

Brokenness is a painful place to be, yet it is also the place where we begin to grow and change. We get so busy with the snaps and breaks of life, just trying to survive through them, that we overlook the benefits that God is bringing about in us through them. Remember:

Psalm 34:18 (NKJV)

"The Lord is close to the brokenhearted and saves those who are crushed in spirit."

I have discovered in my own life that it is in my brokenness that I am drawn closer to God. It is not in the wonderful moments in my life that I tend to pray more, but it is rather in the most painful times that I am seeking God.

Meditate right now on this truth: God sometimes allows us to be broken in order to cleanse us of those things which are hindering our walk with Him. Can you identify the things in your life that feel like they are breaking you?

God doesn't abandon us in our brokenness. No! He is enabling and empowering us to break free! Those chains are snapped! Cracked! Popped! They come crashing down, never to bind us again. Trust God that even in your pain He is setting you free from the things that have bound you for so long. His power is at work within you!

2 Corinthians 4:7 (NKJV)

"We now have this light shining in our hearts, but we ourselves are
like fragile clay jars containing this great treasure. This makes it clear
that our great power is from God, not from ourselves."

Surrender to Him. His hands are holding onto you!

Psalm 34:18 (NKJV)

"The Lord is close to the brokenhearted and saves those who are crushed in spirit."

I want you to reflect upon a time in your life when you felt broken. Maybe it was sickness, health issues, relationship problems, or some spiritual attack you experienced. Maybe you were sitting in jail or recovering in a detox or a rehab. Write about this time in your life:

I know that as I wrote this assignment I can remember how the pain felt, the loneliness, the feeling that things looked so bad at the time. Now though as I look back I am more thankful today that those difficult times don't come to stay. I am thankful that God saw me through those times. I rejoice that having gone through the pain I can better relate to you, as you go through pain. I am thankful through those times of "snaps" and "crackles" that God has placed greater compassion within my heart for others who are struggling. I see how God has taken the brokenness in my life and brought forth faith, strength, and blessing.

Now I want you to reflect upon that time of brokenness you wrote about previously. This time I want you to see the hand of God in your pain.

#1. What did God bring forth out of this time in your life?

#2. What was it about that period of time that you can now be thankful for?

#3. List below ways that God has brightened your light through that brokenness:

God has made some wonderful promises to you as you trust Him. One of my favorites is:

Romans 8:28 (ESV)
"And we know that for those who love God all things work together
for good, for those who are called according to his purpose."

#4. What does that promise mean to you?

> PRAYER: "I come to you Lord, a broken vessel. The world around me seems to think that I may be beyond repair. I know that there are many, many shattered pieces scattered because of my foolish lifestyle. I turn my trust towards you. I know that you are able to do impossible things. When all hope for a better life, a brighter future, and new beginning seems to be beyond my grasp, my heart cries out to you. I believe that you are able to put the pieces back together again. Beauty can rise out of this mess. Lead the way, Lord. I'm ready. In Jesus' name, Amen."

Brokenness and Surrender
Week #28

The two words which comprise the title to this week's lesson are two words that few people associate with success in anything. Under each word below list the words that come to your mind when you read/hear the word:

Brokenness   Surrender

_____   _____

_____   _____

_____   _____

_____   _____

If something is broken then we immediately think it is useless. If surrender is mentioned we think, "I will never surrender! I will be victorious!" Did you realize that God's thoughts and plans are much different from ours?

Isaiah 55:8-9 (NKJV)
"For My thoughts *are* not your thoughts,
Nor *are* your ways My ways," says the LORD.
⁹"For *as* the heavens are higher than the earth,
So are My ways higher than your ways,
And My thoughts than your thoughts."

God tells us that brokenness and surrender before Him are very good things because of where they lead us.

Psalm 51:17 (NKJV)
"The sacrifices of God *are* a broken spirit, A broken and a
contrite heart-- These, O God, You will not despise."

It is through brokenness that God brings us to the end of our own strength and resources. We give up trying to save ourselves and all our futile attempts at self-preservation. It is in this place of brokenness that we are stripped naked and exposed for what we really have been all along. This flesh is a mess! Are you willing to make that confession right now? Are you willing to admit to God that without Him you are nothing? "Yes," you say? Take the test below by simply writing "yes" or "no" beside each number.

#1. ___ I am always ready to allow others to receive the credit for success.

#2. ___ All my rights have been surrendered.

#3. ___ I am willing to be weak.

#4. ___ I am forgiving of all.

#5. ___ I am depending upon Christ for my identity, acceptance, meaning and purpose, and for my strength and victory.

#6. ___ I am seeking the presence of Christ more than His benefits.

#7. ___ I am more concerned with what God thinks than what those around me think.

#8. ___ I am willing to fail.

#9. ___ I am transparent and willing to share weaknesses.

#10.___ I am not performing FOR God but I am allowing Him to work through me.

Okay, how did you do? If you answered "no" to any of the above statements then you have not fully surrendered to God nor are you at the point of brokenness. Maybe you have been clinging to your possessions, your lifestyle, your drugs, alcohol, pornography, or greed. Maybe your car is your idol. Maybe it's your spouse or your partner? You can easily identify your idols by examining what happens when they are removed from your life. Does even the thought of having to live without _____ (you fill in the blank) almost cause a panic attack within you? Are you willing to confess to God right now that you have no righteousness of your own? Have you been stripped naked of yourself? That's brokenness. We must come to the end of ourselves and begin to look to God for all our needs.

How about surrender? There is an old church song, written by Judson W. Van DeVenter, published in 1896 that says:

All to Jesus I surrender;
All to Him I freely give;
I will ever love and trust Him,
In His presence daily live.
Refrain:
I surrender all,
I surrender all;
All to Thee, my blessed Savior,
I surrender all.

Jesus said as recorded in **Matthew 10:39 (NKJV)**

"He that finds his life will lose it; and he that loses his life for my sake will find it."

The writer of that hymn, Judson W. Van DeVenter, ran from God's calling upon his life to be a minister for years. Judson wanted to be an artist instead. It was not until he surrendered his will to God's, answering the call to the ministry, that he discovered great peace and purpose in his life.

My own personal experience has been the same. I knew as a young teenager that God had called me to preach. I didn't know at that point in my life what I wanted to do but one thing I thought I knew; I DID NOT WANT TO BE A MINISTER. My rejection of this calling was a combination of things; #1. I didn't really know any ministers that I thought were not boring. #2. It did not seem like a very good way to get wealthy. #3. I was literally horrified at the thought of public speaking. In fact, when I finally attended bible college and was required to take a public speaking class, I signed up for the 8 AM class. I knew that the early class would be the smallest class. I ran from this calling as fast and as hard as I could, almost killing myself in the process. It was not until 1988 that I stopped running and surrendered to God's plan for my life. I have discovered since that time of surrender that nothing brings me any greater joy or fulfillment than preaching God's truth. Don't you desire that joy and fulfillment as well? It is found through surrender to God.

Take your hands off your life and give it to Him! Surrender your time, talents, your life, your everything. Stop demanding your rights and what you think you deserve and surrender all that to God. It's not about you! Just as Jesus prayed in the Garden of Gethsemane, "Not my will but your will be done," we must have the same heart attitude towards God.

Total surrender = To give up possession or power over; to yield.

Write below some things that come to your mind that you need to surrender to God in each of these areas:

MIND, EMOTION, WILL:

MY BODY:

MY FUTURE PLANS:

MY MARRIAGE:

RECREATION:

MY PLANS FOR SUCCESS:

MY PAST:

HABITS:

POSSESSIONS:

MY TIME:

REPUTATION:

MY HOME:

PROBLEMS:

OTHER AREAS THAT GOD HAS SHOWN YOU TO SURRENDER:

PRAYER: "I confess Oh Lord, you alone are able to take my brokenness and use it for my good and for your glory. I surrender my all to you. The good, the bad, the ugly, everything I am and hope to be. I belong to you. In Jesus' name. Amen."

Turning Failure Into Faith
Week #29

___

We all have a past full of junk, messes that we wish were not there, mistakes, choices, and failures that we have all made. Life is not full of those who have never made mistakes and then the rest of us. No! Everyone has made mistakes! It is the enemy's plot to convince you that you are the only one who has ever struggled.

1 Corinthians 10:13 (NKJV)
"No temptation has overtaken you except such as is common to man; but God is faithful, who will not allow you to be tempted beyond what you are able, but with the temptation will also make the way of escape, that you may be able to bear it."

According to the above promise there is no temptation that can come upon you that is not "common to man," meaning others have struggled with the same thing. Don't listen to the lies that tell you that you are alone in your failures and struggles. There are no new temptations popping up. The same temptations which plague us today are the same ones that existed thousands of years ago. King Solomon, who is known as the wisest man who ever lived, said this:

Ecclesiastes 1:9 (NKJV)
"That which has been is what will be, that which is done is what will be done, And there is nothing new under the sun."

King Solomon said that there is nothing new under this sun. So, if it's true it's probably not new. If it's new, it's probably not true. (I know you follow my reasoning there. Right? Sure you do). The point that I am making is simply this; your current struggles are nothing new. They have been faced, and overcome, before in the past. Since this is true you can overcome them as well. Let's talk about "Turning Failure into Faith."

Judges 16:18-31 (NKJV)
¹⁸ When Delilah saw that he had told her all his heart, she sent and called for the lords of the Philistines, saying, "Come up once more, for he has told me all his heart." So the lords of the Philistines came up to her and brought the money in their hand. ¹⁹ Then she lulled him to sleep on her knees, and called for a man and had him shave off the seven locks of

his head. Then she began to torment him, and his strength left him. [20] And she said, "The Philistines *are* upon you, Samson!" So he awoke from his sleep, and said, "I will go out as before, at other times, and shake myself free!" But he did not know that the LORD had departed from him. [21] Then the Philistines took him and put out his eyes, and brought him down to Gaza. They bound him with bronze fetters, and he became a grinder in the prison. [22] However, the hair of his head began to grow again after it had been shaven. [23] Now the lords of the Philistines gathered together to offer a great sacrifice to Dagon their god, and to rejoice. And they said: "Our god has delivered into our hands Samson our enemy!" [24] When the people saw him, they praised their god; for they said: "Our god has delivered into our hands our enemy, The destroyer of our land, And the one who multiplied our dead." [25] So it happened, when their hearts were merry, that they said, "Call for Samson, that he may perform for us." So they called for Samson from the prison, and he performed for them. And they stationed him between the pillars. [26] Then Samson said to the lad who held him by the hand, "Let me feel the pillars which support the temple, so that I can lean on them." [27] Now the temple was full of men and women. All the lords of the Philistines *were* there--about three thousand men and women on the roof watching while Samson performed. [28] Then Samson called to the LORD, saying, "O Lord GOD, remember me, I pray! Strengthen me, I pray, just this once, O God, that I may with one *blow* take vengeance on the Philistines for my two eyes!" [29] And Samson took hold of the two middle pillars which supported the temple, and he braced himself against them, one on his right and the other on his left. [30] Then Samson said, "Let me die with the Philistines!" And he pushed with *all his* might, and the temple fell on the lords and all the people who *were* in it. So the dead that he killed at his death were more than he had killed in his life. [31] And his brothers and all his father's household came down and took him, and brought *him* up and buried him between Zorah and Eshtaol in the tomb of his father Manoah. He had judged Israel twenty years.

Samson is the superman of the Bible. Here was a man of incredible strength and God-given potential. This was a man who trusted God, who was called by God to serve as a judge, a leader, to God's people of Israel. Samson had been given superhuman strength by God. In Judges 14 we read of how this man killed a roaring loin with his bare hands. In Judges 15 we find this man killing 1000 of his enemies with just the jawbone of a donkey. It is also in chapter 15 that we read of Samson tying the tales of 300 foxes together, in pairs, placing a lit torch between their tails, and sending them forth into the enemy's field to destroy their crops. This guy was so full of potential! He had so much going for him yet in the end he blew it, failed, and his life ended tragically.

I want you to pause right here and write out some of the many resources that God has given you to aid you in recovery (I have already started the list for you-You finish it!):

The church, The Bible, L.I.F.E.,

_____

_____

_____

_____

_____

In week #22 we considered 2 Peter 1:3-4 and we noted from those verses that God has given us:

#1. His divine power

#2. His great and precious promises

#3. His divine nature

Then on top of those great supernatural resources God has given us so many other wonderful tools for us to take advantage of as we walk in freedom.

Samson's life ended with a sad conclusion. This man who had so much going for him ended up wasting his potential and even dying in the end. The reason why Samson was not able to ultimately conquer the enemy was because Samson could not first of all conquer himself. He allowed his weaknesses to control him instead of God.

Samson underestimated:

#1. The power of Satan.

Please be reminded that Satan and demons are real. This enemy seeks to steal, kill, and destroy (John 10:10). The enemy is very perceptive too. He studies you to find your weakness and then he will attack you right there!

Samson's weakness was women. He always had to have a woman on his arm. In Judges 16:1 you can read how Samson would even go hire a "woman of the night" so he would have someone to sleep with and fulfill his selfish desires. Yet, here was a man called by God! In Judges 14 you can read how Samson broke his parent's hearts by demanding a pagan Philistine woman to be given to him. Then as we come to our text today we find Samson with his head in the lap of "delectable Delilah." Delilah had been hired and paid off, by the enemy of the Philistines to find out the secret to Samson's strength. The enemy was plotting to destroy Samson, just as the enemy is plotting to destroy you. Don't underestimate your enemy.

How has the enemy attempted to destroy you in the past?

Samson also underestimated:

#2. The power of self.

Samson was a strong man physically but he was weak morally when it came to resisting the desires of his flesh.

Women were this man's weakness.

Have you identified your weakness? Do you know what the triggers are in your life that usually send you spiraling downward into failure? I know in my own life that I must be on extra guard when discouragement comes my way, or even physical weariness, because I know it is during those times I am prone to fail.

Can you identify some of your weaknesses?

What have been some triggers in the past that have led to failure in your life?

Many people underestimate the power of their own weaknesses by pridefully believing "Oh, I can say no to that." "I can overcome that." "I will never have a problem with that again." I tell you that it will dominate your life if you allow it to. At this point in Samson's story he no doubt thought that he had everything under control. There he was with his head resting on this woman's knees. He should have been on his knees seeking God but instead he had let his guard down and he was resting in the lap of his enemy. Samson was doing what he wanted to do instead of seeking God and asking God what he should do.

Do you have a regular time in your life when you spend time with God seeking His will and direction for your life? Don't think for a minute that you have all you need outside of God's provision for you. Sin will destroy you if you allow it to!

Once Samson revealed to Delilah that if his hair was cut he would lose his strength, the enemy's plot was as good as done. It's important here to understand that Samson's strength was not in his hair. His strength was in the covenant relationship he enjoyed with God and his long hair was a symbol of that relationship. Once his hair was cut he had broken his promise to God and was without God's power upon his life.

Samson underestimated:

#3. The power of sin.

Immediately upon the breaking of his covenant with God, illustrated by the cutting of his hair, Samson was as weak as water and now headed for destruction. This is the power of sin!

Consider what sin cost Samson:

SIN BLINDED HIM. His eyes were gouged out by the enemy. Sin blinds a person to what is true and right. What causes a drunk to fall down and wallow in his own vomit and get right back up and begin drinking again? What would cause a mother to lock her children in another room while she sits in the bathroom and shoots up heroin? Sin blinds you.

What are some ways that you have been blinded to the effects of sin in your past?

SIN BOUND HIM. Sin always binds. Sin never leads to freedom. To the contrary, only truth leads to freedom. (John 8:32). Samson ends up at the end of this story blinded and grinding at the mill like an animal. Sin will grind you down to nothing!

Why would you even entertain the idea of returning to a lifestyle that almost killed you? Many are grinding at the mill today of divorce, physical sickness, imprisonment, broken relationships, poverty, physical pain, etc….because of sin in their life.

Here's the good news: **GOD OFFERS ANOTHER CHANCE.**

In verse 22 it says that Samson's hair began to grow again. He cried out to God in repentance and faith. God gave him another chance, although it was his last chance. It was in Samson's death that he killed more enemies than he did during his lifetime, but Samson died.

God is offering you another chance right now. This could be your final chance as well. Are you taking advantage of the new life that God is offering you? Make the most of this opportunity you are being offered! Your recovery group is here for you, praying for you, lifting you up. God has supplied all you need to succeed. You can do this!

Write out your prayer to God based on what you are thinking right now:

PRAYER: "Looking back on my life there is so much I wish that I could do over again. I would make different choices in many things. I admit that I have made many mistakes in the past. In fact, the truth be told I still fall short. The enemy would have me to live under regret and shame the rest of my life. I refuse to allow that! For I know that you have forgiven me and that you have granted to me another chance at this life. I thank-you for this new life. I refuse to throw it away. It's all because of you, Lord God, that I can rise above my failures and increase my walk of faith. Let it be so. In Jesus' name. Amen."

Getting Past Your Past
Week #30

Philippians 3:13 (ESV)
"Brothers, I do not consider that I have made it my own. But one thing I do: forgetting what lies behind and straining forward to what lies ahead…"

God used the Apostle Paul to write the Book of Philippians to the Church at Philippi. A common theme throughout this short book is "joy." We can have the joy of the Lord regardless of what is going on around us and regardless of what our past has been like. I believe the greatest scheme of the enemy to attempt to discourage us and hold us back in life is bringing up our past. We all have a past! It matters not who you are, or what you may have done, we were all in sin, lost, without Jesus Christ. This week we are studying how we can break free from our past failures and mistakes. I sometimes put it this way, "It doesn't matter what you was. It matters what you is."

Isaiah 43:18-19 (ESV)
"Remember not the former things, nor consider the things of old. Behold, I am doing a new thing; now it springs forth, do you not perceive it? I will make a way in the wilderness and rivers in the desert."

God began a new work in you beginning at that moment in time when you trusted Christ. There is not one single person who can boldly stand and proclaim, "I have now arrived at perfection," but we should all be able to say, "I am not the person I use to be." Your past does not have to define "who" you are today because of "whose" you are now.

The story of the Old Testament Joseph can teach us some important lessons about putting our past behind us. Joseph was one of the 12 sons of Jacob, who is later known as Israel. Jacob's 12 sons would be the beginning of the 12 tribes of Israel. Well, Joseph was his daddy's favorite son. Do you remember in a previous lesson the coat of many colors that Joseph was given by his father? Joseph's brothers were filled with jealousy and they hated Joseph.

Now, as I think about Joseph's past, I am reminded that if anyone had a difficult past to overcome it was this man. Just think of the things that happened to Joseph (Genesis 37-50):

#1. Joseph was his father's favorite son. This was the reason that his father, Jacob, gave to him the coat of many colors. Joseph's eleven brothers were jealous of him and they hated him.

#2. Joseph's brothers attempted to get rid of him by selling him to a caravan that was passing through on their way to Egypt.

#3. Joseph's father was told that Joseph was dead.

#4. Joseph ended up being auctioned as a slave in Egypt. The second highest individual in all of Egypt, Potiphar, purchased Joseph to be his slave.

#5. Joseph was falsely accused by Potiphar's wife of attempting to rape her.

#6. Joseph was thrown in prison, although innocent.

#7. While in prison Joseph befriended Pharoah's chief butler, who was also doing time. Upon the Butler's release he had promised to put in a good word for Joseph but he forgot about him. Joseph was left rotting in prison.

This is just some of the junk that Joseph had to deal with growing up. He could have just sat down and blamed everyone else for his troubles and had a good ole pity party. However, Joseph trusted God and he knew that God was more than able to bring beauty out of the ashes.

What are some of the things in your past, junk that has happened to you, that could hold you back if you allowed it to?

You can learn from Joseph and his brothers how you can rise above your past too. God's hand was upon Joseph. The King of Egypt had a dream and he called for Joseph, who was still in prison, to come and interpret it. Joseph told the king that his dream meant there were seven years of famine coming but they still had time to prepare for it. Pharoah appointed Joseph to be in charge of this preparation. Once the famine began there was no food to be found except in Egypt. Joseph's brothers were sent to Egypt in search of food. Once there they appeared before their brother Joseph since Joseph was the authority in charge of the food distribution. Once Joseph revealed himself to his brothers (Genesis 45) they were fearful that Joseph would seek revenge against them for their wickedness towards him. Joseph however forgave his brothers and promised to take care of them. Joseph then moved his family to Egypt so he could make sure they were all cared for. Then Jacob, Joseph's father, died.

Genesis 50:15-21 (ESV)

When Joseph's brothers saw that their father was dead, they said, "It may be that Joseph will hate us and pay us back for all the evil that we did to him." So they sent a message to Joseph, saying, "Your father gave this command before he died: 'Say to Joseph, "Please forgive the transgression of your brothers and their sin, because they did evil to you."' And now, please forgive the transgression of the servants of the God of your father." Joseph wept when they spoke to him. His brothers also came and fell down before him and said, "Behold, we are your servants." But Joseph said to them, "Do not fear, for am I in the place of God? As for you, you meant evil against me, but God meant it for good, to bring it about that many people should be kept alive, as they are today. So do not fear; I will provide for you and your little ones." Thus he comforted them and spoke kindly to them.

If you are going to get your past in your past **the first thing you must do is BELIEVE THE WORD.** Believe what God says to you! Joseph's brothers were afraid because they really didn't believe what Joseph had promised, as recorded in Genesis 45, that he would take care of them.

Will you believe what God says about you? In Ephesians 1 God calls you a Saint; God says that you are "in Christ." God "chose you," "adopted you," "accepted you," "redeemed you," "forgave you," and "sealed you." Will you believe the Word?

List below some of the things that you have believed about yourself, and your past, that may not be true according to God?

Do you understand the promises of God toward you now that you have accepted Christ? Jesus says that you are forgiven! He still loves you! He accepts you! He promises to take care of you! Don't be afraid. When you fall He will be there to pick you up!

Secondly, if you will, put your past in the past: UNDERSTAND GRACE! In Genesis 50:15 Joseph's brothers were afraid that Joseph was going to pay them back for what they had done against him. God doesn't give you pay back. He offers you grace! Grace is undeserved! You do not get what you deserve but you receive what you do not deserve, like forgiveness and another chance. No one is so unworthy that God will not offer this grace because it's grace!

Thirdly, you must FORGIVE YOURSELF! In Genesis 50:17-18 we see Joseph's brothers begging for forgiveness. Joseph had already forgiven them (Genesis 45) but they had not forgiven themselves. How about you? What do you struggle with in regards to forgiving yourself?

Next, to get past your past, understand that GOD IS BIG ENOUGH TO TRANSFORM YOUR PAST from agony and defeat into a beautiful story of redemption and usefulness. God is able to bring beauty from the ashes! One of the greatest verses in the Bible is:

Genesis 50:20 (NKJV)
"But as for you, you meant evil against me, but God meant it for good, in
order to bring it about as it is this day, to save many people alive."

The place where Joseph was thrown down into the pit by his brothers was called "Dothan." Dothan means "two wells" or "double feast." Here's an awesome truth: When we are in a place where we feel surrounded and put into a corner, with nowhere to go, God is always our rescuer.

Joseph told his brothers, "I know what you did was evil but I forgave you! I see God's intervention in my life. His hand is moving the pieces together. You threw me into a pit but God rescued me." Ultimately God was able to save the nations from starvation through Joseph's leadership. God used all the things that happened to Joseph to bring him to the position where he could be used to save the nations.

GIVE YOUR PAST TO GOD! Trust that somehow, someway God will bring good out of all your junk. He can and will if you trust Him to do it. My life before surrendering to the Lordship of Christ was one lived from one high to the next. If I wasn't using I was planning the next time I would use. My life was a mess. By the time I was in my mid 20's I had already been to jail, lost my license, been divorced and remarried, was addicted to a variety of drugs and hooked on alcohol, and really didn't care. It was not until I surrendered to Christ, and gave Him my life, that my deliverance began. Now as I meet with people who are addicted, or I sit across from someone who has been to jail, or I look a divorcee in the eye, I can minister to them as one who has been there too. If I could go back in time, my friend, there is so much I would change. There were so many stupid decisions that I would reverse. I can't do that but God has already transformed my past into a tool that He uses to help others.

Lastly, YOUR PAST DOES NOT DEFINE WHO YOU ARE NOW!

In relation to this study read the following verse:

Proverbs 4:23 (ESV)
"Keep your heart with all vigilance, for from it flow the springs of life."

Write what you believe this verse is saying that can help you not to allow your past to define you:

I learned a long time ago that you cannot run from your past. There is a way however to get past your past. This begins by understanding you have been forgiven. God now desires to create in you a new creation with a new future and a new life. As I remember who I use to be before I came to Christ I am now filled with thanks that I am not that man anymore. Give Him praise for who He is and what He has done for you!

The title of this lesson, "Getting Past Your Past," is easier said than done, isn't it? If only we could simply hit a "delete" button in our minds like we do a computer and entirely erase our past. If we could simply step into a time machine which would transfer us back into the past so we could do things differently, avoiding the mistakes and steering away from the moments which have brought us pain, shame and regret. Well, there is no delete button, no time machine, but we do have God's Word and His Spirit within us as believers. Here are six truths you must realize if you will get rid of the shame and guilt of yesterday:

#1. Place your faith in Christ.

Cry out to God in your brokenness and believe that He is more than able to heal you. God is able to transform the failures into victories. According to the promise in Romans 8:28 God is able to work ALL things (past, present, future) for your good if you will set your heart upon Him.

Romans 8:28 (ESV)
"And we know that for those who love God all things work together
for good, for those who are called according to his purpose."

#2. Choose to see yourself as God sees you.

Stop believing that you are who you use to be! Stop believing that you are less than what God declares you to be!

Romans 3:23-25 (ESV)

"for all have sinned and fall short of the glory of God,

²⁴ and are justified by his grace as a gift, through the redemption that is in Christ Jesus, ²⁵

whom God put forward as a propitiation by his blood, to be received by faith. This was to

show God's righteousness, because in his divine forbearance he had passed over former sins."

#3. Everytime you have a condemning reminder of your past, place GRACE beside it.

There are 3 sources for your failures to be brought back up; the flesh, the devil, the world. God will not bring up your failures once they are forgiven.

2 Corinthians 5:16-17 (ESV)

"Therefore, if anyone is in Christ, he is a new creation. The

old has passed away; behold, the new has come."

Psalm 103:12 (ESV)

"as far as the east is from the west, so far does he remove our transgressions from us."

Every time the enemy, or your own mind, or someone else tries to bring your past back up, cover it in grace! Then go to God in prayer thanking Him for forgiving you and transforming you!

#4. Renew your mind.

God's Word contains the truth which will set you free (John 8:32).

2 Timothy 3:16-17 (ESV)

"All Scripture is breathed out by God and profitable for teaching, for reproof, for correction,

and for training in righteousness,

¹⁷ that the man of God may be complete, equipped for every good work."

Romans 12:2 (ESV)

"Do not be conformed to this world, but be transformed by the renewal of your mind, that

by testing you may discern what is the will of God, what is good and acceptable and perfect."

Mediating upon what God says will help straighten out your faulty thinking. God's Word offers truth that never changes and a hope that never fades.

#5. Choose to forgive as Christ has forgiven you.

Colossians 3:13 (ESV)
"bearing with one another and, if one has a complaint against another, forgiving each other; as the Lord has forgiven you, so you also must forgive."

Make a choice right now to forgive those who have been involved in your past, including yourself. Let go of the guilt. Give it to Christ.

#6. Look straight ahead and not in the rearview mirror.

Your future is not behind you!

Philippians 3:13-14 (ESV)
"Brothers, I do not consider that I have made it my own. But one thing I do: forgetting what lies behind and straining forward to what lies ahead, I press on toward the goal for the prize of the upward call of God in Christ Jesus."

PRAYER: "Lord, I am determined not to live my life looking in the rearview mirror. I am going to look ahead at the new life you have placed before me. I do believe your word. I thank you for your grace. I choose to forgive myself. I know, Lord God, that you can transform my past into victory. Lord, be glorified as you do just that. In Jesus' name. Amen."

Looking Forward; Trusting God
Week #31

Last week we discussed how we can get the past in the past. Who we were does not have to define who we are. Again, the Apostle Paul put it this way:

Philippians 3:13 (ESV)
"Brothers, I do not consider that I have made it my own. But one thing I do: forgetting what lies behind and straining forward to what lies ahead…"

The Apostle Paul, writing under the inspiration of The Holy Spirit, makes it clear that his current life, and even his life in the future, was not going to be regulated by his past. One of my personal favorite passages of scripture dealing with this issue of putting the past in the past and looking forward to the future is:

1 Corinthians 6:9-11 (ESV)
"Or do you not know that the unrighteous will not inherit the kingdom of God? Do not be deceived: neither the sexually immoral, nor idolaters, nor adulterers, nor men who practice homosexuality, nor thieves, nor the greedy, nor drunkards, nor revilers, nor swindlers will inherit the kingdom of God. And such were some of you. But you were washed, you were sanctified, you were justified in the name of the Lord Jesus Christ and by the Spirit of our God."

The Holy Spirit through Paul writes a long list of habitual lifestyle sins in this passage including **"the sexually immoral, idolaters, adulterers, homosexuality, etc…."** Also in this list are **"drunkards."** The term "drunkards" in the Bible is representative of all substance abuse disorders. The scripture tells us that those who are able to live in these sinful lifestyles will not inherit the Kingdom of God. This does not mean that "quitting" these lifestyles will get you to Heaven. To the contrary, what this does teach is that those who are saved and headed for Heaven will not be comfortable living in these sins. The Holy Spirit convicts and corrects us! God changes us!

The good news is found in verse 11. Now remember Paul is writing to Christians here, to the church at Corinth. He writes, **"And such were some of you. But you were washed, you were sanctified, you were justified in the name of the Lord Jesus Christ and by the Spirit of our God."**

The good news is that this is in the PAST tense! They are not what or who they use to be. The text is clear that it was Jesus Christ and the ministry of the Holy Spirit that had changed them. Once a person places their faith in Christ they are forgiven and justified before God but this is when the change is just beginning. This is why as you look forward you need to trust God to complete what He started in you. This does not mean that this change will come easily or even automatically but change can come.

Sometimes as we set out to take a different direction in life we can become fearful and anxious. Change can make us uncomfortable. Others, and the manner in which they interact with us, can also be discouraging sometimes. You may wonder, "When will they ever trust me again?" If it seems that those closest to you are always giving you the third degree, asking questions concerning where you have been and what you've been doing, and just not believing you, take heart-your future awaits!

As you look forward, trust God and know that things will change. Trust does return. Hurts do heal. Bridges can, many times, be mended. Life can be better than it has ever been before. Your future is full of hope if it is full of God. Also keep in mind during this time that the reason others may struggle to trust you is because of your past behavior. Don't become short and ill with them! It is your fault, based upon your past behavior, that they don't trust you. It will take time for their trust to return and the only way that this will transpire is by you proving yourself to be trustworthy. This takes time and determination.

Today consider this prophetic passage of scripture. God is speaking through Isaiah the Prophet to speak to the Israelites about a time of captivity that was approaching. These were difficult times for Israel yet God reminds them that there is hope for their future.

Isaiah 40:27-31 (NKJV)

"Why do you say, O Jacob, And speak, O Israel: 'My way is hidden from the LORD, And my just claim is passed over by my God?' 28 Have you not known? Have you not heard? The everlasting God, the LORD, The Creator of the ends of the earth, Neither faints nor is weary. His understanding is unsearchable. 29 He gives power to the weak & to *those who have* no might He increases strength. 30Even the youths shall faint and be weary & the young men shall utterly fall, 31But those who wait on the LORD shall renew *their* strength; They shall mount up with wings like eagles, They shall run and not be weary, They shall walk and not faint.'"

"Jacob" and "Israel" both refer to the people of Israel. God is speaking to His people. God is saying "I know that you are going to feel like I am not paying attention to your dilemma, and you may feel like I have simply passed you by, but I have not.

Have you ever had those times in your life when you felt that your way was hidden from the Lord? Those times when you felt as if God was not paying attention to what you were dealing with?

Listen, The Bible teaches that **GOD NEVER IGNORES HIS CHILDREN.** Never forget God's grace! It's not about how well you perform. So often we feel like, "I have failed so many times, why would God pay attention to my life?" It is because of grace, that's why! Grace is you receiving what you do not deserve! Instead of complaining the way that Israel did, why don't you praise Him for His grace? There is power in prayer but there is also great power in praise!

List below those things you should praise God about right now:

Isaiah says in **verse 28, "Have you not heard?"** Why are you having a pity party right now? Get your eyes off your struggles and know that you do have a future. Remember what you have heard and how God has blessed you in your life. He has not changed. He will be in your future just as he is in your today! Trust Him.

In the context for this passage read verse 12: **"Who has measured the waters in the hollow of his hand-measured Heaven with a span and calculated the dust of earth and weighed the mountains in scales and the hills in a balance?"** My friend, you cannot weigh God or measure Him but He weighs and measures everything! He is God and He is bigger than any challenge you may face. God is bigger than your addiction, bigger than your problem, and bigger than your mistakes.

Verse 13 says that God needs no counselors and no advisors. God doesn't need your opinion today. God is asking for your trust. What is it going on in your life right now where you simply need to trust God?

You know something else that should give you strength to "Look Forward and Trust God?" **GOD NEVER GROWS WEARY!** We do but He doesn't. He never faints. I can face my future knowing that God will be ready to help me. God will be there for me. God will have all I need for whatever I may face.

Do you ever feel like your failures must wear God out? Maybe God is up in Heaven saying, "There he/she goes again. I can't believe they did that again. I'm tired and weary of forgiving them." Here is great hope and reason to rejoice because God never gets tired of forgiving us and restoring us. I can face tomorrow knowing that whatever happens He still loves me. He is ready to forgive and ready to restore and ready to remove your sins as far as the east is from the west!

I also want you to know as you move forward that **GOD IS FAITHFUL TO HIS PROMISES.** Read Verse 31, "**But those who wait on the LORD Shall renew *their* strength; They shall mount up with wings like eagles, They shall run and not be weary, They shall walk and not faint.**"

What is God promising in this verse?

This promise is for you! Do you need strength? Do you need power? Look to God for all you need. You can get a life of addiction behind you. You can regain your life. You can overcome in God's strength and power.

I have been clean for over 30 years now. I use to think back when I was getting high that those feeling of euphoria were the best feelings I could ever experience. I now know that was false. As I walk with the Lord in this new life that He has granted me there are times I feel like I am soaring higher than I have ever flown before. The divine presence of the Holy Spirit within me lifts me above my struggles and into another world many times as I worship my Lord. Has this ever happened to you? Sometimes it gets so good I feel as if I could just take off and go on to glory. I also know that as great as those times are in my life now there are even greater things ahead of me.

Look forward, trust God, and make plans for change. Think about what you want in your future. What direction do you desire to move in? Now think about events, places, and practices that need to be eliminated so you can move into your future with hope. List those things that have been part of your life thus far that must not be part of your life now as you move forward:

Look forward, trust God, and make plans for change. List below events, places, and practices that need to be added or increased for change to be realized in your future:

PRAYER: *"Dear Heavenly Father, I love you. I worship you. You are so very good to me. You have rescued me, saved me, given me this new life to live for you. I trust you with my past, present, and with my future. I have already been changed and I am being transformed. The things of my past that have held me captive are falling off. I am being renewed day by day. All because you are my God. I praise your holy name. It is in the name of Jesus I rejoice! Amen."*

Growing In Christ
Week #32

In recent lessons we have discussed putting the past behind us and pressing forward into the future that God has designed for us. If you are currently struggling with these past lessons, please don't become discouraged. Change does not come easily for most. It is not as easy as saying "Just get over it" when it comes to traumatic events in our lives. Healing takes time. Be patient in this process but trust God daily as you move forward.

As I introduce the lesson this week I am reminded of how we are all a work in progress. None of us is exactly where we need to be in our spiritual growth all the time. We all fall short (Romans 3:23). Yet, we should all be able to say that we are more Christ-like today than we have ever been before. Did you know that this is God's goal in our lives?

Romans 8:28-29 ESV
"And we know that for those who love God all things work together for good, for those who are called according to his purpose. For those whom he foreknew he also predestined to be conformed to the image of his Son, in order that he might be the firstborn among many brothers."

What does this verse reveal to us about what God is accomplishing in our lives?

This lesson deals more with the present than it does the past or the future. Change does not happen by accident. The decisions we make today determine the direction that we begin moving in as well. Let's consider where we are now and how we need to allow God's Holy Spirit to change us in areas that we know must change. How does the Holy Spirit guide us?

Meditate upon the following verses and reflect upon how the writers were moved by the Holy Spirit:

Numbers 11:17 (ESV)
"And I will come down and talk with you there. And I will take some of

the Spirit that is on you and put it on them, and they shall bear the burden
of the people with you, so that you may not bear it yourself alone."

In the above passage God is speaking with Moses concerning the leaders of Israel. If those leaders were going to be able to lead the people they needed the Holy Spirit of God. In Numbers 11:17 how were they given the Holy Spirit?

Numbers 27:18 (ESV)
"So the LORD said to Moses, 'Take Joshua the son of Nun, a man
in whom is the Spirit, and lay your hand on him.'"

According to the above verse, how was the Spirit of God able to lead Joshua?

Galatians 5:16-26 (ESV)
"But I say, walk by the Spirit, and you will not gratify the desires of the flesh. [17] For the desires of the flesh are against the Spirit, and the desires of the Spirit are against the flesh, for these are opposed to each other, to keep you from doing the things you want to do. [18] But if you are led by the Spirit, you are not under the law. [19] Now the works of the flesh are evident: sexual immorality, impurity, sensuality, [20] idolatry, sorcery, enmity, strife, jealousy, fits of anger, rivalries, dissensions, divisions, [21] envy, drunkenness, orgies, and things like these. I warn you, as I warned you before, that those who do such things will not inherit the kingdom of God. [22] But the fruit of the Spirit is love, joy, peace, patience, kindness, goodness, faithfulness, [23] gentleness, self-control; against such things there is no law. [24] And those who belong to Christ Jesus have crucified the flesh with its passions and desires. [25] If we live by the Spirit, let us also keep in step with the Spirit. [26] Let us not become conceited, provoking one another, envying one another."

So, you are not to live your life simply gratifying the desires of the _____. If we live our lives simply based on what we want to do, and how we feel, we will not be reflecting Christ-likeness. The long list given in verses 19-21 are not qualities that God desires in our lives. We need to change. This change is possible as we rely on God's power through the Holy Spirit who lives within us as believers. Jesus promised:

John 14:16-17 (ESV)
"And I will ask the Father, and he will give you another Helper, to be with you forever, [17] even the Spirit of truth, whom the world cannot receive, because it neither sees him nor knows him. You know him, for <u>he dwells with you and will be in you.</u>"

> "As I reflect upon what LIFE Ministries has meant to me, I immediately think about how much I have grown in my faith by the tools which Pastor Mike has shared through this ministry. Our lessons are centered around Biblical truth which reminds me that I am not the person I use to be. I have been made new and forgiven! Our weekly meetings help me tremendously to be open, honest, and to move forward in my walk with the Lord."
>
> Michelle House, Whitakers, N.C.

The Apostle Paul wrote:

1 Corinthians 3:16 (ESV)
"Do you not know that you are God's temple and that God's Spirit dwells in you?"

As a way of review from a previous lesson, what three things, revealed to us in the following passage, has God given to us so that we may be everything He desires?

2 Peter 1:3-4 (ESV)
"His divine power has granted to us all things that pertain to life and godliness, through the knowledge of him who called us to his own glory and excellence, [4] by which he has granted to us his precious and very great promises, so that through them you may become partakers of the divine nature, having escaped from the corruption that is in the world because of sinful desire."

God has given us ALL things that pertain to life and godliness. Three things are mentioned:

#1. His _____ power. (Holy Spirit)

#2. His _____ and very great _____.

#3. His divine _____.

We do have the power we need to change!

"Growing in Christ"
Week # 32 assignment

Read and really meditate upon the verses below. Think about what they are teaching you about growing in your faith.

2 Peter 3:18 (ESV)
"But grow in the grace and knowledge of our Lord and Savior Jesus Christ.
To him be the glory both now and to the day of eternity. Amen."

#1. According to the above verse what two things do we need to grow in?

A. _____

B. _____

#2. As we grow in our faith we bring glory to whom?

Hebrews 6:1 (ESV)
"Therefore let us leave the elementary doctrine of Christ and go on to maturity, not
laying again a foundation of repentance from dead works and of faith toward God."

#3. The word "doctrine" is a word which refers to teaching. We should move on in our learning concerning God's truth. We must leave the basic elementary teachings of the Bible and move on into deeper understandings of the scripture. What do you think it means to "go on to maturity?"

#4. If we continue to lay the same foundation over and over again then we are not making progress. The foundation is meant to be built upon! What truths can you identify that you should build upon the foundation of the Gospel, that Christ died and rose again?

1 Peter 2:2 (ESV)
"Like newborn infants, long for the pure spiritual milk,
that by it you may grow up into salvation."

#5. New believers are referred to as newborn _____.

To grow up means that you do not remain where you are right now. Spiritually speaking, what will be your plan for spiritual growth? List some things below that you know will help you grow in your faith.

_____

_____

_____

_____

_____

_____

Now begin to put that plan into action!

Structuring Your Life for Biblical Change
Week #33

The goal in all therapy and all counseling programs is to promote change in a person's life. In most secular environments the goal is simply to promote personal well-being and happiness. While those are not bad goals, they are certainly not the best goals to aim for. Do you remember what we have said should be our bullseye in living? Write your answer below:

I know that everyone desires to live a happy life and to be well but God created us, designed us, saved us, empowered us for an even greater and eternal purpose. God tells us that holiness is much more important to Him than our happiness. I do not want to imply that God is against you being happy. He certainly is not! In fact, God desires good things in your life but those blessings, those good things, are not acquired by chasing after them. God's joy and abundant life is discovered as a result of us living for Him.

Hebrews 12:1-2 (ESV)
"Therefore, since we are surrounded by so great a cloud of witnesses,
let us also lay aside every weight, and sin which clings so closely, and
let us run with endurance the race that is set before us,

² looking to Jesus, the founder and perfecter of our faith, who for the
joy that was set before him endured the cross, despising the shame,
and is seated at the right hand of the throne of God."

According to those verses in order for us to run the race we must first do what?

Who is the founder and perfecter of our faith?

Verse 2 tells us that Jesus, as He went to the cross, was entering into "the joy set before him." What do you think that means?

What are some things in your life that you need to lay aside right now so that you can be everything God desires?

Glenn Howell, a leader in LIFE from its conception, shares in his testimony how after he accepted Christ as His Lord and Savior and immediately he went through his house pouring out bottle after bottle of alcohol. Glenn knew that Christ had forgiven him, saved him, and set him free from his addiction to alcohol. He also knew that he needed to be serious about living this new life for Christ. That meant getting rid of anything that might trip him up and cause him to sin.

Mark 9:43-48 (ESV)

"And if your hand causes you to sin, cut it off. It is better for you to enter life crippled than with two hands to go to hell, to the unquenchable fire. ⁴⁵ And if your foot causes you to sin, cut it off. It is better for you to enter life lame than with two feet to be thrown into hell. ⁴⁷ And if your eye causes you to sin, tear it out. It is better for you to enter the kingdom of God with one eye than with two eyes to be thrown into hell, ⁴⁸ 'where their worm does not die and the fire is not quenched.'"

Jesus is not instructing us to literally start cutting off our hands and feet but He is warning us to be radical about getting out of our lives anything that may cause us to sin. GET SERIOUS ABOUT YOUR RECOVERY! UNDERSTAND RIGHT NOW THAT YOUR RECOVERY IS A MATTER OF LIFE AND DEATH! IT IS A MATTER OF LIVING IN FREEDOM OR LIVING IN BONDAGE! While there may be many helpful techniques and programs that may aid you in recovery, there is only One who can forgive sin. Give thanks to God for all the resources He has provided for you to stay clean but remember to look to Him as your ultimate source to live your new life.

What is it in your life right now that is hindering you?

Ephesians 4:22-24 (ESV)

"to put off your old self, which belongs to your former manner of life and is corrupt through deceitful desires, ²³ and to be renewed in the spirit of your minds, ²⁴ and to put on the new self, created after the likeness of God in true righteousness and holiness."

List below those things, places, people that you must PUT OFF in your life in order to recover:

List below those things, places, and people that you must PUT ON in your life in order to recover:

How has your life changed since seeking recovery?

What has helped you in your recovery?

What has hindered you in your recovery?

What advice would you give to someone who is struggling with a substance use disorder?

PRAYER: "Lord, I need to restructure my life with wisdom. I do not want to return to the life I am leaving behind. Help me to know what changes I must make. I am willing to put off people, places, and things that I might be victorious in this battle. I am committed to this process of change. I desire to bring you glory and honor with my life. Show me the way Lord. In Jesus' name. Amen."

Dealing with Our Emotions
Week #34

A man walked into his Psychiatrist's office for his regular appointment in dealing with stress. The Psychiatrist began by asking, "How do you feel today?" The man replied, "Not too good doctor. Sometimes I feel like a Tee Pee and sometimes I feel like a Wigwam." The doctor replied, "I see the problem. You are two tents." (Translation-You are too tense).

Okay. Okay. I know that's a little corney but it does serve as an excellent lead in for this lesson. In the secular world of counseling and therapy the most important thing seems to be a person's sense of well-being and how they are feeling. The most common phrase used in the secular arena of mental health may well be, "How does that make you feel?" I want to make a clear statement as we begin; Emotions are important but they are not meant to be our focus in life nor are they to determine how we live and respond to life's issues.

First of all, truth **#1: Our emotions are God-given.**

Genesis 1:27 (ESV)
"So God created man in his own image, in the image of God he created him; male and female he created them."

We are created in God's image meaning we have an eternal element to us, our souls, but we are also like God in our ability to think, reason, and experience emotional responses to life's experiences. In the Bible we read where God experienced sorrow (Genesis 6:6), anger (Psalm 30:5), joy (Zephaniah 3:17), love (John 3:16), and the list goes on.

Emotions are God-given attributes of our Heavenly Father. In understanding this truth, we realize that emotions are not sinful or bad since our God is sinless and good. Emotions only become bad or sinful when we allow them to function in our lives in a manner in which they were never intended. Why has God given us emotions?

Truth #2. Emotions are messengers.

We must understand that emotions are not truth communicators. That is not and cannot be their function in our lives. Mankind's fall into sin has affected everything about us in a negative manner. Our bodies hurt because of sin. We struggle to maintain godly thinking because of sin. Our desires are so often turned away from God because of sin. Our emotions too have been affected by our sin nature. Emotions are not trustworthy as a source for truth. Just because you feel a certain way doesn't necessarily mean that it is true.

Most people live according to the unspoken assumption that if I feel it then it must be true. For example, if I feel unloved and unwanted then I must be unloved and unwanted. If I feel like everyone has abandoned me then I must be all alone. Many people live life simply doing whatever their emotions tell them to do. For a depressed person that ultimately means not doing those things that they know they should do simply because they don't feel like doing them. For the angry person this is presented by allowing that emotion to cause them to yell, or to act out in anger. Think of your emotions as messengers in your life, and not to dictate truth or to tell you how you should live.

What are emotions seeking to communicate? Emotions tell me that I have some heart issues going on. When I use the term "heart" I am also including your thought processes and your belief system. If I am fearful then I am reminded that I must not be focused on God's presence in my life. If I am experiencing loneliness, I need to draw close to God who is always with me. If anger begins to rise up within, I am reminded in my heart that this world is not fair, sin is real, and I need to redirect my focus to God who is working all things out for my good (Rom. 8:28). Maybe I am feeling like a failure. That emotion could remind me that I cannot do anything good on my own. I am totally dependent upon the Lord. Your emotions reveal to you that something is going on deep within you and they should motivate you toward God for all you need.

1 Peter 5:6-7 (ESV)
"Humble yourselves, therefore, under the mighty hand of God so that at the proper time he may exalt you, casting all your anxieties on him, because he cares for you."

According to 1 Peter 5:6-7, God desires to exalt us, or to lift us up out of our emotional turmoil. My responsibility in this process is what?

Our emotions, as messengers, should also motivate us towards godly change. In recovery often we experience emotions of regret and shame over our past behavior. These emotions should motivate us to make different choices in life so as not to repeat our past mistakes.

Truth #3. Emotions can help us to enjoy God.

Psalm 16:8-9 (ESV)
"I have set the LORD always before me; because he is at my right hand, I shall not be shaken. Therefore my heart is glad, and my whole being rejoices; my flesh also dwells secure."

In Psalm 16 the writer expresses his worship unto God. He is trusting in God (which deals with fear, anxiety, worry). He writes "my heart is glad." He rejoices (this drives away sadness, depression, complacency)! Worship should include expressing our heartfelt emotions unto God. Emotions are part of who you are and how you think. Sometimes good, sometimes bad, but the next truth is:

#4. Emotions can be managed.

How can you manage how you "feel" to bring God glory? I want to suggest four things that you must practice in order to keep your emotions in check. These are not four easy steps to overcoming or a magic bullet to overcoming emotional struggles. Rather these are guideline truths that can aid us in recovery over our emotions. I am using an acrostic for "FEEL:"

F reely acknowledge and surrender your emotions to God.

E xamine what your emotions are telling you.

E valuate changes that you need to make.

L ook to God as you apply biblical truth.

The first step *Freely acknowledge* is to be honest with God about how you feel. He already knows anyway. Just as God is truthful we need to be as well. Denying our emotions is dangerous to our emotional, mental, and spiritual health. God can handle how you feel, trust me.

Then as messengers *we must examine* what the message is that our emotions are trying to communicate to us. Ask yourself, "Why am I feeling fearful, angry, lonely, sad, etc?

Next you should *evaluate what needs to change* in your thinking or behavior so that you continue to bring glory to God in your life.

Then, *look to God*, trust Him to supply all you need.

#1. What are some "red flags" that you could identify in your life that could indicate that you are suppressing your emotions or denying them? (For example-yelling)

#2. What emotions are you more comfortable in expressing?

#3. Let's consider from scripture how God responds to our emotions when we admit them to Him. Below each scripture write how this verse reveals the manner in which God deals with our emotions:

Psalm 51:17 (ESV)
"The sacrifices of God are a broken spirit; a broken and
contrite heart, O God, you will not despise."

1 Peter 5:7 (ESV)
"..casting all your anxieties on him, because he cares for you."

Following the resurrection of Jesus, Thomas experienced doubt that Jesus had actually risen from the dead. Notice how Jesus responded to his doubt and write it below the verse:

John 20:27-28 (ESV)
"Then he said to Thomas, 'Put your finger here, and see my hands; and put out your hand,
and place it in my side. Do not disbelieve, but believe.'
Thomas answered him, 'My Lord and my God!'"

Matthew 11:28 (ESV)
"Come to me, all who labor and are heavy laden, and I will give you rest."

Philippians 4:5-7 (ESV)
"Let your reasonableness be known to everyone. The Lord is at hand;
do not be anxious about anything, but in everything by prayer and supplication with
thanksgiving let your requests be made known to God.
And the peace of God, which surpasses all understanding, will
guard your hearts and your minds in Christ Jesus."

Isaiah 41:10 (ESV)
"Fear not, for I am with you; be not dismayed, for I am your God; I will strengthen
you, I will help you, I will uphold you with my righteous right hand."

Too often negative emotions are allowed to control us, discourage us, and cause us to turn back. Don't allow this to happen in your life! Relapse is not an option. We gain strength as we understand biblical truth, even as it relates to our emotions. God loves you in spite of your regrets, fears, worries and doubts. You can trust Him! Run to Him! Be honest and real with Him!

Write out your prayer below that expresses your honesty with God concerning how you feel:

PRAYER: "God, my emotions are a mess much of the time. It seems that there is always a lot going on in my life that cause these emotions to rise up from within me. Help me to not allow these feelings to control me. Lord, I want to be controlled by only you. Rescue me from the desires of this flesh. I cannot always trust my emotions but I can always trust you. Help me Lord to stand firm on what you say! Thank-you Lord. In Jesus' name. Amen."

Getting off The Performance Treadmill
Week #35

Galatians 3:11-12 (ESV)
"Now it is evident that no one is justified before God by the law, for 'The righteous shall live by faith.' But the law is not of faith, rather 'The one who does them shall live by them.'"

There was a very old picture of a lady being escorted out of a church service by two men in white coats. This lady evidently had gone crazy and was being removed and committed to an insane asylum. The caption is what caught my eye; The Pastor was quoted as saying to another church member, "We're really going to miss that woman. She did everything in this church." Hmmmm….I didn't know whether I should laugh or cry at that visual bit of humor. It does however point me to a very important truth; If I believe that it is what I do that gives me value, I am going to wear myself out and probably drive me and others crazy in the process. Let's discuss how we can get off the performance treadmill.

I remember growing up in eastern N.C. and always struggling with my self-value. I felt like I never quite measured up to the expectations of those around me. Many things magnified these feelings within me. For example, I had a terrible speech impairment when I was very young. It was so bad that my grandmother could not understand my speech most of the time. Early in my elementary school years I was involved in speech therapy to help correct the problem. Ironic, isn't it, that God would call me to preach? This problem made me feel like I just didn't quite measure up. Other trauma in my young life added to these feelings of inadequacies, which I will not go into here. My personal nature and God-given personality is one of "giving it all I've got" in whatever I choose. So, during my younger years of attempting to withdraw from the world around me because of my feelings of being "less than," I turned to drugs and alcohol as an escape. I was always pushing the limits to get a bigger buzz and a higher high. There was not a drug I would not use if given the opportunity. Some of my drug buddies would put a twist on an old cereal commercial and say, "Give it to Mikey. He'll try it. He'll try anything." (If you remember that old commercial). I felt that I at least had developed an identity with those in addiction.

Once I accepted Christ as my Savior, I immediately was all in. My life was full steam ahead for God, holding nothing back. I was just as much for Jesus as I had been for drugs all those years. It was like going from night to day. My recovery was a huge blessing in my life but I continued to have a problem. I was still equating my personal value and identity with how well I could perform. I wanted people around me to accept and approve of me, and I wasn't sure how to win that approval. Even as a Christian I carried a lot of guilt and shame, thinking that God really could not be very pleased with me.

Jesus has promised us abundant life (John 10:10) but a very common obstacle to living in this abundant life is the belief that our worth and value comes from what we do, or self-effort. I never could seem to do enough where I felt I had reached a satisfactory point of value or worth. The result was increased guilt from constantly falling short. This guilt motivated me to work harder and harder, almost to the point of exhaustion, trying to do better. This belief is all wrong! I discovered that trying to run on the performance treadmill can lead to exhaustion, health problems like headaches and stomach disorders, poor concentration and worry, as well as harming my relationships as I attempted to earn the approval of others. When I first entered the ministry and began preaching I had a stomach issue every Sunday morning because of nervousness. I was so afraid that I was going to fail. I lived for the approval of others. Do you?

Ask yourself these questions and honestly answer them to yourself. If one of these seems especially revealing for you please write a brief answer:

#1. Do you avoid certain people out of fear that they will reject you?

#2. Do you become depressed when others are critical of you?

#3. Do you look for the negative in others?

#4. Do you often feel over controlled by others?

#5. Are you easily manipulated by others?

#6. Do you struggle with anger and resentment towards others?

#7. Do you become anxious when you believe someone might not accept you?

#8. Do you say "yes" when you should say "no?"

#9. Do you feel awkward around others who are different from you?

#10. Do you find yourself trying to impress others?

I know that some of those questions may cause you to really ponder which way you should honestly answer. We are all guilty to some degree but I want you to consider if this is a real issue for you. Do these feelings control you?

There were many times in my life when the fear of rejection controlled me. However, once I began to grow in my faith and understand that my identity is not based upon what I do but what God has already accomplished for me, I began to understand that God loves me and accepts me for who I am. Yes, He desires to change me and He never accepts my sin, but He always accepts me. Wow! That was the moment I began to walk in freedom. I now know that there is nothing I can do that will take the place of having faith in Him to complete me.

TRUTH #1: We can't live up to the Law. Any attempt to do so leads to religion, not relationship.

TRUTH #2: Legalism leads to self-righteousness, not to love.

TRUTH #3: It's not about WHAT I do but it's about WHOSE I am. Have you ever heard the expression, "Christians aren't perfect, just forgiven?" My worth and value is not dependent upon how well I can perform. My value comes from the fact that I belong to God and am now His child.

Don't allow these TRUTHS to bewilder you. We will discuss these later. Let's move into our Bible study:

Matthew 19:16-30 (ESV)

[16] **And behold, a man came up to him, saying, "Teacher, what good deed must I do to have eternal life?"** [17] **And he said to him, "Why do you ask me about what is good? There is only one who is good. If you would enter life, keep the commandments."** [18] **He said to him, "Which ones?" And Jesus said, "You shall not murder, You shall not commit adultery, You shall not steal, You shall not bear false witness,** [19] **Honor your father and mother, and, You shall love your neighbor as yourself."** [20] **The young man said to him, "All these I have kept. What do I still lack?"** [21] **Jesus said to him, "If you would be perfect, go, sell what you possess and give to the poor, and you will have treasure in heaven; and come, follow me."** [22] **When the young man heard this he went away sorrowful, for he had great possessions.** [23] **And Jesus said to his disciples, "Truly, I say to you, only with difficulty will a rich person enter the kingdom of heaven.** [24] **Again I tell you, it is easier for a camel to go through the eye of a needle than for a rich person to enter the kingdom of God."**

[25] **When the disciples heard this, they were greatly astonished, saying, "Who then can be saved?"** [26] **But Jesus looked at them and said, "With man this is impossible, but with God all things are possible."** [27] **Then Peter said in reply, "See, we have left everything and followed you. What then will we have?"** [28] **Jesus said to them, "Truly, I say to you, in the new world, when the Son of Man will sit on his glorious throne,**

you who have followed me will also sit on twelve thrones, judging the twelve tribes of Israel. ²⁹ And everyone who has left houses or brothers or sisters or father or mother or children or lands, for my name's sake, will receive a hundredfold and will inherit eternal life. ³⁰ But many who are first will be last, and the last first.

Now, I want you to pay attention to the question this man asked Jesus as recorded in verse 16. Write the question below:

This man is referred to in verse 22 as having "great possessions." This was a rich man as far as having worldly wealth yet he was living in poverty spiritually. He thought there must be something he could "do" to earn salvation and God's acceptance. When Jesus told this man to keep the commandments He was showing him that keeping the law was not enough. He needed to be willing to surrender (something we have discussed before). Jesus instructed him to give what to the poor?

We know that giving away things to the poor doesn't earn us eternal life so Jesus was teaching something else here. What do you think the message was for this young ruler?

The rich young ruler went away sorrowful because he was not willing to let go of his idols. How about you? See, this is what Jesus requires. He alone desires, and even demands, to be first in our lives. List below some of the most important things/people/activities in your life:

The disciples were flabbergasted at the conclusion of this man's conversation with Jesus. They thought, "If this rich man who was trying to live up to the Law wasn't going to make it, then who would go to Heaven?" Jesus made it clear that God is able to do the impossible, NOT US! God is able to bring us to Heaven, NOT US. It is not about WHAT we do. It's about WHOSE we are!

Even Peter was caught up in doing stuff. In verse 27 Peter said to Jesus, "We have left everything to follow you…" In other words, look what we have DONE. I do not want you to get caught up in doing stuff but I want to encourage you to rest in BEING who you are in Christ. Make sure your focus is on Him and glorifying Him. Don't live your life trying to please people but focus on living your life to please God.

I am not teaching you that works are not important and that it doesn't matter how you live. To the contrary, if you will rest in your identity as God's child who has been redeemed, forgiven, and indwelt with the Holy

Spirit, regardless of what you've done, you have made giant leaps in your relationship with God. Thank God for grace.

Romans 6:1-4 (ESV)

"What shall we say then? Are we to continue in sin that grace may abound? ² By no means! How can we who died to sin still live in it? ³ Do you not know that all of us who have been baptized into Christ Jesus were baptized into his death? ⁴ We were buried therefore with him by baptism into death, in order that, just as Christ was raised from the dead by the glory of the Father, we too might walk in newness of life."

What do you think these verses mean?

PRAYER: *"Lord, I am beginning to understand that my relationship with you has more to do with whose I am now and not necessarily what I do. I belong to you. You love me unconditionally. Help me to not get caught up with doing but to rest in being, just rest in being yours. Thank-you God that I already have your favor. I do not have to work for it. It's by your grace! Oh, how thankful I am! You have accepted me, adopted me, redeemed me, chosen me and you died and rose again for me! I love you Lord. I am eternally blessed to be your child. In Jesus' name. Amen."*

Making Up For Lost Time
Week #36

Joel 2:23-26 (ESV)
"Be glad, O children of Zion, and rejoice in the LORD your God, for he has given the early rain for your vindication; he has poured down for you abundant rain, the early and the latter rain, as before. ²⁴ The threshing floors shall be full of grain; the vats shall overflow with wine and oil. ²⁵ I will restore to you the years that the swarming locust has eaten, the hopper, the destroyer, and the cutter, my great army, which I sent among you. ²⁶ You shall eat in plenty and be satisfied, and praise the name of the LORD your God, who has dealt wondrously with you. And my people shall never again be put to shame."

Do you have any regrets? Most people do. Often as people come out of addictive patterns of living they begin to look back and regret the manner in which they have treated others, as well as simply wishing they had spent their time more wisely. This week's study comes out of a concern a previous LIFE member had on this issue. It is my prayer that it is an encouragement to you as well.

The Book of Joel was written by Joel, a prophet of God, who lived in the area of Jerusalem about 800 years before Christ. Joel calls God's people to repentance (change) after God has sent a devastating plague of locust and drought as judgements because of the people's sin. Joel cries out:

Joel 1:5 (ESV)
"Awake, you drunkards, and weep, and wail, all you drinkers of wine, because of the sweet wine, for it is cut off from your mouth."

The locust had stripped every vine of grapes and the crops in the fields lay barren (1:10). These crop-eating insects represent our enemy. According to John 10:10 our enemy has come to steal, kill, and destroy. What does Joel 1:5 tell us about sin in the sight of God?

Have you ever felt like the judgement of God was upon your life because of sin?

What was your response?

Let us learn from Joel! The prophet Joel calls out to God as recorded in Joel 1:19. Then in response God says:

Joel 2:12-13 (ESV)

[12] "Yet even now," declares the LORD, "return to me with all your heart, with fasting, with weeping, and with mourning; [13] and rend your hearts and not your garments." Return to the LORD your God, for he is gracious and merciful, slow to anger, and abounding in steadfast love; and he relents over disaster."

God desires to bless us, not to correct us. God desires abundance in our lives, not lack. If we will turn (or return) to the Lord with our brokenness He will heal and restore us. We cannot undo our past mistakes but we can decide right now to:

#1. GIVE THEM TO THE LORD.

You cannot change the past. Give your regrets to the Lord. Be determined that you will not continue to make the same mistakes which have led you to the valley of regret. The Lord is waiting for you to come to Him.

#2. TRUST GOD WITH YOUR REGRETS!

Not only did God promise His people through Joel that He would restore the land, sending rain, and removing the locust, God also promised that He would "restore to you the years that the swarming locust had eaten." (2:25) I have discovered in my own personal life that God is more than able to transform my past sins and failures. Today I minister to others who are where I once lived, in the bondage of addiction. My past experiences and struggles are tools that the Holy Spirit is using in my life to help others now. That's how mighty God is! All the time that I wasted on things that really did not matter was time gone. I cannot get that time back. Many things in life can be replaced like houses, cars, money and material possessions but time cannot be replaced. Once time is spent, it is spent. What does lost time mean to you?

For some, regrets concerning the past have to do with living selfishly. We get so caught up in our own world that we neglect to be blessing to others or even to serve the Lord. For others, lost time relates to losing a loved one in death. We look back and we regret that we didn't have time with that person to do the things we had planned and hoped to do. Personally, my regrets concerning lost time have to do with living a "Christ-less life." I wish I could roll time back and begin living my life for Christ much sooner than I have. Once time is lost, it's gone. We cannot do anything to get it back. But God is able to do what we cannot! How does God restore the years that we have lost?

#1. God deepens our relationship with Him to a degree we have never known before. Why don't you ask Him right now to do this for you? Pray and confess to God that you have wasted precious time, asking Him to restore to you a deeper love for Him, and a richer walk in His truth.

#2. God can multiply your fruitfulness in your time remaining. In the Book of Joel the people went four years with crop devastation. However, when God restored the years that the locust had eaten they were given bumper crops! You can look to God, asking Him, "Lord, please multiply your fruitfulness in my life that I may be used by You in a greater way than ever before."

#3. Trust God to take your short-term loss and produce long term gains! God's faithfulness has seen you through the difficult years. He has been faithful to bring you to where you are right now. Jesus had only 3 short years of public ministry before going to the cross. Isaiah 53:8 says that "He was cut off." This passage speaks of the cross. In the prime of His life, at the age of 33, Jesus died on the cross. His ministry had just begun and yet it ended, it would seem, so abruptly. Yet we know His ministry is eternal. Why don't you turn to God and ask Him to do through you a ministry that will last forever in the brief time that you are here.

We serve a God who is able to restore us in every way.

1 Peter 5:10 (ESV)
"And after you have suffered a little while, the God of all grace, who has called you to his eternal glory in Christ, will himself restore, confirm, strengthen, and establish you."

According to the above promise in 1 Peter 5:10:

#1. God is the God of all _____.

What do you believe the word "grace" means?

Joel called the people in the southern kingdom to return to God. Hosea was used by God to call the people in the northern kingdom to repentance. This is what Hosea said:

Hosea 6:1-2 (ESV)
[1] "Come, let us return to the LORD; for he has torn us, that he may heal us; he has struck us down, and he will bind us up.
[2] After two days he will revive us; on the third day he will raise us up, that we may live before him."

My friend, we cannot do anything about the past but there is much we can do about the present which helps determine our future. How will you, right now, begin to make the most out of your remaining time? List some ways that you have determined to change:

Write a prayer below asking God to restore the time you have lost. Also give Him praise for what He has promised to do in restoring the time.

The Importance of Accountability
Week #37

Hebrews 3:13
"But exhort one another daily, while it is called 'Today,'
lest any of you be hardened through the deceitfulness of sin."

God has not created us to be independent creatures in need of nothing, but we are created as very dependent beings. In fact, we are very needy. We need food, water, shelter, and companionship. We need oxygen to breathe. We need a controlled climate, not too hot and not too cold. We need God. There is only One Sovereign being in the universe and that is God Almighty. **Psalm 103:19 declares, *"The LORD has established His throne in heaven, And His kingdom rules over all."*** We are creatures totally dependent upon the Creator.

We also need one another. In the creation account recorded in Genesis, God created everything within a six day period of time, resting on the seventh day. At the end of the first five days of creation, God spoke a benediction in relation to what He created. A benediction is a blessing. That benediction or blessing that God spoke was *"and it was good."* The Bible records God making that statement at the end of each of the first five days of creation (Genesis 1:4, 10, 12, 18, 21 and 25).

However, at the end of the sixth day, God spoke a malediction. A malediction is not a blessing, but a curse. God created man during that sixth day of creation. He then looked upon man and declared, ***"It is not good."* (Genesis 2:18).** What is not good? That man is alone. What was God's answer to this problem? God created a companion that was especially for Adam. We all need companionship. We all need support from one another.

LIFE Ministries has always existed as a "safe haven" for those struggling to come and find acceptance, healing, and love. One of the men who serves in security for the LIFE chapter in Edgecombe County, who has been present at many meetings over the years, shares this truth:

"I personally have seen God move in the lives of many men and women struggling to return from the grip of addiction. Not only have those people experienced individual successes, but they are welcomed into a new, supportive family with the love of Christ at its core. One of the most powerful ministries that I have ever been involved in!" Jeff Eatmon

We all need a support system around us. It is this support system that helps us live out the Christian life. We know that salvation is a gift that God gives to the believing sinner. That is the process of justification which is a sovereign act of God. We receive that act of justification from God by grace through faith. The work of sanctification, however, requires our ongoing and active participation. Sanctification, unlike justification, is a process and not an act. Sanctification is a lifelong process where the believer is learning and growing in the faith. We are ever becoming and never fully arriving. We can help one another in this change process.

The Christian life is referred to in the Bible as a *walk* and not a *rest*. Sanctification requires not only our own personal participation, but many times the participation of others in our lives to aid us in this growth process. Listen to how Paul writes this:

Romans 10:14-17 (NKJV)
"How then shall they call on Him in whom they have not believed? And how shall they believe in Him of whom they have not heard? And how shall they hear without a preacher? And how shall they preach unless they are sent? As it is written: 'How beautiful are the feet of those who preach the gospel of peace, Who bring glad tidings of good things!' But they have not all obeyed the gospel. For Isaiah says, 'Lord, who has believed our report?' So then faith comes by hearing, and hearing by the word of God."

We need others in our lives who are sent to proclaim God's truth that we might believe. How will we hear unless someone tells us the Truth of the Gospel?

The local church should serve a vital purpose in the life of every believer. Each member of that local church is important and intrinsically interconnected with the other members. You are important to the body of Christ. There is a special place within the body where God desires you to serve alongside other believers. You have been saved and equipped to minister in your specific area of service. As each member within the church serves by exercising their spiritual gifts, the church is enabled to be the living, and world-changing organism, that God desires. There is a place for you in the church! Your fellow believers need you just as you need them.

The parallel comparison that scripture gives us of this truth uses the example of the human body. Every member of your body is connected and dependent upon the other members. What good is a hand without an arm? How about a foot without a leg? A body without a heart?

1 Corinthians 12:12-27 (NKJV)

For as the body is one and has many members, but all the members of that one body, being many, are one body, so also is Christ. For by one Spirit we were all baptized into one body--whether Jews or Greeks, whether slaves or free--and have all been made to drink into one Spirit. For in fact the body is not one member but many. If the foot should say, "Because I am not a hand, I am not of the body," is it therefore not of the body? And if the ear should say, "Because I am not an eye, I am not of the body," is it therefore not of the body? If the whole body were an eye, where would be the hearing? If the whole were hearing, where would be the smelling? But now God has set the members, each one of them, in the body just as He pleased. And if they were all one member, where would the body be? But now indeed there are many members, yet one body. And the eye cannot say to the hand, "I have no need of you"; nor again the head to the feet, "I have no need of you." No, much rather, those members of the body which seem to be weaker are necessary. And those members of the body which we think to be less honorable, on these we bestow greater honor; and our unpresentable parts have greater modesty, but our presentable parts have no need. But God composed the body, having given greater honor to that part which lacks it, that there should be no schism in the body, but that the members should have the same care for one another. And if one member suffers, all the members suffer with it; or if one member is honored, all the members rejoice with it. Now you are the body of Christ, and members individually.

The context in which Paul penned those words was one of great division within the church at Corinth. They were divided into small cliques and special interest groups. They were even refusing to fellowship with one another during a common meal! Paul addressed these believers and reminded them of how they needed one another.

Often, we read in the Bible the phrase *one another* which speaks of our interconnectedness. Read below a few of those[8]:

- John 13:14: *"Wash one another's feet."*

- Romans 12:10: *"Be kindly affectionate to one another..."*

- Romans 12:10: *"Giving preference to one another."*

- Romans 12:16: *"Be of the same mind one toward another."*

---

8   Adrian Rogers, The Adrian Rogers Legacy Collection, The Church-The Body of Christ, New testament, 1 Corinthians 12. © 2011 Rogers Family Trust. (Database © 2011 WORDsearch Corp).

- <u>Romans 14:13</u>: *"Do not judge one another."*

- <u>James 4:11</u>: *"Do not speak evil one of another."*

- <u>Romans 14:19</u>: *"Edify one another."*

- <u>Romans 15:7</u>: *"Receive one another."*

- <u>Romans 15:14</u>: *"Admonish one another."*

- <u>1 Corinthians 12:25</u>: *"Care for one another."*

- <u>1 Peter 4:10</u>: *"Minister gifts one to another."*

- <u>1 Corinthians 16:20</u>: *"Greet one another."*

- <u>Galatians 5:13</u>: *"Serve one another."*

- <u>Galatians 6:2</u>: *"Bear one another's burdens."*

- <u>Ephesians 5:21</u>: *"Submit one to another."*

- <u>1 Thessalonians 4:18</u>: *"Comfort one another."*

- <u>Hebrews 3:13</u>: *"Exhort one another."*

- <u>Hebrews 10:24</u>: *"Consider one another."*

- James 5:16: *"Confess your faults one to another."*

- <u>James 5:16</u>: *"Pray one for another."*

- <u>1 Peter 4:9</u>: *"Use hospitality one to another."*

- <u>1 John 1:7</u>: *"Fellowship with one another."*

My friend, when you made the decision to follow Christ, that was your final independent decision. From that point onward, every decision you face should be approached by asking God, "What do you want me to do?"

First of all, get involved in a local church serving our Lord with fellow believers as you exercise your spiritual gifts. The local church is here for your benefit. The writer of **Hebrews 10:25** exhorts us **"not forsaking the assembling of ourselves together, as is the manner of some, but exhorting one another, and so much the more as you see the Day approaching."** We need to assemble together as the church to exhort, which means to comfort, entreat, and to invite to come near. The majority of the time that the word *church* appears in the Bible it refers to a local church. God has placed the church among us to help us.

Secondly, have a time set aside each day when you study God's Word and pray. You need to grow in your faith. Growth cannot take place apart from nourishment. Donald Whitney, in his book *Spiritual Disciplines for the Christian Life* says, "There is simply no healthy Christian life apart from a diet of the milk and meat of Scripture."[9] There are many Bible studies available, just like this one, to aid you in your deliverance from addiction. Many helpful resources can be found on the Internet. Get involved in a regular Bible study program.

Thirdly, surround yourself with godly people. If you are constantly associating with your old friends who are living lives of idolatry, you will struggle to live out this new life of freedom. The Psalmist declared in **Psalm 119:115 (NKJV), "Depart from me, you evildoers, For I will keep the commandments of my God!"** The writer of Proverbs tells us in **Proverbs 4:14-15 (NKJV), "Do not enter the path of the wicked, And do not walk in the way of evil. Avoid it, do not travel on it; Turn away from it and pass on."** There is an ancient Oriental proverb that says, "If you lie down with dogs you will rise up with fleas." Be careful concerning the company you keep.

Be careful that your friends are striving to walk in holiness as you are. **Amos 3:3 "Can two walk together, unless they are agreed?"** Those you associate with should be in agreement with you concerning how to live. Those around you can either build you up or they can tear you down. **Proverbs 27:17** teaches **"As iron sharpens iron, So a man sharpens the countenance of his friend."**

Lastly, allow others to hold you accountable. This requires that you confide in a few close friends whom you know you can trust. Be real. Be honest about your struggles and the wonderful work that God is doing in your life. **James 5:16, "Confess your trespasses to one another, and pray for one another, that you may be healed."** Ask these close friends, or family members, to pray for you. Also invite them to ask you on a regular basis how you are doing. These need to be loved ones who sincerely care about you and want to see you succeed in living out your new victorious life for Christ.

You are accountable to God. You should be living your life to obey and serve Him.

You should also be accountable to others, as you receive and offer accountability.

---

9   Donald S. Whitney, Spiritual Disciplines For the Christian Life, (Colorado Springs, Colorado; 19910, p.24.

Who is your accountability partner?

PRAYER: *"Dear God in Heaven, I confess that I am not an independent and self-sufficient creature. I need You every minute of every day and night. You have all that I need. I need you. I also need to be a faithful part of Your body as represented in the local church. Please guide my path to that community of believers that You want me to serve alongside of. Lord, I need the support of others and I desire to offer that same support to those around me. My desire is to be a healthy and active member of Your body. Show me where You would have me to serve and what You would have me to be. I am asking, seeking, and knocking. In Jesus' name, Amen."*

"The Importance of Accountability"
Week #36 assignment

1. Attend a Bible-believing and Bible-preaching church at least once each week.

2. Spend a daily time in prayer, asking God to help you walk in victory.

3. Ask a Christian friend of the same sex to help hold you accountable. If you do not know who to ask, pray about this and ask God to give you discernment. This person should be trustworthy and willing to check on you occasionally.

4. As a member of the body you should function in a manner which helps the other members. Look for ways that you can minister to others this week. Every member is important and should be serving faithfully in ministry.

5. Read **Hebrews 13:17 (ESV) "Obey your leaders and submit to them, for they are keeping watch over your souls, as those who will have to give an account. Let them do this with joy and not with groaning, for that would be of no advantage to you."**

According to that verse, what is God telling us to do?

6. **Hebrews 10:23-25 (ESV) "Let us hold fast the confession of our hope without wavering, for he who promised is faithful. And let us consider how to stir up one another to love and good works, not neglecting to meet together, as is the habit of some, but encouraging one another, and all the more as you see the Day drawing near."**

According to this verse, as it relates to you holding someone else accountable, what should you aim for in dealing with the other person?

The Power of Thankfulness in Recovery
Week #38

Have you ever seen a bumper sticker or heard someone say, "There's power in prayer?" I am sure that we would all agree with that statement as long as it is God's people who are praying to Him. However, have you ever really pondered the truth that there is power in praise and thanksgiving?

We are commanded:

1 Thessalonians 5:16-18:
"Rejoice always, pray without ceasing, give thanks in all circumstances;
for this is the will of God in Christ Jesus for you."

What does that verse mean to you?

God is telling us to be thankful and to rejoice even in the difficult times in life! That is so hard for us to do because we just don't feel like it. We should be thankful and offer God our praise even when we don't necessarily "feel" like doing so. We will either choose to be obedient to 1 Thessalonians 5:16-18 or we will choose to be disobedient. This is a big deal!

List below some of the things that you are thankful for right now:

It's easy to give thanks and to praise God when life is going the way we want it. It is during those more difficult times however that we find ourselves feeling a little "less than" grateful when we struggle. Consider the experience of Paul and Silas as recorded in Acts 16. These missionaries were traveling around preaching, teaching, and healing people in the power of the Holy Spirit. They had just encountered a demon possessed girl and Paul cast that demon out of her. As long as the demon was living within her she was out of her mind. Some men had taken advantage of this girl by charging people to come into contact with the demon possessed girl claiming she had the power to tell their fortunes. Once the young girl was delivered, and her mind returned to normal, these men had lost their source of income. Outraged, the men brought charges against Paul and Silas and had them thrown into prison. How would you feel if you were imprisoned for a crime that you had not committed?

Acts 16:25-34 (ESV)

[25] About midnight Paul and Silas were praying and singing hymns to God, and the prisoners were listening to them,

[26] and suddenly there was a great earthquake, so that the foundations of the prison were shaken. And immediately all the doors were opened, and everyone's bonds were unfastened.

[27] When the jailer woke and saw that the prison doors were open, he drew his sword and was about to kill himself, supposing that the prisoners had escaped.

[28] But Paul cried with a loud voice, "Do not harm yourself, for we are all here."

[29] And the jailer called for lights and rushed in, and trembling with fear he fell down before Paul and Silas.

[30] Then he brought them out and said, "Sirs, what must I do to be saved?"

[31] And they said, "Believe in the Lord Jesus, and you will be saved, you and your household."

[32] And they spoke the word of the Lord to him and to all who were in his house.

[33] And he took them the same hour of the night and washed their wounds; and he was baptized at once, he and all his family.

[34] Then he brought them up into his house and set food before them. And he rejoiced along with his entire household that he had believed in God.

Paul and Silas suffered persecution as a result of doing good! I believe that would be the most difficult time to maintain a thankful spirit. We tend to tell ourselves in such situations, "I don't deserve this." Yet whenever we have this attitude we forget what we do deserve! We actually deserve much worse! We deserve to be separated from God forever in an eternal place of judgment called Hell.

First, we are all guilty:

Romans 3:23 (ESV)

"for all have sinned and fall short of the glory of God,"

Secondly, we all deserve eternal judgement:

Romans 6:23 (ESV)

"For the wages of sin is death, but the free gift of God is eternal life in Christ Jesus our Lord."

So, especially in those times when you feel that you don't deserve the problem that you are dealing with, keep things in perspective and remember that you deserve much worse. When I remember this truth I am free to deal with my struggles with a heart of gratitude. I know that although I am having to deal with the junk of life I do not, and will not, receive what I deserve in the end.

I see a pattern in the biblical account of Paul and Silas:

Suffering led to praises which led to preaching which led to production which led to securing protection!

These men were beaten with rods (Acts 16:23) and placed in stocks within the prison. In response to the suffering we see them offering praises unto God (Acts 16:25). As a result of their praises, God sent an earthquake which caused the prison doors to open. This gave Paul and Silas an audience before the guard who was about to take his own life fearing the prisoners had fled. The missionaries preached salvation to the guard (Acts 16:31). The result (production) was that the guard and his entire household were saved (Acts 16:33-34). The account ends with protection:

Acts 16:35-40 (ESV)

[35] But when it was day, the magistrates sent the police, saying, "Let those men go."

[36] And the jailer reported these words to Paul, saying, "The magistrates have sent to let you go. Therefore come out now and go in peace."

[37] But Paul said to them, "They have beaten us publicly, uncondemned, men who are Roman citizens, and have thrown us into prison; and do they now throw us out secretly? No! Let them come themselves and take us out."

[38] The police reported these words to the magistrates, and they were afraid when they heard that they were Roman citizens.

[39] So they came and apologized to them. And they took them out and asked them to leave the city.

[40] So they went out of the prison and visited Lydia. And when they had seen the brothers, they encouraged them and departed.

Once these officials learned that the missionaries were Roman citizens they were afraid because according to their own law they were not to treat a Roman citizen in the manner in which they had treated Paul and Silas. This gave Paul and Silas the upper hand. Notice they visited Lydia in her home and they visited with the church, all within Philippi. These missionaries didn't have to hurry out of town now because they were given protection in light of their Roman citizenship.

I wonder how differently this story might have ended had these two men not given thanks and praises to God in the midst of their pain? THERE IS POWER IN PRAISING GOD REGARDLESS OF WHAT YOU MAY BE DEALING WITH! Recovery is not an easy process for most of us. The old sins want to hold onto us and pull us back. Sometimes we feel like it is one difficult day after another, one temptation after another, one struggle after another. We pray that God would deliver us! We cry out to Him as Paul did:

Romans 7:24-25 (ESV)
"Wretched man that I am! Who will deliver me from this body of death?
25 Thanks be to God through Jesus Christ our Lord!"

Prisons can come in many different types. More so than a physical place of incarceration we may find ourselves in a prison of addiction, drugs, alcohol, or some other type of addictive lifestyle sin. We want to desperately to break free. We pray, study, and try as hard as we can to break the restraints that seem to bind us without success. Maybe what God is waiting for is your heartfelt praise and gratitude unto Him. It is interesting that before the earthquake came there was praise and prayer unto God from Paul and Silas.

Psalm 50:23 (ESV)
"The one who offers thanksgiving as his sacrifice glorifies me; to one
who orders his way rightly I will show the salvation of God!"

How can thanksgiving be a sacrifice?

Stop telling yourself that you don't deserve the struggle that you are dealing with! Instead apply Romans 6:17-18:

Romans 6:17-18 (ESV)
"But thanks be to God, that you who were once slaves of sin have become obedient from the
heart to the standard of teaching to which you were committed,
18 and, having been set free from sin, have become slaves of righteousness."

Get focused on what is really happening! You are saved if you have trusted Jesus as your personal Savior. You are being delivered from sin right now! Thank God for that! Realize that you are not receiving what you deserve because of God's grace and mercy.

#1. Why is God so concerned with us being thankful?

#2. What are some times when you tend to be unthankful?

#3. List below many of your blessings. What do you have to be thankful for?

#4. What has changed in your understanding about thankfulness in this study?

PRAYER: *"I praise you Lord! I am overflowing with thanksgiving and worship unto you for what you do and for who you are! You have indeed blessed me beyond anything I could have ever hoped for. My cup overflows. My blessings far exceed my difficulties in life. Help me God to be more focused upon my praises than I am upon my troubles. I realize that there is great power in praise. You alone are worthy of all my praise. I thank-you Lord. In Jesus' name. Amen."*

A THANKFULNESS EXERCISE

Sometimes it is difficult to maintain a thankful attitude but it is necessary in recovery and in living obedient unto God.

1 Thessalonians 5:18 (NKJV)
"Give thanks in all circumstances; for this is the will of God in Christ Jesus for you."

Make a thanksgiving list using each letter of the alphabet as the first letter for each:

A	
B	
C	
D	
E	
F	
G	
H	
I	
J	
K	
L	
M	
N	
O	
P	
Q	

R	
S	
T	
U	
V	
W	
X	
Y	
Z	
Extra:	
Extra:	
Extra:	
Extra:	

Goal-Setting and My Recovery
Week #39

---

1 Corinthians 10:31 (NKJV)
"Therefore, whether you eat or drink, or whatever you do, do all to the glory of God."

At this point, unless you are very new to the LIFE program, you are familiar with our bullseye verse above. Our goal in life, and the motivating factor in the manner in which we live, should be aimed at bringing God honor and glory.

Looking at 1 Corinthians 10:31, are there any activities which are exempt from this goal?

What do you think it means to bring "glory to God?"

The word "glory" in the Old Testament involves the idea of greatness of splendor. In the New Testament, the word translated "glory" means "dignity, honor, praise and worship." When we put those two definitions together, we find that glorifying God means to acknowledge His greatness and give Him honor by praising and worshiping Him, mainly because He, and He alone, deserves to be praised, honored and worshipped by us. God alone is worthy of our praise and honor.

Now the question arises, "How do we accomplish this goal in our lives? How do we go about bringing God glory?" Let's see if we can begin to answer this question by examining 1 Chronicles 16:28-29:

1 Chronicles 16:28-29 (NKJV)
"Give to the LORD, O families of the peoples, Give to the LORD glory and strength. Give to the LORD the glory *due* His name; Bring an offering, and come before Him. Oh, worship the LORD in the beauty of holiness!"

Three times in those two verses we read the word "give," and as well as the words "bring" and "come." These verbs require us to "do something." We are to give God glory through the bringing of an offering. What is this offering? The Apostle Paul wrote:

Romans 12:1 (NKJV)
"I beseech you therefore, brethren, by the mercies of God, that you present your bodies a living sacrifice, holy, acceptable to God, *which is* your reasonable service."

The offering you should bring to God is the offering of yourself in full surrender to Him. You must understand that your life is not your own. You have been bought with a price.

1 Corinthians 6:19-20 (NKJV)
"Or do you not know that your body is the temple of the Holy Spirit *who is* in you, whom you have from God, and you are not your own?
For you were bought at a price; therefore glorify God in your body and in your spirit, which are God's."

You must come to that point in your life where you realize and confess that you really do not know what is best for your life, but God does. You surrender your life, your body, your all to His will. To live your life with the goal of glorifying God means that you agree with God, submit to God, and you live in obedience to God.

AGREE with God that you need Him.

SUBMIT to God your will, your plans, your dreams, your all.

BE OBEDIENT to God in everything He commands you.

We say we love God yet so often we fail to really agree, submit, and walk in obedience to God. Jesus said:

John 14:15 (NKJV)
"If you love Me, keep My commandments."

My greatest goal in life should be to express my love for the Lord through the manner in which I live my life. I desire to bring Him glory. I challenge you to aim for this goal. This should be our long-term goal in life. Then we should all set short term goals which help us achieve our long term goal. Let's consider goal-setting in your recovery process.

If you are going to walk in soberness, stay clean, and live out the abundant life that Christ offers you must aim for that in your life. It will not be by accident that you celebrate 6 months clean. It will not be by chance that you regain your life of sobriety and live a productive life because the enemy desires to steal, kill, and destroy. If our lives are simply left to happenstance we will waste our existence on useless pursuits and end up with only regrets at the end of the road.

A major key to overcoming substance abuse or addiction is to keep your eyes on that goal of bringing glory unto God and recovery will come! Paul certainly understood the necessity of being goal-oriented. If you **"seek first the kingdom of God" (Matthew 6:33)** and align your other goals with this powerful vision, God will faithfully help you with all your goals. Stay focused and you will walk out of your addiction, one day at a time.

Philippians 3:13-14
"Brethren, I do not count myself to have apprehended; but one thing I do, forgetting those things which are behind and reaching forward to those things which are ahead, I press toward the goal for the prize of the upward call of God in Christ Jesus."

That verse says that Paul was "reaching forward to those things which are ahead." What things are you reaching for? It is very difficult to realize your goals if you are not clear on what those goals are. Also, you must identify your goals in order to measure your progress towards fulfilling those goals. I want you to really pause and consider your answer to these two questions before you proceed in this assignment:

What is it exactly that you are trying to achieve in life?

What steps are you taking to accomplish that goal?

A few common answers that I hear are, "I want to get sober." "I want to repair family relationships." "I want to have some stability in my life." "I desire to become productive again." The key is to break these goals down into smaller, more manageable goals, that you can begin to reach now.

Think about your goals right now. Can you list a few below?

This week I desire to:

Before the end of this year I want to have accomplished:

Five years from now I want to:

Ten years from now I plan to:

My forever goals are:

Now, let's think about goal-setting with a purpose. If your long-term goal is to bring glory to God through your life, how will you set your goals to reflect that? For example, I know that living my life sober glorifies God because He tells me in Titus 2:12 that I am to live soberly and godly. As I think of some small steps I can take now, I identify these as my short-term goals;

#1. I will stop attending places where drugs and alcohol are available.

#2. I will begin associating with sober people.

#3. I will begin to take one day at a time and structure my life to stay clean today.

Let's reverse the assignment you just did a bit:

STEP 1: WRITE DOWN YOUR GOAL IN AS FEW WORDS AS POSSIBLE

STEP 2: MAKE YOUR GOAL DETAILED. WHO? / WHAT? / WHEN? / WHERE?

HOW WILL YOU REACH THIS GOAL? LIST THREE ACTION ITEMS (BE SPECIFIC)

1. _____

2. _____

3. _____

STEP 3: MAKE YOUR GOAL MEASURABLE. MEASUREMENTS / TRACKING DETAILS

I will measure/track my goal by using the following numbers or methods:

I will know I've reached my goal when:

STEP 4: WHAT RESOURCES DO YOU NEED FOR SUCCESS?

Items I need to achieve this goal:

How I'll make the time:

Things I need to learn more about:

People I can talk to for support:

STEP 5: MAKE YOUR GOAL REALISTIC. LIST WHY YOU WANT TO REACH THIS GOAL

STEP 6: MAKE YOUR GOAL TIME-BASED. LIST WHEN YOU PLAN TO REACH THIS GOAL

I will reach my goal by (date): ___ / ___ / ___

Additional dates and milestones: _____

PRAYER: *"Dear Heavenly Father, please help me set goals that are honoring to you. Give me power to reach these goals in my recovery. Show me Lord your will for my life that I might walk in it. In Jesus' name. Amen."*

Jesus, Our Deliverer
Week #40

Matthew 1:18-25 (ESV)

[18] Now the birth of Jesus Christ took place in this way. When his mother Mary had been betrothed to Joseph, before they came together she was found to be with child from the Holy Spirit. [19] And her husband Joseph, being a just man and unwilling to put her to shame, resolved to divorce her quietly. [20] But as he considered these things, behold, an angel of the Lord appeared to him in a dream, saying, "Joseph, son of David, do not fear to take Mary as your wife, for that which is conceived in her is from the Holy Spirit. [21] She will bear a son, and you shall call his name Jesus, for he will save his people from their sins." [22] All this took place to fulfill what the Lord had spoken by the prophet: [23] "Behold, the virgin shall conceive and bear a son, and they shall call his name Immanuel" (which means, God with us). [24] When Joseph woke from sleep, he did as the angel of the Lord commanded him: he took his wife, [25] but knew her not until she had given birth to a son. And he called his name Jesus.

Often, we think of the season of Christmas when we reflect upon the birth of Jesus. It really does not matter what time of year it is as you work through these lessons, the birth of Jesus relates to our recovery. I love the record in scripture of God becoming a man, in Jesus, to be our deliverer. No one else could have paid for our sins upon the cross. He was the "God-man" meaning He was 100% God but also 100% man. He is the only one to walk this earth who was without sin. Our deliverer had to be someone with no sin, yet someone like us, who could pay the penalty for our wrongs. This is the importance of the virgin birth. If Jesus had been born into this world just as anyone else, through the relationship of a man and a woman, He would have borne within Himself the sin nature that we all have. God, through bypassing man's part in conception, came through the virgin Mary, thus being the only sinless man. Wow! People say that this is impossible and they are exactly right. God however accomplishes impossible things. Allow that truth to sink into your soul right now. Whatever you are facing or dealing with right now in your recovery, God is able to bring deliverance to pass in your life. He can do the impossible.

Matthew 19:26 (ESV)
But Jesus looked at them and said, "With man this is impossible, but with God all things are possible."

Jesus said that "with God all things are possible." How does that truth help you right now?

In our text from Matthew 1 we read of an angel appearing to Joseph, and informing him that the baby within the womb of Mary was a miracle child. I believe that all babies are miracles, and all children are gifts from God. However, this baby within Mary would be special in many ways. The angel instructed Joseph to name the child "Jesus."

List some names that are very special to you, including your own name:

Do you know what any of these names mean? If you know what your name means, or if you can google it right now, write the meaning below:

I use to work in sales before entering the ministry, and I remember we were taught in training that the number one word that people like to hear is their own name spoken. This is one reason why it is important to remember names of new acquaintances, so that you can call them by name the next time you meet. Salespeople are always trying to connect with customers in any way that they can, calling others by their name is a great start.

The name Jesus comes from the Hebrew name "Yeshua," meaning "to deliver, to rescue." Jesus is the sweetest name I know! I love the name Melissa, that's my wife's name, and my daughters; Sarah, Michaela, and Hannah, these are all special names to me. The greatest name of all though is the name of Jesus. He alone is my deliverer! Jesus is the only One who can deliverer you from the penalty and the power of sin. He alone has the power to accomplish that in your life!

You can choose deliverance today through Jesus. You don't need a movie star, a famous singer, a great politician, a well-known artist, but the One you need is Jesus, **"for He will save His people from their sins."**

Every single one of us needs that deliverance and salvation. No one is so good that they need not be saved and no one is so bad that they can't be saved. That my friend is the power of God!

What are some things you need deliverance from in your own life?

Eternal life is not simply about the length of life (living forever in the sweet by and by) but it is just as much about living now in deliverance (in the sour now and now). Remember Jesus promised "abundant life." (John 10:10). Take time to remember why Jesus came. God did not have to leave Heaven to come down to man. He didn't have to die on the cross. He didn't have to go through all that He did but He chose to because of His great love for us. He desires that we come into His abundant and eternal life! A clear illustration of bondage, and the power of God to deliver is seen in the Book of Exodus. The Egyptians had taken the people of Israel into slavery. God's people were made to work for the Egyptians in making blocks for building. This was extremely hard labor. Moses cried out to God to deliver them out of this bondage.

Exodus 3:7-8 (NKJV)
"And the LORD said: 'I have surely seen the oppression of My people who are in Egypt, and have heard their cry because of their taskmasters, for I know their sorrows. So I have come down to deliver them out of the hand of the Egyptians, and to bring them up from that land to a good and large land, to a land flowing with milk and honey.'"

Sometimes my circumstances are too stressful for me, yet knowing that God sees what I am suffering is a great relief. Just as God saw the oppression of His people in Egypt, heard their cry and knew their sorrows, He sees, hears, and knows our struggles too.

Egypt is used as a symbol of spiritual bondage when the Pharaoh held God's people captive. Egypt represented harsh servitude for the Hebrews. Likewise, our addictions kept us in bondage too. We became enslaved and were held captive by its power. God saw our oppression. The Lord is watching. He is however doing more than just watching. Note what God says:

#1. "I have surely seen…"

#2. "and have heard their cry"

#3. "for I know their sorrows"

#4. "I have come down to deliver them"

Those four truths are taught in Exodus 3! How does that help you?

Sometimes you may feel like no one really sees what you are dealing with. No one really listens to you when you try to explain your struggles. You feel like you are the only one who is dealing with the things you are fighting against. Well, God does and He takes it one step further, for verse 8 says, "I have come down to deliver them." We need more than just sympathetic understanding from friends. We need someone who is able to step in and help us. Remember, God is faithful. He hears and delivers all who call upon Him.

Take time to mediate on Psalm 18:1-19.

Psalm 18:1-19 (ESV)
¹ I love you, O LORD, my strength.

² The LORD is my rock and my fortress and my deliverer, my God, my rock, in whom I take refuge, my shield, and the horn of my salvation, my stronghold. ³ I call upon the LORD, who is worthy to be praised, and I am saved from my enemies. ⁴ The cords of death encompassed me; the torrents of destruction assailed me; ⁵ the cords of Sheol entangled me; the snares of death confronted me. ⁶ In my distress I called upon the LORD; to my God I cried for help. From his temple he heard my voice, and my cry to him reached his ears. ⁷ Then the earth reeled and rocked; the foundations also of the mountains trembled and quaked, because he was angry. ⁸ Smoke went up from his nostrils, and devouring fire from his mouth; glowing coals flamed forth from him. ⁹ He bowed the heavens and came down; thick darkness was under his feet. ¹⁰ He rode on a cherub and flew; he came swiftly on the wings of the wind. ¹¹ He made darkness his covering, his canopy around him, thick clouds dark with water. ¹² Out of the brightness before him hailstones and coals of fire broke through his clouds. ¹³ The LORD also thundered in the heavens, and the Most High uttered his voice, hailstones and coals of fire.

¹⁴ And he sent out his arrows and scattered them; he flashed forth lightnings and routed them. ¹⁵ Then the channels of the sea were seen, and the foundations of the world were laid bare at your rebuke, O LORD, at the blast of the breath of your nostrils. ¹⁶ He sent from on high, he took me; he drew me out of many waters. ¹⁷ He rescued me from my strong enemy and from those who hated me, for they were too mighty for

me. [18] They confronted me in the day of my calamity, but the LORD was my support. [19] He brought me out into a broad place; he rescued me, because he delighted in me.

PRAYER: "All praise and honor and glory belong to my Savior, Jesus, the Christ. You came into this sin plagued earth so long ago to rescue mankind from their own failure into sin. Lord, you were not obligated, you did not have to do what you did, but you came offering up your sinless life upon a cruel Roman cross. You paid a debt that we owed but a debt that we could never have paid. A debt that demanded mankind be separated from you forever. You have rescued and delivered us! Whoever will look and believe in faith can be forgiven. I praise your holy name for the blessing of forgiveness. This indeed is the greatest blessing ever known to mankind. Praise Jesus! Praise Jesus! In His holy name I pray. Amen."

A Testimony of Deliverance by Jessica Getsinger:

I would do anything for my next fix. I lived this way for about six months, from January 2019 until July of 2019. During this time, I caught over 10 charges, went to jail weekly, and did whatever I could for my high for the next rock, or next shot. I lost everything behind this drug, my cars, my home, my kid, myself and even my freedom. On July 8, 2019 I went to prison for 8-10 months due to my drug addiction and again in February of 2020.

When they say people do as they're raised, that isn't true. I was brought up in a church going, loving family, but my depression sent me into drug use and addiction. I do not blame my problems on others. NO! I have accepted full responsibility for all of my actions. Do I say my recovery came from the help of others? YES! But, most of all my Savior helped me. GOD was the only person I had late nights in a cold, lonely cell. I prayed for God to take the taste from my mouth, take the addiction away from me. and also to stay with me and never leave. All the nights I had drug dreams I praised and prayed to the Lord asking for his guidance. I got through my time in prison because of God and I know it is because of Him that I am even alive today. How do I know it's real? He was the only one I had, everyone else was gone. I was in this alone, because of my choices. God spoke to me one night and told me to follow him. That night I gave my life to Christ. I haven't had a drug dream, not even a thought of relapse. As of today 3-10-2020 I have 8 months and 3 days clean. I cannot explain why we go through situations that we do, but the Lord has a plan for all of us and without him we are NOTHING. It is my experience and belief that addiction cannot be overcome without help from the Lord. I'm so thankful for my relationship with the Lord and also my LIFE MINISTRIES family, along with my biological family who has been there and supported me for the past 3 years. I believe prison and my Savoir is why I am now clean. I am so thankful for finding myself and the LORD. This is my testimony of the LIFE I now have as a recovering addict.

Amen!

Jessica Getsinger

Congratulations! Here's A New Commitment for a New You

Winston Churchill's last words were, "I'm bored with it all." According to Steve Jobs' sister Mona, the Apple founder's last words were, "Oh wow. Oh wow. Oh wow." As basketball great "Pistol" Pete Maravich collapsed during a pickup game, his last words were: "I feel great." Leonardo da Vinci was also overly modest, saying, "I have offended God and mankind because my work did not reach the quality it should have." I guess that masterpiece known as the Mona Lisa wasn't good enough?

What would be your last words concerning this forty lesson journey through scripture? How have these lessons helped you?

Congratulations on making it! Now you may be asking, "What's next?" This is not the end of your recovery journey but this is just the beginning. I urge you however to look past this life! Look into eternity! Consider your own mortality. Please understand that you will not live forever on this earth. Eternity awaits each one of us! If today was your final day on earth, what would you spend it doing? If your next few words spoken would be your final words before you died, what would you want to say? What would you tell your family? What would be your last words to loved ones before you leave and pass into eternity?

The man Joshua found himself in that exact situation. Joshua knew that his passing was near so he called the people of Israel together and he spoke these last words to those he loved:

Joshua 24:14-15 (NKJV)
"Now therefore, fear the LORD, serve Him in sincerity and in truth, and put away the gods which your fathers served on the other side of the River and in Egypt. Serve the LORD! And if it seems evil to you to serve the LORD, choose for yourselves this day whom you will serve, whether the gods which your fathers served that *were* on the other side of the River, or the gods of the Amorites, in whose land you dwell. But as for me and my house, we will serve the LORD."

My dear friends, please hear this challenge from Joshua. Joshua reminds us in verse 14 that we are to "fear the Lord."

What does this phrase mean to you? What does it mean for you to "fear the Lord?"

According to scripture, a *REVERENT FEAR of God* means to live with the "awe" and "awareness" of who God is. He is not "the man upstairs" or "the big Kahuna." No, He is God almighty! As you set your resolutions and goals for the rest of your life make certain that a conscious awareness of who God is prevails within each one of those goals. As we are focused on "WHO" God is we quickly understand that we are far from where we need to be. My own personal prayer is that God will make me more like Him. My desire is to walk in holiness and to become more of the godly person that He desires for me to be.

What are some of your goals for your new life free of addiction?

How does your personal understanding of God affect your stated goals?

Joshua reminds us that not only are we to fear the Lord but we must also SERVE Him in sincerity. Find a bible believing church and get involved! You need to be serving the Lord through His church.

Joshua 24:14 (NKJV)
"Now therefore, fear the LORD, serve Him in sincerity and in truth, and put away the gods which your fathers served on the other side of the River and in Egypt. Serve the LORD!"

The word "serve" in verse 14 means "to worship." The word "sincere" means "without blemish." This is a word that refers to the animals that were used for sacrifice that were to be whole and complete, lacking nothing. We are to present our bodies as a living sacrifice, holy, acceptable unto God.

Finally, Joshua commands the people to "put away the gods which your fathers served." Cast aside those idols! Here is a challenge to each one of us to make sure that we have no false Gods in our lives! The Apostle Paul put it like this:

Philippians 1:20-21 (ESV)
"For to me to live is Christ, and to die is gain."

How would you fill in the blank below, not with Paul's answer, but with your honest answer?

"For to me to live is _____."

What are you living for? Family? Money? Fame? Recognition? Are you living just for the sake of pleasure? How would you honestly fill in that blank? Would it be your children or your job or your hobby? Maybe sobriety or recovery or cleanness?

If you answer is anyone/anything other than Christ than you will have to complete that verse like this, **"For me to live is** *your answer here* **and to die is LOSS."** Think about it: When you breathe your final words everything else is left behind. Your family, your money, your fame, your possessions, and yes, even your self-efforts at sobriety, as you pass into eternity.

This is a great point in time to recommit yourself to the Lord. You have completed a 40 week biblical study, renewing your mind with God's truth along the way. You have been given tools to help you think right so that you can now act right. You will face temptations. There may be times ahead of you where you may struggle. However, by God's grace and through His power you can overcome. Chains do fall off. If you have been clean and sober from your idols during the past 40 weeks you may already be experiencing freedom from your addiction. If not, that freedom is waiting for you straight ahead! You cannot do anything to change the past but you can make stronger, more godly commitments right now, that will affect your future.

"We will all have ups and downs, but seriously, with Christ, there is this amazing peace you can have and a promise that he will never leave you or forsake you. Being a child of God comes with the knowledge that He will provide for you and His strength can get you through anything. Get ready for the best life you can have!"

Dana Brown, author of "Desperate for a Fix," published July 27, 2016, page 189

Dana was delivered from her addictions by Christ, who rescued her off the streets of New York City. Dana and her husband Mark are the founders of ZOE Freedom Center, a 501c3 nonprofit www.tzoefc.com

Suggested Group Study Guidelines

It is my prayer that this forty-week journey in recovery will be a blessing to you as an individual, but also to the group that you may be a part of. While this worktext is designed to be completed within a forty-week period, it may take longer for your group to complete it. That's alright. Don't stress about getting each lesson thoroughly taught each week. If one lesson carries over into another week that's fine. Welcome discussions and interaction within your group as we can learn from one another.

These are tips I have learned from leading groups:

#1. Be flexible. Again, encourage interaction and discussion from your group but also guard against getting off track.

#2. Encourage everyone to be involved but don't place individuals on the spot. Try to get everyone actively involved. People retain only 10% of what they hear. They retain 90% of what they hear, see, and do.

#3. Ask those participating to bring their Bibles, a notepad, and a pen to each session. Have some bibles on hand for those who do not have a bible.

#4. Contact group members between meetings. Between meetings, try to contact each member by email, telephone call, text, or postcard simply to encourage them to press on.

#5. Instruct the participants to read the lesson at least once and complete the assignment for that lesson prior to each group meeting.

#6. Prayer is essential. Pray for each participant by name each week. Ask God to speak to hearts and change lives. Pray concerning the upcoming meeting that our Lord would be honored in every way. Ask God to lead and guide your group to victorious Christian living.

Begin each meeting with prayer: Ask if there are any prayer needs among the members about which you can pray. Take time here to really listen to needs and pray about these as a group. Be sensitive to those who may need special prayer. Be willing to take the time to gather around those individuals, laying on hands, and praying out loud.

#7. Make the meeting room as warm and inviting as possible. A meal or a time of refreshments may be desirable to create an atmosphere of fellowship.

#8. Be certain your meeting environment is one that honors privacy. Your participants need to know that this is a safe environment where they can share their struggles with fellow believers.

#9. Stay on schedule. It will only discourage and confuse your group if meetings are continually cancelled and/or rescheduled. Stay within the time frame agreed upon as well, for the duration of the meeting. Start on time. End on time. Respect the time of others.

#10. A smaller group size of ten or less usually works best. This keeps the meetings more personal and allows time for each to share if desired. If your group is larger consider a time of small groups at the end of your meetings. You could have gender-based groups as your small group time.

May our Lord fill you with His Spirit as you step forward to be used by Him. Be real with your group. Be honest concerning how you have struggled in the past. Offer the hope that is found only in the Gospel of Jesus our Lord. Continue to bring the group discussions back to what scripture teaches and offer the encouragement found there. Only God can heal the human heart.